SPAIN BY CAR

SPAIN BY CAR

A Comprehensive Guide to
Places to Stay on the Major Roads

NORMAN RENOUF

Quiller Press
London

Any reader who has suggestions for new hotels to be added for future editions, please write in with all details to Norman Renouf, c/o Quiller Press, 46 Lillie Road, London SW6 1TN. Can we attribute your entry to your name?

First published in 1992 by
Quiller Press Ltd, 46 Lillie Road, London SW6 1TN

ISBN 1 870948 572

Produced by Hugh Tempest-Radford *Book Producers*

Typeset by Goodfellow & Egan Phototypesetting Ltd, Cambridge

Printed in Great Britain by St Edmundsbury Press

CONTENTS

1 INTRODUCTION

If there is one thing that travellers by car in Spain have in common it is that, sooner or later, they will be looking for a place to stay at night. Through personal experience, over 25,000 miles driven in Spain over the last three-and-a-half years, I have found that this is not quite so simple as it sounds. Although there are many hotels and other classifications of accommodation alongside the roads, there is no guarantee there is going to be one nearby when you want to stop. Even if there is, it may be too expensive, too down market, does not have a pool or is simply full. This last point is very important during certain times of the year and also during fiestas, when every hotel for miles around will be fully booked, sometimes many months ahead.

In my experience there are three types of hotel guides already in existence but they all fail, for one reason or another, to cater adequately for the car traveller in Spain. Firstly there are specialist guides; an example are the ones for the Parador Nacional chain. These are beautiful hotels that have every modern facility and are often located in historic buildings but they have been excluded from this guide for two reasons.

Firstly they are well signposted for many miles ahead all over Spain, and secondly they are prohibitively expensive for the average traveller – a double room usually starts at around 12,000 pesetas. Another and more common type of guide is the selective one where the author 'selects' hotels according to certain criteria. It is my experience that these hotels are usually fairly upmarket and generally located in cities and towns. As a consequence there is not a wide range of hotels listed and, anyway, they are not along the routes which the car travellers have to use to get to their destination. The third type are those issued by the Spanish National Tourist Office and

these are in a different format altogether. They are by province
with the hotels in the provincial capital listed first, by
descending order of classification, and then the rest are listed
by town in alphabetical order. These are not at all helpful for
car travellers, as a long journey will inevitably mean that one
passes through many different provinces and, also, they are
not comprehensive. For example on the short NIII route,
between Madrid and Valencia, the official guide identifies only
two-thirds of the places that appear in this guide.

Given all of these facts I decided that it was time to write a
hotel guide tailored to the requirements of car travellers. The
criteria are simple. Firstly, as car travellers have to use the
roads that exist, these form the basis of the guide. Secondly
every hotel, of whatever classification from de luxe five-star
ones to humble guest houses, along each of the most
important roads, is included. There is an overview of each
route and then every hotel is listed in the order it appears on
the road, along with all the basic information such as address,
telephone number, parking facilities, prices, distance from the
next hotel, a brief comment and, in most instances, a
photograph. There is also an index for each route detailing the
reference number of the hotel, the town, the name of each
hotel, the parking facilities available, the distance from the
beginning of the route, and then, at the end of the guide, the
location of petrol stations, highlighting lead-free, and an A–Z
of helpful hints. With this information travellers can either
plan their journey in advance, decide during each day where
they might like to stay that night and call ahead, or simply use
it on an *ad hoc* basis every day. These features make this guide
unique, in that it allows the traveller to select from a
comprehensive list of both routes and hotels.

Personally I find the information invaluable on my travels in
Spain. As I never know exactly how far I am going to go on
any particular day, I wait until early afternoon, select where I
want to stay, and call the hotel to reserve a room. If it is full, I
simply choose another. This alleviates all problems and makes
for a less stressful journey.

Unlike other guides this also pays for itself – in two ways.
First, financially: by ensuring that you are aware of where the
less expensive hotels are located, it is quite possible to save the
cost of the guide every night you need accommodation.

Second, by providing peace of mind: this is less quantifiable but often equally important. Nothing is guaranteed to spoil a day's journey more than not knowing where the next hotel is and how safe the car will be. At the end of a long hot day, with tired and bored children in the back seat, this is a sure cause of tension.

Finally, let me wish you many pleasant journeys in this vast and intriguing country or, as the Spanish say, *buen viaje*.

G   A   L   E   R   I   A   S

Key to Symbols

🅿	PARKING
✗	RESTAURANT
☕	CAFETERIA
⚊	SWIMMING POOL
🛏	DOUBLE BEDS
🛏	SINGLE BEDS

2 HOW TO USE THIS GUIDE

The Routes

It is obviously not practical or even necessary to include every route in this, the third largest country in Europe. The six main roads that emanate from Madrid, the NI to NVI, form the backbone of the Spanish road system and are therefore detailed first. The remainder of the roads have been chosen because they connect cities and places that are most likely to be visited by tourists.

There are two types of route which are generally excluded from this guide: toll motorways (*autopistas*) and those roads that run through very popular coastal tourist resorts. Autopistas are not detailed because quite often they run parallel to a regular road, where the hotels will be located, and also because they are very expensive. In any event there are not that may autopistas to be considered. There is less need to detail those roads that run through coastal tourist areas, for example the Costa del Sol, as there are numerous hotels in those places. There is one long section where both of the above criteria apply, between Alicante and Barcelona, and that is why the eastern coastal route has not been covered.

The routes that are included are shown on the Contents page in the numerical order of the road, beginning with the NI.

The Roads

The three types of road that most travellers will use are as follows:

Autopista

This is a toll (*peaje*) motorway and is identified by the A prefix. There are not many of these in Spain and most are in the north. In almost every instance autopistas have been excluded from this guide for the reasons given above.

Autovia

This is a toll-free dual carriageway that is almost to motorway standard. In the last few years there has been a huge investment in road bulding in Spain. As a consequence many of the main roads that used to be single carriageway, and therefore slow, have been improved to this standard. By 1992 most of these roadworks will be completed and this will make travelling much easier as well as faster. For example it will take several hours less to get from Irun to Malaga.

N Roads

Those that have not been improved vary considerably in quality; some are very good while others are close to deplorable. About the only way of knowing how good they are depends on the size of the map being used. The small road maps issued free by the Spanish National Tourist Office are on a scale of 1/1,500,000 and show all N roads as being of the same quality. This is highly misleading and I would recommend that maps on a scale of 1/400,000 are used: they give a much more realistic picture of the roads and terrain. Another beneft is that many of the hotels are located in small towns that do not appear on smaller scale maps.

Accommodation

This is a complex subject in Spain. There are many different types of accommodation and most of these have their own individual classifications which are dependent upon the facilities they offer. To complicate matters even further, minimum standards are regulated by the central government but they may be changed upwards by each of the autonomous regional governments.

The regulations are extremely lengthy and detailed; they even dictate the size of the alcoves in five-star hotels and therefore will not be repeated here. The types, their classifications and the abbreviation used in the guide are shown below in descending order, along with one or two comments.

It is not always easy to know what standard to expect: obviously the higher a place is rated the better it should be, but even this is not that simple; for example a HR ** is likely to be better than a H *. At the lower end it is even more complex as there can be very little difference between Hostals and Pensións, other than size.

Remember there is a 6% tax on all rooms and this is increased to 12% for five-star hotels.

Hotel *, **, *, ****, *****

4/5-star hotels have to have air-conditioning while in the others it is dependent upon climatic conditions.

Abbreviation: H *, H **, H ***, H ****, H *****

Hotel-Residencía *, **, *
Hostal-Residencía *, **, *

These are only obliged to offer breakfast but they must have a cafeteria.

Abbreviation: HR *, HR **, HR ***

Motel *, **, *

These are not always what would typically be thought of as motels.

Abbreviation: M *. M **, M ***

Hostal *, **, *

A * star hostal does not have to have a washbasin in each room but there has to be a common bathroom on every floor or for every ten rooms.

A** star hostal has to have a washbasin in each room and at least one common bathroom for every ten rooms.

As a rule of thumb, double rooms are more likely to have a private bath/shower than singles. Also some places charge extra for use of the common bathroom.

Abbreviation: Hostal *, Hostal **, Hostal ***

Pensión *, **, *

These are similar to Hostals but can have no more than twelve rooms. Sometimes they can be an integral part of people's houses. The standards are similar to Hostals.

Abbreviation: P *, P **, P ***

Casa de Huéspedes (Guest House)

These are usually rather small and basic.

Abbreviation: CH

Fondas

These are few and far between and like CHs usually small and basic.

Abbreviation: F

Location

The address in most instances is the town and province. The majority of the buildings are located alongside the road and are not actually in the town, which is usually just a short distance away. Those that are in a town have a street address as well.

Car Parking

The car parking facilities available are identified as follows (other details are added where relevant):

Excellent (E)
This constitutes a place that has private lockup garages and usually a price will be stated. The remaining facilities are generally Very Good or Good.

Very Good (VG)
This constitutes a place that has private parking within its own grounds.

Good (G)
This constitutes a place that has space for parking around it but off the street.

On Street (O/S)
This indicates that cars have to be left on the street. In small provincial towns this is quite safe, but it is certainly not advisable in large cities.

Beds

In Spain a double room almost always means twin beds: if a double bed is desired request a *matrimonial*. Extra beds can usually be supplied for a small additional charge. Most rooms already have a built-in extra bed that children find absolutely fascinating, the clothes closet. As these often have extra blankets and pillows, the only problem, if you have more than one child, is who gets to use it.

Restaurants/Cafeterias/Bars

Restaurants
Unless notified to the contrary every hotel will have a restaurant. Beware though: the hours of opening are very different from the UK, or even France. At lunchtime they are usually open between 1330 and 1600. At night do not expect to find one open before 2100 at least; in the south it is possibly as late as 2200. Evening meals are not that expensive and in the smaller places can be as low as 750 pesetas. That includes a bottle of wine for every two people, which is often already on the table. In other places there will be a choice: a bottle of wine

or a bottle of mineral water. A word of warning here: the wine
you will given is of table quality, most probably red and very
strong. It is easy to drink too much without realising the effect
it is having. The Spanish way of getting around this is to mix
the wine with a bottle of lemonade called *Casera* to form a long
cool drink.

Cafeterias
Some places have cafeterias and this is important if you plan to
stop between lunchtime and dinnertime, as it is the only way
you can guarantee getting something to eat. It's a long wait if
you decide to stop at 1700 and the restaurant does not open
until 2200.

Bars
I have only ever seen one Spanish hotel, of whatever type, that
did not have a bar. However there are many variations; some
are very simple while others are much more elaborate and
have open grills for sandwiches (*bocadillos*) etc.

Swimming Pools

Surprisingly, given the usual climatic conditions, very few
places have a swimming pool (*piscina*) and these are noted on
an individual basis.

However most Spanish towns, regardless of size, have a
piscina municipal. These are generally well signposted, cheap
and clean. During the summer they are often open up to
2130/2200 and make a refreshing break after a long hot day on
the road.

**Please do not hesitate to write in with your
comments and suggestions for hotels. Be sure to let
me have details as per the entries in this guide and
say whether I can acknowledge your name as the
information source.**
**Write to NORMAN RENOUF c/o QUILLER PRESS,
46 LILLIE RD, LONDON SW6 1TN.**

3 NI MADRID–BURGOS–VITORIA–SAN SEBASTIÁN–IRÚN (FRANCE)

The Route

This is a journey of just over 480 km (about 300 miles) and for the first half, from Madrid to Burgos, there are no options. From Burgos it is possible to take the autopista toll road, but as this takes an indirect route and is expensive it is not an option I would consider. In any event by the time this guide is published the NI will have been upgraded to an autovia standard and the days of being stuck behind trucks will be over.

The first 50 km are not that interesting, the large Aguila brewery and the motorcycle race track – close to 25 km – being the only landmarks. Not far past here, at the 30.8 km mark off the northbound carriageway, is an intriguing restaurant, the Terramar, with a very large pool. It would make for a relaxing stop on a hot day. There used to be a hotel at the end of the pool but, unfortunately, it has been closed for some time. The road climbs for a little after 60 km and the Sierra de Guadarrama mountains become more clearly visible to the north-west. It then descends and passes through a wide valley enclosed by mountains, before beginning to climb up to the Puerto de Somosierra, at a height of 1,444 metres (approximately 4,500 feet). From the Puerto to Aranda de Duero it crosses an open plateau and the views of the sierras to the south-east are magnificent. The next part of the trip to Burgos is unexceptional and only Lerma is worth a mention. The Duke of Lerma was an important figure in the early 17th century and the old part of town is worth a visit. There is another mountain range, the Sierra de la Demanda, to the north-east and this is a winter sports area for the Spanish.

If you are not planning to visit the city of Burgos there is a fast way around the outside. As soon as the tower of the Landa Palace becomes visible, shortly before the city, move to the right of the road and take the exit to the autopista. After a few km take the exit off by the Ciudad de Burgos hotel, and rejoin the N1. From the north repeat this process, only in reverse.

The NI and A1 autopista then run parallel to each other for about 90 km and, until Pancorbo, there is nothing to see. Here the old town is protected by large jagged mountains before the road passes through the ravine (*desfiladero*). This is one of the places where the French and Wellington's forces clashed in 1813. Once past Pancorbo the road is comparatively flat even though there are mountains in the distance; after Vitoria it becomes far more mountainous. From Alsasua the N1 begins to climb and reaches its highest point at Idiazabal; here the scenery is reminiscent of the lower alpine regions in France and Switzerland. The next 15 km are very slow as the road twists and turns down to the coastal area. Although the scenery is quite nice on the run into San Sebastián it is spoilt as the towns are very industrial. San Sebastián is rather different to most Spanish seaside resorts; it is very elegant with promenades around the beaches and an interesting small harbour near the old town, which is famous for its restaurants. It is an unfortunate fact of life here that that the Basque nationalists are an important force. The most obvious and least harmful signs, to people, are the slogans that are painted everywhere. Violence also plays its part and one never knows when and how it will erupt; there are occasional street shootings and so refrain from sensitive political conversations in public places. From San Sebastián the last part of the route to Irún is not long and apart from the squalid industrial port area, it is quite scenic. There is a Mamout hypermarket at Oyarzun and this is convenient for stocking up on your favourite Spanish goodies: it saves carrying them all across Spain.

Warning

Spain has the image of being a sun-drenched country and, in the summer, this is certainly true. However, unlike the UK, it has a Continental climate and as a consequence the seasons are extreme. There are two mountain passes on this route, the Puerto de Somosierra 99 km from Madrid, and the region around Idiazabal at 405 km. These can be closed because of snow in the winter, so pay attention to the weather forecasts between November and April.

Route Planner

REF	TOWN	NAME	PKG	KMs FROM MADRID
NI/1	Madrid	Ramon de la Cruz	E	0
NI/2	Alcobendas	Grand Prix	G	16.5
NI/3	Alcobendas	El Fronton	G	16.6
NI/4	Fuente del Fresno	Pamplona	G	25
NI/5	San Agustin del Guadalix	El Figon de Raul	O/S	28
NI/6	El Molar	CH	G	43.2
NI/7	La Cabrera	Mavi	G	58
NI/8	La Cabrera	El Cancho del Aguila	G	60
NI/9	Loyozuela	Los Pinos	G	68
NI/10	Gascones	Venta Mea	G	77
NI/11	Horcajo de la Sierra	La Matilla	VG	88.6
NI/12	Puerto de Somosierra	Mora	G	92.5
NI/13	Santó Tome del Puerto	Misasierra	VG	99
NI/14	Santó Tome del Puerto	Venta Juanilla	G	100
NI/15	Cerezo de Abajo	Langa	G	103
NI/16	Castillejo de Mesleon	El Ancla	E	110
NI/17	Boceguillas	Centro	G	115
NI/18	Boceguillas	Tres Hermanos	G	115
NI/19	Boceguillas	Cardenal Cisneros	G	117
NI/20	Boceguillas	Castill	G	118
NI/21	Carabias de Pradales	Cristobal	G	130
NI/22	Carabias de Pradales	La Antigua Viña	G	130
NI/23	Honrubie de la Cuesta	Las Campanas Milario	VG	135
NI/24	Fuentespina	Area Tudanca	VG	153
NI/25	Aranda de Duero	Tres Condes	E	157
NI/26	Aranda de Duero	Julia	O/S	160
NI/27	Aranda de Duero	Aranda	O/S	160
NI/28	Aranda de Duero	Los Bronces	E	160
NI/29	Aranda de Duero	Montehermoso	VG	163
NI/30	Gumiel de Hizan	Los Hermanos	G	171
NI/31	Lerma	Casa Angeles	O/S	200
NI/32	Lerma	Docar	O/S	200
NI/33	Lerma	Alisa	E	202
NI/34	Villagonzalo-Perdanales	La Varga	G	232
NI/35	Villagonzalo-Perdanales	Area Castil	G	233

REF	TOWN	NAME	PKG	KMs FROM MADRID
NI/36	Burgos	Landa Palace	E	236
NI/37	Burgos	Ciudad de Burgos	VG	249
NI/38	Quintanapalla	Quintanapalla	G	254
NI/39	Briviesca	Sanmar	G	278
NI/40	Briviesca	El Vallés	VG	280
NI/41	Calzada de Bureba	Juli	G	290
NI/42	Santa Maria Rivarredona	La Espiga de Oro	G	296
NI/43	Pancorbo	De Pancorbo	G	302
NI/44	Pancorbo	Poli	G	302
NI/45	Pancorbo	El Desfiladero	G	305
NI/46	Pancorbo	El Molino	E	306
NI/47	Miranda de Ebro	Tudanca	G	318
NI/48	Elburgo	Olaona	G	364
NI/49	Ilarduya	Asparrena	G	385
NI/50	Eguino	Las Ventas	G	387
NI/51	Ciordia	Iturrimurri	G	389
NI/52	Olazaguita	Ederrena	G	391
NI/53	Alsasua	Hendia	O/S	395
NI/54	Alsasua	Leku-Ona	G	396
NI/55	Alsasua	Alaska	G	402
NI/56	Idiazabal	Ongi-Etorri	G	405
NI/57	Idiazabal	Alai	G	405
NI/58	Idiazabal	Beunos Aires	G	405
NI/59	Olaberria	Castillo	VG	419
NI/60	Legorreta	Izarra	O/S	428
NI/61	San Sebastián	Avenida	VG	469
NI/62	San Sebastián	Pellizar	VG	472
NI/63	Oyarzun	Lintzirin	E	475

G   A   L   E   R   I   A   S

The Hotels

NI/1 HR** Ramon de la Cruz

Madrid

☎ (91) 401.72.00

🅿 E		✗	✓
🍴 ✗		⚲	✗
🛏 6,300		🛌 4,000	

Madrid: 0 km

Located close to the plaza of Manuel Becerra, and only about 5 minutes from the motorway through the city (exit Alcalá/Ventas), this is quite nice and the surrounding area is an interesting mixture of shops and apartments. There is a private car park just behind the hotel: it costs about 1,400 a day. Do not book in without checking the car park for vacancies and the same applies the other way round.

NI/2 H** Grand Prix

Alcobendas, Madrid

☎ (91) 652.46.00

🅿 G		✗	✓
🍴 ✗		⚲	✗
🛏 3,900		🛌 2,500	

Madrid: 16.5 km

This is rather nice but unfortunately it is on a very busy fast corner and general environment could be better as well. Accessible mainly from the northbound carriageway.

NI/3 Hostal** El Fronton

Alcobendas, Madrid

☎ (91) 652.34.37

🅿 G		✗	✓
🍴 ✗		⚲	✗
🛏 3,500		🛌 ✗	

Madrid: 16.6 km

Somewhat smaller than the Grand Prix, which is almost next door, this is all right but the comments on the surroundings also apply here.

NI/4 Pamplona

Fuente del Fresno, Madrid

☎ (91) 857.02.34

🅿 G		✗	✓
🍴 ✗		⚲	✗
🛏 3,500		🛌 2,000	

Madrid: 25 km

Located on the northbound carriageway and very close to the road, this is just past the large Aguila brewery. It is small and not that nice. Personally I think it is expensive.

NI/5 H** El Figon de Raul

San Agustin del Guadalix, Madrid

📞 (91) 841.90.11

🅿	✗ O/S	✗	✓
🍵	✓	🛏	✗
🛎	6,000	🍴	4,500

Madrid: 28 km

Off the N1 in the town of San Augustin, it is a very attractive and distinguished hotel but unfortunately the parking is not good.

NI/6 CH

El Molar, Madrid

📞 (91) 841.10.09

🅿	G	✗	✓
🍵	✗	🛏	✗
🛎	2,500	🍴	✗

Madrid: 43.2 km

A rather ordinary, plain place.

NI/7 H** Mavi

La Cabrera, Madrid

📞 (91) 868.80.00

🅿	G	✗	✓
🍵	✗	🛏	✗
🛎	3,200	🍴	2,000

Madrid: 58 km

On the north side of the road this is quite a large, pleasant hotel in an area close to where Madrileños like to come to relax.

NI/8 P** El Cancho del Aguila

La Cabrera, Madrid

📞 (91) 868.83.74

🅿	G	✗	✓
🍵	✗	🛏	✗
🛎	2,500	🍴	1,600

Madrid: 60 km

This is a very large building for a pension, even a two-star one. It is in the same location as the Mavi.

NI/9 HR* Los Pinos

Loyozuela, Madrid

📞 (91) 869.40.63

🅿	G	✗	✓
🍵	✗	🛏	✗
🛎	3,500	🍴	✗

Madrid: 68 km

Quite small, this is far easier to reach from the southbound carriageway although there is a *cambio de sentido* – change of lanes – from the other side. The name means The Pine Trees.

NI/10 HR** Los Ares

Gascones, Madrid

📞 (91) 868.03.91

🅿 G		✗	✓
🍷 ✗		🛏 ✗	
🛏 3,000		🛏 1500	

Madrid: 77 km

A very small place that has character, having been much improved over the last two years.

NI/11 Hostal* La Matilla

Horcajo de la Sierra, Madrid

📞 (91) 869.90.06

🅿 VG		✗	✓
🍷 ✗		🛏 ✗	
🛏 3,600		🛏 1800	

Madrid: 88.6 km

Located just before the road begins to climb up to the Puerto de Somosierra, this is a large hostal. It has a very extensive menu of set meals, though some of the prices are rather high.

NI/12 H** Mora

Puerto de Somsosierra, Madrid

📞 (91) 869.90.16

🅿 G		✗	✓
🍷 ✗		🛏 ✗	
🛏 4,500		🛏 3,000	

Madrid: 92.5 km

Located at the summit of the Puerto de Somosierra this is not a bad hotel. It is surprising for how much of the year the nearby peaks are snow-covered.

NI/14 CH Venta Juanilla

Santo Tomé del Puerto, Segovia

📞 (911) 55.50.66

🅿 G		✗	✓
🍷 ✗		🛏 ✗	
🛏 1,200		🛏 800	

Madrid: 100 km

Positioned next to a club this is a small and not very nice place. It is basic and the rooms are about the worst I have seen anywhere.

NI/13 H*** Misasierra

Santo Tomé del Puerto, Segovia

📞 (911) 55.50.05

🅿 VG	✗ ✓
☕ ✓	🛏️ ✗
🛏️ 5,400	🛏️ 3,500

Madrid: 99 km

A large hotel that has all modern facilities, including an interesting shop, and nice views into the bargain.

NI/16 Hostal** El Ancla

Castillejo de Mesleon

📞 (911) 55.50.46

🅿 E	✗ ✓
☕ ✗	🛏️ ✗
🛏️ 2,600	🛏️ ✗

Madrid: 110 km

In an isolated, landlocked position The Anchor is rather a strange name for the location. It is on the northbound carriageway and is quite nice. The private garages are 750 per night extra.

The next four places are now bypassed by a new road: to reach them, take either the north or south exit for Boceguillas

NI/15 HR* Langa

Cerezo de Abajo, Segovia

📞 (911) 55.50.33

🅿 G	✗ ✓
☕ ✗	🛏️ ✗
🛏️ 2,150	🛏️ 1,500

Madrid: 103 km

Situated at the bottom of a small hill this is a modern pleasant hostal that is not over priced.

NI/17 HR** Centro

Boceguillas, Segovia

📞 (911) 54.37.92

🅿 G	✗ ✓
☕ ✓	🛏️ ✗
🛏️ 2,500	🛏️ ✗

Madrid: 115 km

This, like the next three places is now bypassed as the main road has been substantially improved here. This hostal is nothing special and next door to the Tres Hermanos.

NI/18 Hostal* Tres Hermanos

Boceguillas, Segovia

☎ (911) 54.30.40

🅿 G		✗	✓
☕	✗	🍴	✗
🛏 3,750		🛏 2,500	

Madrid: 115 km

Called Three Brothers, this is the largest of the places here. It is quite nice but I consider the restaurant to be overpriced. A short walk away in the town is a much cheaper restaurant with a more local atmosphere.

NI/20 P* Castill

Boceguillas, Segovia

☎ (911) 54.37.16

🅿 G		✗	✓
☕	✗	🍴	✗
🛏 1,900		🛏 1,000	

Madrid: 118 km

A very basic pension where the singles do not have a bath/shower.

NI/21 Hostal** Christobal

Carabias de Pradales, Segovia

☎ (911) 54.37.08

🅿 G		✗	✓
☕	✗	🍴	✗
🛏 2,100		🛏 1,295	

Madrid: 130 km

An unusually shaped hostal that is perhaps a little basic. I tried to stay here once but it was full – so best to book.

NI/19 HR** Cardenal Cisneros

Boceguillas, Segovia

☎ (911) 54.30.82

🅿 G		✗	✓
☕	✗	🍴	✗
🛏 2,600		🛏 1,400	

Madrid: 117 km

This hostal has some charm even though its location behind a service station is not the best. The single rooms do not have a bath/shower.

NI/22 Hostal** La Antigua Viña

Carabias de Pradales, Segovia

☎ (911) 54.37.00

🅿 G	✗	✓
☕ ✗	🛏 ✗	
🛏 3,500	🛏 ✗	

Madrid: 130 km

Set back about 100 yards off the southbound carriageway, on the same side as the Cristobal, this has an old-fashioned atmosphere and appears rather nice.

NI/23 M*** Las Campanas de Milario

Honrubia de la Cuesta, Segovia

☎ (911) 53.30.00

🅿 VG	✗	✓
☕ ✗	🛏 ✗	
🛏 4,500	🛏 3,500	

Madrid: 135 km

Located off the northbound carriageway this is only accessed from the other direction by a footbridge. It is a pleasant enough place but I feel that it is on the expensive side.

NI/24 M*** Area Tudanca

Fuentespina, Burgos

☎ (947) 50.60.11

🅿 VG	✗	✓
☕ ✓	🛏 ✓	
🛏 4,500	🛏 3,600	

Madrid: 153 km

A very modern complex with many facilities and large shops, it has a brother in Miranda de Ebro about 160 km up the road. Although certainly it does not have any traditional character about it.

N/26 H* Julia

Aranda de Duero, Burgos

☎ (947) 50.12.00

🅿 O/S	✗	✓
☕ ✗	🛏 ✗	
🛏 4,200	🛏 1,790	

Madrid: 160 km

Located in the centre of town this is nice but there is next to no parking. The town is interesting to wander around, and makes a change from staying in hotels close to the road.

NI/27 Hostal** Aranda

Aranda de Duero, Burgos

☎ (947) 50.16.00

🅿 O/S		✗	✓
🍴	✗	🛏	✗
🛏 3,500		🛏 2,000	

Madrid: 160 km

Half way between the centre of town and the Los Bronces this is a very pleasant hostal and I rather like it. There are some parking places in a small plaza next to the hostal and also in the *plaza de toros* car park across he road. Otherwise street parking is not bad.

NI/25 HR*** Tres Condes

Aranda de Duero, Burgos

☎ (947) 50.24.00

🅿 E		✗	✓
🍴	✓	🛏	✗
🛏 4,500		🛏 3,500	

Madrid: 157 km

For such a large hotel this is in a strange location, the southern suburbs of the town. Take the Valladolid exit, south of town, towards Aranda, and you can't miss it. It is very nice and related to the Los Bronces just north of the town. Private parking is 1,000 extra.

G A L E R I A S

NI/28 H*** Los Bronces

Aranda de Duero, Burgos

📞 (947) 50.08.50

🅿 E		✗ ✓
☕ ✓		💈 ✓
🛏 4,900		🍴 3,500
Madrid: 160 km		

Just off the N1 near the northern exit from Aranda this is a large hotel with many facilities. The restaurant especially is very nice – but not cheap – and the regional speciality, Lamb roasted in a Horno de Asar, is prominent. However having stayed here I was a little disappointed with the standard of the rooms given that it is not inexpensive.

NI/29 H*** Montehermoso

Aranda de Duero, Burgos

📞 (947) 50.15.50

🅿 VG		✗ ✓
☕ ✓		💈 ✗
🛏 4,500		🍴 3,000
Madrid: 163 km		

This is a very large and impressive hotel off the southbound carriageway of the N1. It has many facilities.

NI/30 Hostal* Los Hermanos

Gumiel de Hizan, Burgos

📞 (947) 54.40.09

🅿 G		✗ ✓
☕ ✗		💈 ✗
🛏 1,800		🍴 1,000
Madrid: 171 km		

Named The Brothers, this is a short distance north of Aranda and is rather basic.

NI/31 HR** Docar

Lerma, Burgos

📞 (947) 17.09.62.

🅿 O/S		✗ ✗
☕ ✗		💈 ✗
🛏 1,700		🍴 1,200
Madrid: 200 km		

This, and the Casa Angeles, are located in the plaza just off the N1 in the centre of Lerma and the parking is not good. It is a charming place and the rooms are really nice. The fact that there is no restaurant is not a problem given its position in town.

NI/33 H** Alisa

Lerma, Burgos

☎ (947) 17.02.50.

🅿 E		✗ ✓
🍵 ✓		🛁 ✗
🛏 4,200		🛄 2,500
Madrid: 202 km		

Only a km or so north of Lerma this is a large, modern, impressive hotel where there are many facilities and everything is very nice. The restaurant is not too expensive for the set menu but the portions are not large. Surprisingly, even though it is set well back from the road, the noise of the trucks speeding past carries to the rooms.

NI/32 HR* Casa Angeles

Lerma, Burgos

☎ (947) 17.10.73.

🅿 O/S		✗ ✓
🍵 ✗		🛁 ✗
🛏 3,000		🛄 2,000
Madrid: 200 km		

A most strange place that has a very narrow frontage and seems to be like a maze inside. The rooms are not that good either.

NI/35 H** Area Castil

Villagonzalo-Pedernales, Burgos

☎ (947) 20.68.00.

🅿 G		✗ ✓
🍵 ✗		🛁 ✗
🛏 4,255		🛄 2,200
Madrid: 233 km		

Somewhat smaller than the La Varga, this is not too bad. The area was undergoing expensive road improvements the last time I was here, so it is difficult to envisage where these last two places will end up in relation to the new road.

NI/34 HR*** La Varga

Villagonzalo-Pedernales, Burgos

☎ (947) 20.16.40.

🅿 G		✗ ✓
🍵 ✗		🛁 ✗
🛏 5,000		🛄 ✗
Madrid: 232 km		

This is a few km south of Burgos and does not appear too bad, although a touch expensive.

NI/36 H***** Landa Palace

Burgos, Burgos

☎ (947) 20.63.43.

🅿 E		✗ ✓
☕ ✓		🍴 ✓
🛏 13,900		🛏 8,800

Madrid: 236 km

There are few hotels that I have seen that can match this one; it is really splendid in all respects. The lobby is part of an ancient castle and outside there is a collection of antique carts. All extras are rather expensive and there is of course 12% to add for IVA (Spanish VAT).

NI/37 H*** Ciudad de Burgos

Burgos, Burgos

☎ (947) 43.10.41

🅿 VG		✗ ✓
☕ ✗		🍴 ✗
🛏 4,300		🛏 2,600

Madrid: 249 km

This large hotel is dominant in its isolated position. It is very nice and especially good value – a single room here is only £3 or so more than in the next place and, from personal

experience in both, there is absolutely no comparison. Every room has a colour TV included in the price.

NI/38 HR* Quintanapalla

Quintanapalla, Burgos

☎ (947) 43.10.22

🅿 G		✗ ✓
☕ ✗		🍴 ✗
🛏 3,000		🛏 2,000

Madrid: 254 km

Positioned on the edge of this village it is no more than adequate; in fact when it is compared wiht the Ciudad de Burgos it is very bad value indeed.

NI/39 H** Sanmar

Briviesca, Burgos

☎ (947) 59.07.00

🅿 G		✗ ✓
☕ ✗		🍴 ✗
🛏 3,700		🛏 2,300

Madrid: 278 km

A large building with glass covered terraces on the front. This also has a club on the premises so it is likely to attract a rough clientele.

NI/40 H** El Vallés

Briviesca, Burgos

☎ (947) 59.00.25

🅿 VG		✗	✓
🍴 ✗		🛏 ✗	
🛏 4,675		🛏 3,737	

Madrid: 280 km

I like this hotel as it has a very distinguished atmosphere without being too formal, the public rooms are nice and there are also gardens.

NI/42 Hostal** La Espiga de Oro

Santa Maria Rivarredonda, Burgos

☎ (947) 35.41.36

🅿 G		✗	✓
🍴 ✗		🛏 ✗	
🛏 2,500		🛏 2,000	

Madrid: 296 km

I have been fascinated by this extremely unusually shaped hostal ever since I first saw it. Even its name is unusual, The Golden Ear, and it could refer to an ear of corn. The last time I was in the area I determined to take a closer look and possibly even stay. Unfortunately I was

disappointed – the attitude of the staff left a lot to be desired and in reality it is a little run-down, so I chose somewhere else instead.

NI/41 Hostal** Juli

Calzada de Bureba, Burgos

☎ (947) 59.50.00

🅿 G		✗	✓
🍴 ✗		🛏 ✗	
🛏 3,500		🛏 1,700	

Madrid: 290 km

This is a large unusually shaped building that appears to be frequented by truck drivers.

NI/43 Hostal** De Pancorbo

Pancorbo, Burgos

☎ (947) 35.40.00

🅿 G		✗	✓
🍴 ✗		🛏 ✗	
🛏 2,500		🛏 1,800	

Madrid: 302 km

Although the views at the back overlooking the old town and mountains are very dramatic it does not compensate for the front. This is close to the busy and noisy road. The hostal itself is reasonable but nothing special.

NI/44 HR** Poli

Pancorbo, Burgos

☎ (947) 35.40.76

🅿 G		✗ ✓
🛏 ✗		⚘ ✗
🍽 2,500		🛏 1,800
Madrid: 302 km		

The same applies here as for the De Pancorbo, the only difference is that this is not so nice and smaller.

NI/45 Hostal** El Desfiladero

Pancorbo, Burgos

☎ (947) 35.40.27

🅿 G		✗ ✓
🛏 ✗		⚘ ✗
🍽 2,800		🛏 1,700
Madrid: 305 km		

Just through the Pancorbo ravine this is an isolated, attractive area and has a rustic atmosphere. There is a wooden terrace, with some games, and also a camping site.

NI/46 H*** El Molino

Pancorbo, Burgos

☎ (947) 35.40.05

🅿 E		✗ ✓
🛏 ✓		⚘ ✓
🍽 4,950		🛏 2,575
Madrid: 306 km		

Named The Windmill, this is a very nice hotel with modern facilities. It cannot be missed when approached from the north as there is a windmill on the hill just before it.

NI/48 HR** Olaona

Elburgo, Alava

☎ (945) 30.70.04

🅿 G		✗ ✓
🛏 ✗		⚘ ✗
🍽 3,450		🛏 2,185
Madrid: 364 km		

In an isolated location, this is quite large but also a little bland.

NI/47 HR*** Tudanca

Miranda de Ebro, Burgos

☎ (947) 31.18.43

🅿 G	✗	✓
🍽 ✓	🛏	✗
🕏 4,950		🛏 3,465
Madrid: 318 km		

This is a very large place on the road through the town; the location is not too good. The facilities are excellent and include a well stocked shop. For my taste it is a little too commercial, as is it brother in Fuentespina about 160 km closer to Madrid.

NI/49 HR** Asparrena

Ilarduya, Alava

☎ (945) 30.41.28

🅿 G	✗	✓
🍽 ✗	🛏	✗
🕏 2,400		🛏 1,200
Madrid: 385 km		

An odd place with scenic views that is modern but has a garage taking up most of the ground floor.

NI/50 Hostal* Las Ventas

Eguino, Alava

☎ (945) 30.40.28

🅿 G	✗	✓
🍽 ✗	🛏	✗
🕏 2,700		🛏 1,500
Madrid: 387 km		

Quite a nice small hostal but unfortunately it is a little close to the road and might be noisy.

NI/51 H** Iturrimurri

Ciordia, Navarra

📞 (948) 56.25.63

🅿 VG		✖ ✓
🍺 ✓		🍴 ✗
🛏 4,800		🛏 2,800
Madrid: 389 km		

This is rather pleasant with many modern facilities and it also has a brother in Haro, La Rioja, on the N232 not far away.

NI/52 Hostal* Ederrena

Olazaguita, Navarra

📞 (948) 56.05.25

🅿 G		✖ ✓
🍺 ✗		🍴 ✗
🛏 2,000		🛏 ✗
Madrid: 391 km		

Located on a side road, this is rather basic and has a rural atmosphere. It is just before the town of Alsasua and the views are attractive, if you ignore the local light industry.

NI/53 HR* Hendia

Alsasua, Navarra

📞 (948) 56.20.07

🅿 O/S		✖ ✓
🍺 ✗		🍴 ✗
🛏 4,000		🛏 ✗
Madrid: 395 km		

A rather difficult place to find. From the south exit of the N1 drive towards the town and then turn left on the bridge and follow the road in the direction of the train station. From the north there is a hotel roadsign so follow that. Once there the parking is on the street but appears safe and the place itself is interesting. I arrived at lunchtime and it was full which is always a good sign.

NI/54 Hostal** Leku-On

Alsasua, Navarra

📞 (948) 56.24.52

🅿 G		✖ ✓
🍺 ✗		🍴 ✗
🛏 3,000		🛏 ✗
Madrid: 396 km		

This is a not unattractive hostal surrounded by trees and the views are not bad. It has the figure of a chef outside advertising its restaurant.

NI/55 H* Alaska**

Alsasua, Navarra

☎ (948) 56.28.02

🅿 G	✗ ✓
☕ ✓	🛏 ✗
🛏 3,500	⊨ 2,500
Madrid: 402 km	

The nicest of the hotels in this scenic area, it is quite attractive but a bit close to the road.

NI/56 Hostal* Ongi-Etorri

Idiazabal, Guipúzcoa

☎ (943) 80.12.81

🅿 G	✗ ✓
☕ ✗	🛏 ✗
🛏 2,800	⊨ ✗
Madrid: 402 km	

The first of three places next door to each other and they all have different characteristics.

The scenery is particularly nice and it is very reminiscent of the lower alpine districts of France and Switzerland. This one is on the modern side and seems to have erratic opening times as I have been past on one or two occasions when it was closed.

NI/57 Hostal* Alai

Idiazabal, Guipúzcoa

☎ (943) 80.12.83

🅿 G	✗ ✓
☕ ✗	🛏 ✗
🛏 2,800	⊨ 1,500
Madrid: 405 km	

The largest of the three places, this is a stop for bus tours and can change from being very quiet to being crowded out in a matter of minutes. The restaurant is large also.

NI/58 HR* Buenos Aires

Idiazabal, Guipúzcoa

☎ (943) 80.12.82

🅿 G		✗ ✓
☕ ✗		🛁 ✗
🛏 2,500		🚪 1,500
Madrid: 405 km		

This is my choice of the three: it is the smallest and has the most character, rather like a large chalet in style. The rooms do not have bath/shower and are perhaps a little basic. There is a small children's playground in the gardens.

NI/60 Hostal* Izarra

Legorreta, Guipúzcoa

☎ (943) 80.60.44

🅿 O/S		✗ ✓
☕ ✗		🛁 ✗
🛏 1,500		🚪 800
Madrid: 428 km		

Although small and basic this is not a bad hostal, though there is one major problem – the location. It is on a bend and only a pavement's width from this busy road. As a consequence it is noisy and the parking, on street, is very bad and not close to the hostal.

NI/59 H*** Castillo

Olaberria, Guipúzcoa

☎ (943) 88.19.58

🅿 VG		✗ ✓
☕ ✓		🛁 ✗
🛏 5,500		🚪 3,600
Madrid: 419 km		

A stylish hotel is called the Castle, there are most facilities that one would want. Unfortunately, as is often the case, the surroundings do not do it justice.

NI/61 HR*** Avenida

San Sebastián, Guipúzcoa

☎ (943) 21.20.22

🅿 VG		✗ ✓
☕ ✗		🛁 ✓
🛏 7,000		🚪 4,500
Madrid: 469 km		

A delightful hotel located on a hill overlooking this very elegant and stylish city. From the pool there is a

lovely view of the famous La Concha
(The Shell) bay and it is obvious how
it came by the name. The car parking
area is not large, on a steep incline,
and not easy to get in and out, but
otherwise this is a relaxing place to
stay.

NI/62 HR** Pellizar

San Sebastián, Guipúzcoa

☎ (943) 28.12.11

🅿 VG	✗ ✓
🍵 ✗	🛏 ✗
🛏 6,000	⇌ 4,000

Madrid: 472 km

On the north side of town and about
500 metres off the road towards
France this is a modern place that is
pleasant but lacks character. It has
most facilities one would want and is
in a residential area.

NI/63 H** Lintzirin

Oyarzun, Guipúzcoa

☎ (943) 49.20.00

🅿 E	✗ ✓
🍵 ✓	🛏 ✗
🛏 5,300	⇌ 3,390

Madrid: 475 km

The last hotel before the border town
of Irún this is large and modern. It is
also close to the Mamout
hypermarket, a good place to do last
minute shopping in Spain and related
to the Mammouth stores in France.

G   A   L   E   R   I   A   S

4 NII MADRID–ZARAGOZA–BARCELONA–LA JUNQUERA (FRANCE)

The Route

The NII (N two not N eleven) is the longest of the six main roads from Madrid and its route takes it through Zaragoza and Barcelona to the border of La Junquera, about 800 km (nearly 500 miles) away. It is convenient to break the route into three sections, and these are detailed below.

Section 1: Madrid to Zaragoza

This section covers a distance of about 318 km (200 miles) and, apart from short distances at either end, the road – in 1991 – is just single carriageway. However by 1992 the whole section will have been improved to autovia standard, either by upgrading the existing road or building new stretches. Where the latter is the case, for example the bypass around La Almunia de Doña Godina, the km count may change but the hotels listed will still be the closest to the new road. Alhama de Aragón, at a height of 664 metres, is an interesting place to visit as it is a spa town and there are a variety of cures available, most at reasonable prices.

The scenery from Madrid to Alhama is not that interesting and after Alhama there is an agricultural valley. By Calatayud it begins to change dramatically and becomes very hilly, with a strange lunar-like landscape. It is very arid and the final run in to Zaragoza is across a plateau.

Section 2: Zaragoza to Barcelona

From Zaragoza to Barcelona there are two options; either the A2 autopista or the old NII. In fact untl Lérida (Lleida) the two run parallel and all the hotels are actually on the NII. After Lérida the A2 takes a more southerly route and joins the A7 just north of Tarragona, on the Mediterraean coast. The NII continues due east straight to Barcelona and the distance is about 300 km, roughly 190 miles.

As far as hotels are concerned the opening of the A2, as an alternative and faster route, seems to have cut the prices. There are many attractive hotels that are reasonably priced. For the initial 20 km the A2 and NII are the same road, to an autovia standard. At Alfajarin the road splits and the A2 becomes an autopista toll road. The scenery on this route is rather drab and boring; the arid barren flatness is not broken up until the road enters the Provincia de Huesca at around 395 km. By 428 km a plain can be seen through the hills and the road then descends into Fraga. After a further 10 km the aridity suddenly gives way to a wide fertile valley and aptly the first hotel is called the Oasis. This valley is the beginning of an important agricultural area that lasts for about 80 km: you will see many roadside stalls offering a wide range of produce. The scenery becomes more varied as the road climbs to a height of 703 metres at La Panadella. It becomes much more dramatic at El Bruc, near the junction of the Montserrat road, where there is a particularly recommended hotel.

The rest of the journey into Barcelona is very boring but, if you are interested in football, the Nou Camp stadium is well worth a visit. It is just down the hill from the Princess Sofia hotel – which cannot be missed – on the outskirts of the city.

Section 3: Barcelona to La Junquera (France)

This last, and shortest, section of only 160 km (100 miles) also has two options. There is the A7 autopista as well as the NII but these run parallel for a great part of the journey. The NII runs along the coast for the first 35/40 miles, however the scenery would be much nicer if a railway line was not between it and the sea. As there are many hotels on this stretch I have not listed every one, just enough to give a cross-section. It is of interest to note that from Madrid to Barcelona, 620 km, there are only 49 hotels but on this section, of only 160 km, there are 23 and that is only a selection. The coastal towns along here have changed dramatically in the last quarter of a century. In the 1960s places like Callella were small self contained villages and a room in a beach front hotel cost only 50 pence a night.

Shortly past Calella the road turns inland and heads for

Gerona (Girona) and the French border. This is a rather pleasant journey through rolling hills, and at Pont de Molins there are views to the distant mountains.

For last minute shopping La Junquera is a must. This is a small border town that appears only to exist for duty free shopping; the shopkeepers seem to assume that everybody is French or Spanish as all the prices are in francs and pesetas. Store after store offer all kinds of alcoholic drinks at very reasonable prices. My particular favourite is the draught Sangria: this is stored in wooden barrels and you help yourself. At about 250 pesetas a litre, it is a bargain (this includes the plastic bottle) as it is the best and strongest that I have ever tasted.

Route Planner

REF	TOWN	NAME	PKG	KMs FROM MADRID
NII/1	Madrid	Avion	VG	14.2
NII/2	Guadalajara	Husa Paz	VG	57
NII/3	Trijueque	Liébana	G	78
NII/4	Ledanca	Km. 95	G	95
NII/5	Almadrones	Venta de Almadrones	G	103
NII/6	Sauca	Sauca	G	125
NII/7	Alcolea del Pinar	El Pinar	G	132
NII/8	Esteras de Medinaceli	Estrs. de Medinaceli	G	143
NII/9	Medinaceli	Catalan	O/S	150
NII/10	Medinaceli	Duque de Medinaceli	O/S	150
NII/11	Medinaceli	Nico Hotel 70	G	151
NII/12	Lodares de Medinaceli	Torremar	G	154
NII/13	Arcos de Jalon	Stilo	G	167.5
NII/14	Arcos de Jalon	Los Castillejos	G	170
NII/15	Alhama de Aragon	Parque	G	
NII/16	Alhama de Aragon	Guajardo	E	
NII/17	Calatayud	Calatayud	E	237
NII/18	Calatayud	Marivella	G	240
NII/19	La Almunia de Doña Godina	Rio Grio	G	263
NII/20	La Almunia de Doña Godina	Mularroya	G	263.7

REF	TOWN	NAME	PKG	KMs FROM MADRID
NII/21	La Almunia de Doña Godina	Doña Godina	G	271
NII/22	La Almunia de Doña Godina	Manolo	G	271
NII/23	La Almunia de Doña Godina	Mesón de la Ribera	G	272
NII/24	Zaragoza	El Cisne	G	309
NII/25	Zaragoza	Ramiro 1	E	320
NII/26	Alfajarin	Rausan	G	341
NII/27	Alfajarin	Casino de Zaragoza	VG	343
NII/28	Villafranca de Ebro	Pepa	G	347
NII/29	Osera de Ebro	Portal de Monegros	G	354
NII/30	Bujaraloz	El Cíervo	G	381
NII/31	Bujaraloz	Español	G	390
NII/32	Bujaraloz	Los Monegros	G	392
NII/33	Candasnos	El Pilar	G	410
NII/34	Candasnos	La Cruzanzana	G	412
NII/35	Fraga	Casanova	E	436
NII/36	Fraga	Oasis	G	445
NII/37	Lerida	Reina Isabel	E	461.5
NII/38	Lerida	Jamaica	G	462.5
NII/39	Lerida	Bimba	G	462.5
NII/40	Lerida	Condes de Urgel	VG	463
NII/41	Lerida	Ilerda	G	464
NII/42	Els Alamus	King	G	471
NII/43	Bellpuig	Bellpuig	G	497
NII/44	Villagras	Del Carmen	G	504
NII/45	La Panadella	Bayona	G	535
NII/46	La Panadella	Vell	G	535
NII/47	Argensola	La Quinta Forca	G	536
NII/48	Igualada	America	G	556.2
NII/49	El Bruc	Bruc	VG	568
NII/50	Barcelona	Mesón Castilla	E	621
NII/51	Mataro	Castell de Masta	G	649
NII/52	San Andreu de Llavaneras	Las Palmeras	G	652
NII/53	San Andreu de Llavaneras	Santa Gemma	G	652
NII/54	Sant pol de Mar	Gran Sol	G	664
NII/55	Vidreres	Margarita	G	692
NII/56	Sils	Del Rolls	G	698
NII/57	Sils	Touring	G	698
NII/58	Fornells de la Silva	Fornells Park	VG	712
NII/59	Gerona	Costa Bella	E	718
NII/60	Sarria de Ter	Jo. C. Ana	O/S	720.5
NII/61	San Julia de Ramis	Les Claus	G	721
NII/62	Mediña	Mediña	G	726

NII/63	Vilademuls	Sausa	G	732
NII/64	Bàscara	Fluvia	G	740
NII/65	Pontós-Bàscara	Santa Ana	G	741
NII/66	Pont de Molins	La Masia	G	762
NII/67	Pont de Molins	Serra	G	762
NII/68	Capmany	La Mercè Park	G	769
NII/69	Pont de Molins	Ceramica Jordi	G	773
NII/70	La Junquera	Vista Alegre	G	774
NII/71	La Junquera	Frontera	G	776
NII/72	La Junquera	Junquera	G	777
NII/73	La Junquera	Puerta de España	G	777

The Hotels

NII/1 M*** Avion

Madrid, Madrid

☎ (91) 747.62.22

🅿 VG		✗ ✓
🍽 ✓		🛏 ✓
🛏 7,900		🛏 6,500
Madrid: 14.2 km		

This motel is reached more easily from the Madrid-bound carriageway although it is possible to get there via the Puente de San Fernando from the northbound carriageway. It is quite a large complex where there are tennis courts, squash courts and a large pool, altogether rather impressive.

NII/2 H*** Husa Pax

Guadalajara, Guadalajara

☎ (911) 22.18.00

🅿 VG		✗ ✓
🍽 ✓		🛏 ✓
🛏 6,000		🛏 4,800
Madrid: 57 km		

A rather nice modern hotel with all expected facilities. Surprisingly there is an extra charge for a room with colour TV. It is well back from the autovia and therefore should not be noisy.

NII/3 Hostal** Liébana

Trijueque, Guadalajara

☎ (911) 32.00.65

P G	✗ ✓
🍷 ✗	🛏 ✗
🛏 2,800	🍴 ✗

Madrid: 78 km

A small hostal located in an isolated position, it is only accessed from the Madrid-bound carriageway.

NII/4 Hostal** Km 95

Ledanca, Guadalajara

☎ (911) 28.50.01

P G	✗ ✓
🍷 ✗	🛏 ✗
🛏 1,500	🍴 ✗

Madrid: 95 km

This has the same attributes as the Liebana, except that it is next to a service station.

NII/5 H* Venta de Almadrones

Almadrones, Guadalajara

☎ (911) 28.50.11

P G	✗ ✓
🍷 ✗	🛏 ✗
🛏 3,800	🍴 2,600

Madrid: 103 km

Only accessed from the Madrid-bound carriageway, this is of reasonable size and has large shops.

NII/6 M** Sauca

Sauca, Guadalajara

☎ (911) 30.01.29

P G	✗ ✓
🍷 ✗	🛏 ✗
🛏 4,240	🍴 2,650

Madrid: 125 km

This is an isolated position on the north side of the road but is easily reached from the south carriageway via the *cambio de sentido* – change of lanes. It is quite large and there is also a service station.

NII/7 Hostal** El Pinar

Alcolea del Pinar, Guadalajara

📞 (911) 30.00.49

🅿 G		✗	✓
🍷 ✗		🛏 ✗	
🛏 5,000		🚪 3,500	

Madrid: 132 km

A rather large and impressive looking hostal that is located on the northbound carriageway. I thought this looked attractive and stayed here one night; although the food was quite good I was disappointed with the room. All in all I consider it to be somewhat expensive.

NII/9 HR** Catalan

Medinaceli, Soria

📞 (975) 32.60.01

🅿 O/S		✗	✓
🍷 ✗		🛏 ✗	
🛏 2,800		🚪 ✗	

Madrid: 150 km

Located in the town, this is small and likely to be noisy.

NII/8 HR** Esteras

Esteras de Medina, Soria

📞 (975) 32.60.07

🅿 G		✗	✓
🍷 ✗		🛏 ✗	
🛏 3,200		🚪 1,700	

Madrid: 143 km

Relatively small and close to the road, it could be noisy.

NII/10 HR* Duque de Medinaceli

Medinaceli, Soria

📞 (975) 32.61.11

🅿 O/S		✗	✓
🍷 ✗		🛏 ✗	
🛏 5,400		🚪 4,320	

Madrid: 150 km

This hostal has some style; it is an attractive building and even has a doorman. Parking is not good, and it might be noisy at the front.

NII/11 H*** Nico Hotel 70

Medinaceli, Soria

☎ (975) 32.60.11

🅿 G		✗	✓
🍴 ✗		🛌 ✗	
🛏 6,600		🚪 4,800	
Madrid: 151 km			

A rather modern building and quite a nice hotel. Unfortunately it appears to be a place where tourist buses stop, and this spoils it somewhat.

N11/12 HR*** Torremar

Lodares de Medinaceli, Soria

☎ (975) 32.60.50

🅿 G		✗	✓
🍴 ✗		🛌 ✗	
🛏 3,500		🚪 1,750	
Madrid: 154 km			

This is quite a large building but looks a little old-fashioned. It is very close

to a natural water (*agua potable*) outlet which is ideal for filling a large cooler, preferably adding ice. This is much cheaper and healthier than buying cokes from petrol stations all day.

NII/13 Hostal* Stilo

Arecos de Jalon, Soria

☎ (975) 32.02.01

🅿 G		✗	✓
🍴 ✗		🛌 ✗	
🛏 3,500		🚪 2,000	
Madrid: 167.5 km			

A reasonable hostal but likely to be noisy, and the singles are without a bath.

NII/14 HR* Los Castillejos

Arcos de Jalon, Soria

☎ (975) 32.00.50

🅿 G		✗	✓
🍴 ✓		🛌 ✗	
🛏 3,710		🚪 ✗	
Madrid: 170 km			

Located in a pleasant open area, this has only doubles. The hotel is in a separate building from the bar.

NII/15 H*** Parque

Alhama de Aragón, Zaragoza

📞 (976) 84.00.11

🅿 G	✗ ✓
☕ ✗	🛏️ ✗
🛏️ 5,550	🚪 3,750
Madrid:	

In a thermal spa town this particular hotel is large and grand; there is even a walkway over the road to a very pleasant park. Remedies at various prices are available, but the facilities close at 1930 in the summer.

NII/16 Hostal** Guajardo

Alhama de Aragón, Zaragoza

📞 (976) 84.00.02

🅿 E	✗ ✓
☕ ✗	🛏️ ✗
🛏️ 2,600	🚪 1,150
Madrid:	

This hostal is just past the previous much larger hotel. It is very old-fashioned and rather unusual; unfortunately the singles are without a bath/shower. A private lockup

garage is available for an extra 300 pesetas a night, and as there is no nearby on-street parking this is a necessity if you stay here.

NII/17 H*** Calatayud

Calatayud, Zaragoza

📞 (976) 88.52.71

🅿 E	✗ ✓
☕ ✓	🛏️ ✗
🛏️ 5,500	🚪 3,400
Madrid: 237 km	

A particularly nice large hotel that is located just to the north of town. There are private garages for 300 a night extra and there is a large *piscina municipal* just across the road.

NII/18 HR** Marivella

Calatayud, Zaragoza

📞 (976) 88.12.37

🅿 G	✗ ✓
☕ ✗	🛏️ ✗
🛏️ 3,300	🚪 2,700
Madrid: 240 km	

Rather a nice place in a quiet location. It is a shame that the pool next door is private.

NII/19 H** Rio Grio

La Almunia de Doña Godina,
Zaragoza

☎ (976) 60.00.01

🅿 G		✗ ✓
☕ ✗		🛏 ✗
🛎 4,558		🍴 3,074
Madrid: 263 km		

This is a very nice hotel that has a
ceramic and garden centre next door.

NII/20 HR* Mularroya

La Almunia de Doña Godina,
Zaragoza

☎ (976) 60.00.55

🅿 G		✗ ✓
☕ ✗		🛏 ✗
🛎 3,000		🍴 1,600
Madrid: 263.7 km		

Just past the previous place, this is
quite interesting although smaller.

NII/21 HR* Doña Godina

Avda. Generalisimo, 22, La Almunia
de Doña Godina, Zaragoza

☎ (976) 60.02.69

🅿 G		✗ ✓
☕ ✗		🛏 ✗
🛎 2,500		🍴 1,200
Madrid: 271 km		

Off the NII, and in the town, this will
be much quieter. It is a nice place,
but the singles do not have a bath: a
double without is only 2,000.

NII/22 HR* Manolo

Avda. Zaragoza, 12, La Almunia de
Doña Godina, Zaragoza

☎ (976) 60.11.38

🅿 G		✗ ✓
☕ ✓		🛏 ✗
🛎 2,000		🍴 1,300
Madrid: 271 km		

Again this is on the main road in
town; it is slightly old-fashioned but
relatively inexpensive. Rooms
without bath are 1,000 and 1,700
respectively.

NII/23 HR* Mesón de la Ribera

La Almunia de Doña Godina,
Zaragoza

☎ (976) 60.00.92

🅿 G	✗ ✓
☕ ✗	⚬ ✗
🛏 1,200	🚪 600
Madrid: 272 km	

Just off the new road, this is on the
edge of a town. The rooms are very
basic but if you just want a night's
sleep and are not too concerned
about the surroundings this is the
place. When I stayed here several
years ago, the food was not bad at all.

NII/25 H*** Ramiro 1

Zaragoza, Zaragoza

☎ (976) 89.27.20

🅿 E	✗ ✓
☕ ✗	⚬ ✗
🛏 6,000	🚪 4,500
Madrid: 320 km	

A city centre hotel, fully air-
conditioned, with colour TV in every
room. Private parking facilities are
nearby.

NII/24 H*** El Cisne

Zaragoza, Zaragoza

☎ (976) 33.20.00

🅿 G	✗ ✓
☕ ✓	⚬ ✓
🛏 6,000	🚪 4,000
Madrid: 309 km	

Located on the northbound
carriageway, 10 minutes south of
Zaragoza, this is called The Swan. The
restaurant advertises that it has
typical Aragon food, and there is also
a go-cart track.

NII/26 HR** Rausan

Alfajarin, Zaragoza

☎ (976) 10.00.02

🅿 G	✗ ✓
☕ ✗	⚬ ✗
🛏 3,360	🚪 2,465
Madrid: 341 km	

This is just to the north of Zaragoza,
by Exit 1 of the A2 autopista. As
might be expected it is similar to a
service area on a motorway, large
and bland.

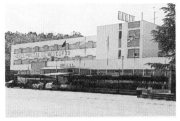

NII/29 HR* Portal de Monegros

Osera de Ebro, Zaragoza

☎ (976) 16.72.12

🅿 G		✗	✓
🍽	✓	🛏	✓
🛏 4,500		🚗 3,200	

Madrid: 354 km

This is a little old, but nice; it has a pool and children's zone, and is next to a service station.

NII/27 H**** Casino de Zaragoza

Alfajarin, Zaragoza

☎ (976) 10.00.04

🅿 VG		✗	✓
🍽	✓	🛏	✓
🛏 11,000		🚗 8,500	

Madrid: 343 km

Yes, this really is a casino: it advertises itself as 'spectacular' and that it certainly is. Besides the casino there is a shooting range, pool, tennis, sauna, solarium and also massage facilities. The rooms are as grand as you might expect. Turn off the NII at the sign, go up the hill to the north and this is on its own at the top.

NII/30 H** El Cíervo

Bujaraloz, Zaragoza

☎ (976) 17.30.11

🅿 G		✗	✓
🍽 ✗		🛏	✗
🛏 3,200		🚗 2,000	

Madrid: 381 km

Called The Stag, this has a style that fits the name. It is isolated and has a rustic, hunting atmosphere; the prices are reasonable.

NII/28 HR** Pepa

Villafranca de Ebo, Zaragoza

☎ (976) 10.05.00

🅿 G		✗	✓
🍽 ✗		🛏	✗
🛏 3,000		🚗 1,500	

Madrid: 347 km

Located in a fairly isolated position, this is of medium-size and has games and a shop in the bar. Access to the A2 for Zaragoza is Exit 1 and for Barcelona it is Exit 2 at Pina de Ebro.

NII/31 P** Español

Bujaraloz, Zaragoza

☎ (976) 17.31.92   .

🅿 G		✗ ✓
☕ ✗		🍴 ✗
🛏 3,150		🛏 1,750
Madrid: 390 km		

A medium-size place that appears modern from the outside. It is close to Exit 3 of the autopista.

NII/32 HR* Los Monegros

Bujaraloz, Zaragoza

☎ (976) 17.30.21

🅿 G		✗ ✓
☕ ✗		🍴 ✗
🛏 2,600		🛏 1,400
Madrid: 392 km		

On the north side of the road, this is a strange building that has a small service station just outside.

NII/33 CH El Pilar

Candasnos, Huesca

☎ (974) 46.30.17

🅿 G		✗ ✓
☕ ✗		🍴 ✗
🛏 1,800		🛏 800
Madrid: 410 km		

Located in a very small town, this is small and close to the road. The singles do not have a bath/shower.

NII/34 H* La Cruzanzana

Candasnos, Huesca

☎ (974) 46.30.25

🅿 G		✗ ✓
☕ ✗		🍴 ✗
🛏 3,000		🛏 1,500
Madrid: 412 km		

Located in an isolated position, this has a charming style both inside and out. The prices are very reasonable.

NII/35 H* Casanova

Fraga, Huesca

☏ (974) 47.01.50

🅿 E		✗	✓
☕ ✓		⚹	✗
🛏 3,500		🍽 2,000	

Madrid: 436 km

This is a large nice place right in the centre of Fraga, and therefore could possibly be noisy. Private garage facilities are an extra 1,000.

NII/36 Hostal** Oasis

Fraga, Huesca

☏ (974) 47.06.54

🅿 G		✗	✓
☕ ✗		⚹	✗
🛏 3,700		🍽 1,400	

Madrid: 445 km

A suitably-named place, as the arid countryside suddenly gives way to a green fertile valley, even in August. The singles do not have a bath/shower.

NII/37 H* Reina Isabel

Lérida, Lérida

☏ (973) 26.01.51

🅿 E		✗	✓
☕ ✗		🍽 1,800	
🛏 3,000		⚹	✗

Madrid: 461.5 km

I quite like this isolated hotel where the set meals are 800, and private garage facilities 300 extra.

NII/38 H** Jamaica

Lérida, Lérida

☏ (973) 26.51.00

🅿 G		✗	✓
☕ ✗		⚹	✗
🛏 4,500		🍽 2,200	

Madrid: 462.5 km

This is a large hotel that has a slightly old-fashioned style.

NII/39 Hostal* Bimba

Lérida, Lérida

☎ (973) 26.00.26

🅿 G	✗ ✓
☕ ✗	🧹 ✗
🛏 2,200	🛏 1,100

Madrid: 462.5 km

This hostal is very run down indeed; it does, though, have a large *Horno de Asar* (open brick oven) in the restaurant.

NII/40 H**** Condes de Urgel

Lérida, Lérida

☎ (973) 20.23.00

🅿 VG	✗ ✓
☕ ✓	🧹 ✗
🛏 7,142	🛏 4,464

Madrid: 463 km

A very large four-star hotel with all expected facilities except a pool.

NII/41 H** Ilerda

Lérida, Lérida

☎ (973) 20.07.50

🅿 G	✗ ✓
☕ ✓	🧹 ✗
🛏 3,800	🛏 2,500

Madrid: 464 km

Another large impressive hotel, part Renault showroom. For an extra 1,000 single, and 900 double, you get air-conditioning, TV, cable video and background music.

NII/42 H* King

Ela Alamus, Lérida

☎ (973) 19.91.88

🅿 G	✗ ✓
☕ ✗	🧹 ✗
🛏 4,500	🛏 2,700

Madrid: 471 km

Just to the east of Lérida this is a very nice modern place that is only spoilt by its bland location.

NII/43 Hostal** Bellpuig

Bellpuig, Lérida

📞 (973) 32.02.25

🅿 G		✕ ✓
💬 ✗		🛁 ✗
🛏 2,600		🍴 1,600

Madrid: 497 km

A large hostal with a big bar, located behind a service station.

NII/44 Hostal* Del Carmen

Villagras, Lérida

📞 (973) 31.10.00

🅿 G		✕ ✓
💬 ✗		🛁 ✗
🛏 5,000		🍴 2,500

Madrid: 504 km

Another large hostal, it is very nice, but possibly a touch expensive.

NII/45 H* Bayona

La Panadella, Barcelona

📞 (93) 809.20.11

🅿 G		✕ ✓
💬 ✗		🛁 ✗
🛏 3,500		🍴 2,100

Madrid: 535 km

Much larger than the other hotel here, it is nice but does not have such a pleasant atmosphere. The location is about 730 metres above sea level.

NII/46 Hostal** Vell

La Panadella, Barcelona

📞 (93) 809.20.08

🅿 G		✕ ✓
💬 ✗		🛁 ✗
🛏 3,000		🍴 1,500

Madrid: 535 km

Just past the Bayona, this does not look much from the outside but it is a different story inside. The open brickwork and wooden panelling give it a charming atmosphere.

NII/47 Hostal* La Quinta Forca

Argensola, Barcelona

☎ (93) 809.20.52

🅿 G	✗ ✓
☕ ✗	✂ ✗
🛏 2.400	🛏 1,200
Madrid: 536 km	

A rather delightful small hostal that is set well back from the road in a location that has pretty views. It is also very reasonably priced so, if you fancy it, book ahead to ensure a room.

NII/48 H*** America

Igualada, Barcelona

☎ (93) 803.10.00

🅿 VG	✗ ✓
☕ ✓	✂ ✓
🛏 6,950	🛏 4,700
Madrid: 556.2 km	

A very large hotel that has all modern facilities and a children's playground.

NII/49 H*** Bruc

El Bruc, Barcelona

☎ (93) 771.00.61

🅿 VG	✗ ✓
☕ ✓	✂ ✓
🛏 5,500	🛏 3,900
Madrid: 568 km	

This is a truly amazing place close to the Montserrat road with a background of spectacular mountains. There are five saloons with space for over 1,000 people, two discos and a beautiful swimming pool complex that is partly covered by a huge marquee. Set in an isolated position, this is most impressive and not too expensive.

NII/50 H*** Mesón Castilla

Calle Valldoncella 5, Barcelona, 08001

☎ (93) 735.04.61
Fax: (93) 318.21.82

🅿 E	✗ ✓
☕ ✗	✂ ✗
🛏 7,350	🛏 4,825
Madrid: 621 km	

In Barcelona one is spoilt for choice where hotels are concerned; however those with private parking facilities, which are a must, are usually very expensive. I have chosen this one because it is part of the Husa chain; it is central – close to the Ramblas, Plaza Catalunya and the cathedral – also it is quiet and not too expensive. A drawback is that it is in a back street and a little difficult to find: but once there, put the car in the garage next door at only 1,100 a day, and go out to explore the city.

NII/51 H*** Castell de Masta

Mataro, Barcelona

☎ (93) 790.10.44

🅿 G	✕ ✓
🍵 ✓	🛏 ✓
🛏 6,400	🛏 5,000

Madrid: 649 km

Called the Masta Castle, this is very nice with much style: it advertises that it has a 16th century atmosphere. It is also close to the sea.

NII/53 HR** Santa Gemma

San Andreu de Llavanaras, Barcelona

☎ (93) 792.61.25

🅿 G	✕ ✓
🍵 ✗	🛏 ✗
🛏 5,000	🛏 3,500

Madrid: 652 km

Next to the previous hostal, this is also on a hill with good sea views.

NII/52 HR** Las Palmeras

San Andreu de Llavaneras, Barcelona

☎ (93) 792.60.02

🅿 G	✕ ✓
🍵 ✗	🛏 ✓
🛏 5,000	🛏 3,500

Madrid: 652 km

This is somewhat different. The hostal and pool are on a hill with good sea views, while the restaurant is down close to the busy NII.

NII/54 H*** Gran Sol

Sant Pol de Mar, Barcelona

☎ (93) 760.00.51

🅿 G	✕ ✓
🍵 ✓	🛏 ✓
🛏 7.450	🛏 5.200

Madrid: 664 km

A very nice modern hotel located above the village of Sant Pol de Mar, every room having magnificent views over the Mediterranean (see below). A double room for single use is 5,960 and all rooms have colour TV; if I have one complaint it is that the rooms are a little too small. Dinner and lunch are 1,800: breakfast is 650.

NII/55 H* Margarita

Vidreres, Gerona

☎ (972) 85.01.12

🅿 G		✖ ✓
☕ ✗		🍴 ✗
🛏 4,000		🛏 2,640
Madrid: 692 km		

Located in an isolated position, this is slightly old-fashioned but nice. It is close to Exit 7 of the A7.

NII/56 Hostal* Del Rolls

Sils, Gerona

☎ (972) 85.32.29

🅿 G		✖ ✓
☕ ✓		🍴 ✗
🛏 3,500		🛏 1,750
Madrid: 698 km		

A very large and impressive building that is also nice inside. Singles without bath are 1,000.

NII/57 H* Touring

Sils, Gerona

☎ (972) 85.30.66

🅿 G		✖ ✓
☕ ✗		🍴 ✗
🛏 6,000		🛏 4,000
Madrid: 698 km		

This is not so large as the Del Rolls next door, but it is very nice and classy as shown in the prices. There are tennis courts and a children's park.

NII/58 H*** Fornells Park

Fornells de la Silva, Gerona

☎ (972) 47.61.25

🅿 VG		✖ ✓
☕ ✓		🍴 ✓
🛏 7,500		🛏 5,100
Madrid: 712 km		

Located just south of Gerona this is a very gracious hotel with a pool and children's playground, surrounded by woods and gardens.

NII/59 H*** Costa Bella

Gerona, Gerona

☎ (972) 20.22.03

🅿 E	✗ ✓
🍽 ✗	🛏 ✗
🛏 8,200	🚪 5,700

Madrid: 712 km

A little north of the city, across from the hospital, this is a good modern hotel. Private parking is 800 extra.

NII/60 H** Jo. C. Ana

Sarria de Ter, Gerona

☎ (972) 20.74.02

🅿 O/S	✗ ✓
🍽 ✗	🛏 ✗
🛏 4,500	🚪 2,500

Madrid: 720.5 km

The parking here is really bad, and due to its location directly across from a Coca Cola bottling plant and close to the main road it is likely to be noisy. It is more easily accessible from the northbound carriageway.

NII/61 Hostal* Les Claus

San Julia de Ramis, Gerona

☎ (972) 21.40.19

🅿 G	✗ ✓
🍽 ✗	🛏 ✗
🛏 2,200	🚪 1,500

Madrid: 721 km

Accessible more easily from the northbound carriageway, this is rather a strange place. It is full of antiques, clocks and miniatures. The back room has a pool table. Rather noisy.

NII/62 H** Mediña

Mediña, Gerona

☎ (972) 49.80.00

🅿 G	✗ ✓
🍽 ✗	🛏 ✗
🛏 3,200	🚪 1,500

Madrid: 726 km

In an interesting location, across from an old bridge, this is a medium-size hotel.

NII/63 Hostal** Sausa

Vilademuls, Gerona

☎ (972) 56.01.55

🅿 G	✗ ✓
🍴 ✓	🛏 ✓
🛏 4,000	🛏 2,000
Madrid: 732 km	

I am rather taken by this place; it is nice and modern and there is a lovely selection of food laid out in the bar. The tank full of lobsters looked particularly tempting.

NII/64 Hostal* Fluvia

Bàscara, Gerona

☎ (972) 56.00.14

🅿 G	✗ ✓
🍴 ✗	🛏 ✗
🛏 3,000	🛏 2,200
Madrid: 740 km	

A small clean modern hostal, where rooms without bath are 1,500 and 2,500 respectively.

NII/65 H* Santa Anna

Pontós-Bàscara, Gerona

☎ (972) 56.00.22

🅿 G	✗ ✓
🍴 ✗	🛏 ✗
🛏 2,200	🛏 1,000
Madrid: 741 km	

This is quite large with an old style. It is in an isolated position.

NII/66 H* La Masia

Pont de Molins, Gerona

☎ (972) 50.33.40

🅿 G	✗ ✓
🍴 ✗	🛏 ✗
🛏 4,100	🛏 3,200
Madrid: 762 km	

This is in an isolated position, and is not large. The mountains in the background provide pretty views.

NII/67 HR* Serra

Pont de Molins, Gerona

☎ (972) 52.83.93

🅿 G		✗	✓
☕ ✗		🛏	✗
🛏 2,100		🛏 1,250	

Madrid: 762 km

In an isolated position, this again has pleasant views to the mountains.

NII/69 P* Ceramica Jordi

Pont de Molins, Gerona

☎ (972) None

🅿 G		✗	✓
☕ ✗		🛏	✗
🛏 2,900		🛏	✗

Madrid: 773 km

Strangely, this is a pension located above a ceramic and souvenir shop, a most unusual combination.

NII/68 H** La Mercè Park

Capmany, Gerona

☎ (972) 54.90.38

🅿 G		✗	✓
☕ ✓		🛏	✗
🛏 6,200		🛏 4,800	

Madrid: 769 km

A large hotel in a pleasant location. A river runs behind but do not expect to find water in it all year. There is a 'typical' restaurant and even a chapel. Rooms with front views are 3,100 and 5,500 respectively.

NII/70 Hostal* Vista Alegre

La Junquera, Gerona

☎ (972) 55.40.78

🅿 G		✗	✓
☕ ✗		🛏	✗
🛏 2,500		🛏 1,250	

Madrid: 774 km

Located on the outskirts of town this is likely to be noisy as it is close to the road and also a service station.

NII/71 H** Frontera

La Junquera, Gerona

☎ (972) 55.40.50

🅿 G		✗	✓
🍷	✓	🛏	✗
🛏 3,500		🚪 2,000	

Madrid: 776 km

Also close to the town, this has a money exchange. A double with only a shower is 250 less.

NII/72 H** Junquera

La Junquera, Gerona

☎ (972) 55.41.00

🅿 G		✗	✓
🍷	✗	🛏	✗
🛏 3,700		🚪 2,450	

Madrid: 777 km

Another medium-sized place that also has a money changing office.

NII/73 H*** Puerta de España

La Junquera, Gerona

☎ (972) 55.41.20

🅿 G		✗	✓
🍷	✓	🛏	✗
🛏 6,307		🚪 4,134	

Madrid: 777 km

Named the Gate of Spain, this is either the first or last hotel in Spain, depending upon your direction. It is right next to the border control in a busy noisy area. There is a shop and all rooms have TV but, for me, it is expensive and I would prefer a nicer location.

NIII MADRID-VALENCIA

The Route

At only 330 km (just over 200 miles) this is the shortest, and
least interesting, of the six main routes from Madrid. It is also
the road that has been least improved as, except for short
stretches at either end, it is single carriageway.

About the only thing that is different in the first 180 km or
so is the reservoir that is just to the north of the Hotel Claridge
at Pantano de Alarcon. The most interesting and spectacular
view is at Minglanilla by the Hotel Mirador de Contreras
(Viewpoint of Contreras), this is well worth a stop for a few
minutes. On one side is the Contreras reservoir and on the
other a deep valley; of particular note is the old road that
winds down the hills to a bridge.

After Minglanilla the road enters the area of Utiel and
Requena, which is famous for its wine, and then passes into a
heavily wooded area before descending into the industrial
town of Buñol. Chiva, the next town, has an attractive
location on a hill, and after that the only point of interest
before the airport and suburbs of Valencia is the large
university complex to the north.

Route Planner

REF	TOWN	NAME	PKG	KMs FROM MADRID
NIII/1	Fuentidueña	Miralrio	G	62.5
NIII/2	Tarancon	Sur	G	82
NIII/3	Tarancon	Pilcar	G	83
NIII/4	Tarancon	Stop	G	83.5
NIII/5	Saelices	Araceli	G	101.5
NIII/6	Montalbo	Castilla	G	116
NIII/7	Montalbo	El Valencia	G	116
NIII/8	Montalbo	Casablanca	G	116

REF	TOWN	NAME	PKG	KMs FROM MADRID
NIII/9	Villares del Saz	El Pilar	G	131
NIII/10	Villares del Saz	SolySombra	G	132
NIII/11	Cervares del Llano	San Fermin	G	141
NIII/12	La Almarcha	San Cristobal	G	154
NIII/13	Honrubia	Marino	G	167
NIII/14	Honrubia	Jose	G	167
NIII/15	Pantano de Alarcon	Claridge	G	184.6
NIII/16	Motilla del Palancar	Cuenca	G	198.5
NIII/17	Motilla del Palancar	Del Sol	VG	199
NIII/18	Motilla del Palancar	Tres Hermanos	O/S	199
NIII/19	Motilla del Palancar	Gijón	G	199.5
NIII/20	Castillejo de Iniesta	Montes	G	211
NIII/21	Castillejo de Iniesta	La Estrella	G	212
NIII/22	Graja de Iniesta	Pepe	G	219
NIII/23	Graja de Iniesta	San Jorge	G	220
NIII/24	Graja de Iniesta	Pepe II	G	220
NIII/25	Minglanilla	Miralles	G	226
NIII/26	Minglanilla	La Casona	G	229
NIII/27	Minglanilla	Mirador de Contreras	G	235
NIII/28	Utiel	Potajero Chico	G	263
NIII/29	Requena	Sol II	G	272
NIII/30	Requena	Sol	O/S	276
NIII/31	Requena	Patilla	G	277
NIII/32	Requena	Requena	G	284
NIII/33	Siete Aguas	Los Alamos	G	294
NIII/34	Buñol	Hajo Jilton	G	305.7
NIII/35	Chiva	Ignacio	G	311.5
NIII/36	Chiva	Loma del Castillo	G	321
NIII/37	Chiva	La Carreta	E	330

G   A   L   E   R   I   A   S

The Hotels

NIII/1 HR* Miralrio

Fuentidueña de Tajo, Madrid

☎ (91) 872.81.98

🅿 G	✗ ✓
☕ ✗	✂ ✗
🛏 2,200	⇄ 1,500

Madrid: 62.5 km

This has an unusual exterior and is not very large. It can only be accessed from the Valencia-bound carriageway.

NIII/2 H** Sur

Tarancon, Cuenca

☎ (966) 11.06.00

🅿 G	✗ ✓
☕ ✗	✂ ✗
🛏 4,350	⇄ 2,800

Madrid: 82 km

A medium-sized hotel that has a large restaurant.

NIII/3 HR* Pilcar

Tarancon, Cuenca

☎ (966) 11.06.25

🅿 G	✗ ✓
☕ ✗	✂ ✗
🛏 2,700	⇄ 1,500

Madrid: 83 km

A rather small undistinguished hostal-residencía.

NIII/4 HR* Stop

Tarancon, Cuenca

☎ (966) 11.01.00

🅿 G	✗ ✓
☕ ✗	✂ ✗
🛏 2,300	⇄ 1,350

Madrid: 83.3 km

This name appears now and again and personally I do not like it. However this Stop appears to be quite pleasant; it has a two-fork restaurant.

NIII/5 HR* Araceli

Saelices, Cuenca

☎ (966)

🅿 G		✗	✓
☕ ✗		🛏 ✗	
🏠 2,800		🍴 1,450	

Madrid: 101.5 km

Located just to the west of the town this has an unusual shape. It is not very large but is kept clean and neat.

NIII/6 H** Castilla

Montalbo, Cuenca

☎ (966) 13.00.14

🅿 G		✗	✓
☕ ✗		🛏 ✗	
🏠 2,780		🍴 1,140	

Madrid: 116 km

A nice new hotel that has a pleasant bar. The prices are very reasonable.

NIII/7 P* El Valencia

Montalbo, Cuenca

☎ (966) 13.01.36

🅿 G		✗	✓
☕ ✗		🛏 ✗	
🏠 1,600		🍴 800	

Madrid: 116 km

This is a little older than the others in Montalbo, but to compensate, it has more atmosphere as well as an attractive restaurant. The single rooms do not have a bath or shower.

NIII/8 P** Casablanca

Montalbo, Cuenca

☎ (966) 13.03.03

🅿 G		✗	✓
☕ ✓		🛏 ✗	
🏠 6,000		🍴 4,000	

Madrid: 116 km

Called the Whitehouse, it is quite large and also sells hams and cheeses. However the price appears to be far too expensive for what it is.

NIII/9 CH El Pilar

Villares del Saz, Cuenca

📞 (966) 29.81.59

🅿 G	✗ ✓
🍷 ✗	🛗 ✗
🛏 2,000	🚪 1,000

Madrid: 131 km

A small guest house that is basically just rooms above a bar and restaurant. I would be surprised if the singles have a bath/shower.

NIII/10 Hostal* SolySombra

Villares del Saz, Cuenca

📞 (966) 29.80.84

🅿 G	✗ ✓
🍷 ✗	🛗 ✗
🛏 1,600	🚪 800

Madrid: 132 km

Unusually named Sun and Shade, this is rather a plain hostal that has games in the bar.

NIII/11 Hostal* San Fermin

Cervera del Llano, Cuenca

📞 (966) 29.40.10

🅿 G	✗ ✓
🍷 ✗	🛗 ✗
🛏 2,200	🚪 1,000

Madrid: 141 km

In an isolated position, the building is modern but plain, and it is attractive inside.

NIII/12 HR* San Christobal

La Almarcha, Cuenca

📞 (966) 29.10.24

🅿 G	✗ ✓
🍷 ✗	🛗 ✗
🛏 1,400	🚪 700

Madrid: 154 km

Located close to the junction of the Belmonte/Cuenca road, this is rather basic. The singles do not have a bath/shower.

NIII/13 P* Marino

Honrubia, Cuenca

☏ (966) 29.20.33

🅿 G		✕	✓
☕	✗	🛁	✗
🛏 2,500		🛏	✗

Madrid: 167 km

A small neat pension that only has double rooms.

NIII/14 P* Jose

Honrubia, Cuenca

☏ (966) 29.20.08

🅿 G		✕	✓
☕	✗	🛁	✗
🛏 1,900		🛏 700	

Madrid: 167 km

This is rather basic. The singles do not have a bath/shower.

NIII/15 H*** Claridge

Pantano de Alarcon, Cuenca

☏ (966) 33.11.50

🅿 G		✕	✓
☕	✓	🛁	✓
🛏 4,790		🛏 3,330	

Madrid: 184.6 km

Located in a very isolated position, with views across to a large reservoir, this is an impressive hotel that has been strangely designed. It has rather an odd name for this part of the world.

NIII/16 CH Cuenca

Motilla del Palancar, Cuenca

☏ (966) 33.10.44

🅿 G		✕	✓
☕	✗	🛁	✗
🛏 2,200		🛏 1,100	

Madrid: 198.5 km

There is nothing special about this small basic guest house.

NIII/17 H** Del Sol

Motilla del Palancar, Cuenca

☎ (966) 33.10.25

🅿 VG	✗ ✓
☕ ✗	⚙ ✗
🛏 3,750	🛏 2,200
Madrid: 199 km	

This is fairly large and has a delightfully old-fashioned style. There are many outbuildings, which are used as car parks. It is just before the junction with the main Cuenca road. It appears to be very good value for money.

NIII/18 HR* Tres Hermanos

Motilla del Palancar, Cuenca

☎ (966)

🅿 O/S	✗ ✓
☕ ✗	⚙ ✗
🛏 2,525	🛏 1,450
Madrid: 199 km	

Situated at the junction of the Cuenca road this is small and likely to be particularly noisy. It has an interesting selection of local goods for sale.

NIII/19 H** Gijón

Motilla del Palancar, Cuenca

☎ (96) 33.10.01

🅿 G	✗ ✓
☕ ✓	⚙ ✗
🛏 3,220	🛏 2,575
Madrid: 199.5 km	

Located in the centre of town, next to a small park, this is modern and has some style, I do not know the significance of the name, as Gijón is a long way away in northern Spain.

NIII/20 F Montes

Castillejo de Iniesta, Cuenca

☎ (96) 218.73.08

🅿 G	✗ ✓
☕ ✗	⚙ ✗
🛏 1,700	🛏 800
Madrid: 211 km	

A large building for a Fonda. This has a very basic bar and a petrol station is close by. The singles do not have a bath/shower.

NIII/21 P* La Estrella

Castillejo de Iniesta, Cuenca

☎ (96) 218.73.04

🅿 G	✘ ✓
☕ ✘	🔧 ✘
🛏 2,100	🛏 1,050
Madrid: 212 km	

A small neat pension that has a barbecue and sells hams and cheeses. Rooms without baths are 825 and 1650 for singles and doubles respectively.

NIII/22 Hostal* Pepe

Graja de Iniesta, Cuenca

☎ (96) 218.73.28

🅿 G	✘ ✓
☕ ✘	🔧 ✘
🛏 3,000	🛏 1,500
Madrid: 219 km	

Located on a corner between two roads this is quite large and has plenty of car parking space. The people were very friendly and that made for a pleasant atmosphere. There is a Pepe II just up the road which is much smaller.

NIII/23 HR* San Jorge

Graja de Iniesta, Cuenca

☎ (96) 218.77.04

🅿 G	✘ ✓
☕ ✘	🔧 ✘
🛏 3,000	🛏 1,500
Madrid: 220 km	

This is small and perhaps somewhat expensive.

NIII/24 Hostal* Pepe II

Graja de Iniesta, Cuenca

☎ (96) 218.72.00

🅿 G	✘ ✓
☕ ✘	🔧 ✘
🛏 2,000	🛏 1,000
Madrid: 220 km	

Small, and in an isolated position. The people here were very unfriendly on the day I visited.

NIII/25 HR* Miralles

Minglanilla, Cuenca

☎ (96) 218.70.18

🅿 G	✗ ✓
🍴 ✗	🛏 ✗
🛏 1,900	🍴 1,070

Madrid: 226 km

Located at the bottom of a hill, just outside town, this is quite nice but the large building seems a little run down. It has a small shop and is reasonably priced.

NIII/26 H** La Casona

Minglanilla, Cuenca

☎ (96) 218.79.00

🅿 G	✗ ✓
🍴 ✗	🛏 ✗
🛏 3,400	🍴 1,700

Madrid: 229 km

A very nice modern hotel in an isolated position. There are large reception rooms for weddings and banquets so it might be noisy at weekends.

NIII/27 H* Mirador de Contreras

Minglanilla, Cuenca

☎ (96) 218.61.71

🅿 G	✗ ✓
🍴 ✗	🛏 ✗
🛏 2,540	🍴 1,600

Madrid: 235 km

Located in a strange and isolated position this hotel has truly spectacular views on either side of the road. The building is not unattractive either.

NIII/28 HR** Potajero Chico

Utiel, Valencia

☎ (96) 217.00.09

🅿 G	✗ ✓
🍴 ✗	🛏 ✗
🛏 2,200	🍴 1,100

Madrid: 263 km

A large plain hostal set back a little from this busy road. It sells local produce, including rice.

NIII/29 Motel Sol II

Requena, Valencia

☎ (96) 230.00.58

🅿 G		✗ ✓
🍷 ✗		🍴 ✗
🛏 4,000		🛏 3,500

Madrid: 272 km

Located in the heart of the wine
producing area, the restaurant
overlooks vineyards. The rooms are
in a separate modern building.

NIII/30 P* Sol

Requena, Valencia

☎ (96) 230.00.90

🅿 O/S		✗ ✓
🍷 ✗		🍴 ✗
🛏 1,400		🛏 700

Madrid: 276 km

This is very odd. From the outside it
does not look at all good, but inside it
is much more interesting and has a
selection of local produce for sale.
It is basic, single rooms do not have
a bath/shower, and could be noisy as
it is close to the road.

NIII/31 Hostal* Patilla

Requena, Valencia

☎ (96) 230.00.60

🅿 G		✗ ✓
🍷 ✗		🍴 ✗
🛏 2,000		🛏 1,000

Madrid: 277 km

On the eastern side of Requena, this
hostal is most easily accessed from
the Valencia-bound carriageway.
It could be noisy, especially at the
front, and the rooms do not have
bath/showers.

NIII/32 Hostal* Requena

Requena, Valencia

☎ (96) 230.09.82

🅿 G		✗ ✓
🍷 ✗		🍴 ✗
🛏 4,500		🛏 3,000

Madrid: 284 km

Located in an isolated position this is
rather basic for the prices.

NIII/33 HR** Los Alamos

Siete Aguas, Valencia

☎ (96) 234.00.57

🅿 G	✗ ✓
☕ ✗	🛏 ✗
🛏 3,000	🚻 2,000
Madrid: 294 km	

Set back from the road behind a petrol station in a reasonably modern building, on the edge of an attractive wooded area.

NIII/35 CH Ignaciao

Chiva, Valencia

☎ (96) 252.00.08

🅿 G	✗ ✓
☕ ✗	🛏 ✓
🛏 1,800	🚻 900
Madrid: 311.5 km	

This is located in a service road off the Valencia-bound carriageway. For a guest house it is very large and there is a reasonably large pool; however it is close to the busy road and is probably noisy.

NIII/36 Hostal* Loma del Castillo

Chiva, Valencia

☎ (96) 252.00.09

🅿 G	✗ ✓
☕ ✗	🛏 ✓
🛏 2,650	🚻 1,700
Madrid: 321 km	

A reasonably sized place with interesting views over the town. The food is not at all bad. If you are looking for a pool check first: it was drained when I was there. The rooms are not great but are adequate.

NIII/34 CH Hajo Jilton

Buñol, Valencia

☎ (96) 250.11.50

🅿 G	✗ ✓
☕ ✗	🛏 ✗
🛏 1,500	🚻 750
Madrid: 305.7 km	

A very small guest house that, besides being likely to be noisy, is located in a heavily industrialised area. The singles do not have a bath/ shower.

NIII/37 M*** La Carreta

Chiva, Valencia

☎ (96) 251.11.00

🅿 E		✕ ✓
☕ ✓		🍴 ✓
🛏 6,148		🛏 3,952

Madrid: 330 km

This is a beautiful motel that has grace and style; it is called The Waggon. There is a disco and a good-sized pool.

G   A   L   E   R   I   A   S

6NIV MADRID–BAILÉN–CÓRDOBA–SEVILLA–JEREZ–CÁDIZ

The Route

This route of 663 km (approximately 415 miles) is not of much interest scenically or in any other way. One advantage though is that it is a fast easy road that is toll-free and the only option is between Sevilla and Cádiz where the autopista is a faster, but expensive, alternative to the NIV. There are 102 hotels, more than on any other route.

The road traverses the Madrid plateau for the first 70 km and the only point of interest is the large monument to the east of the road, about 15 km south of Madrid. It then descends on to the plains of La Mancha and the countryside is more or less flat all the way to the border with Andalucia, nearly 160 km (100 miles) away. There is an exception at Puerto Lápice, at 134 km; here there are two large hills on either side of the road and one is topped by those windmills made famous by Don Quixote. The road bypasses the two largest towns, Manzanares and Valdepeñas, that are important for the wine they produce. Although the majority is ordinary table wine that does not have a good reputation there are many wines that are of better quality. To taste, and perhaps buy, visit any of the bodegas in the area. Many hotels sell bottles and other examples of local (Manchego) produce, notably ham (*jamon*) and cheese (*quéso*).

Almuradiel, where the scenery begins to change, is a town with a hunting emphasis which explains some of the names of the hotels. Just after Almuradiel, near 249 km, the road enters Andalucia and then the carriageways divide and go their separate ways through the dramatic pine covered mountains of the Desfiladero de Despeñaperros. After a few km the carriageways rejoin at the small town of Santa Elena, while at La Carolina there is a large monument and views of more

mountains to the south-east, across a valley. The NIV turns
sharply to the west at Bailén and around here you will see
numerous roadside shops selling brightly coloured ceramics.
If you look closely when passing the town you will see black
smoke coming from many locations at all times of the year.
There is a connection between this and the ceramic shops;
Bailén is the centre for ceramic production and the smoke
emanates from the kilns. From Andújar to Córdoba the road
more or less follows the course of the Guadalquivir river with
the hills of the Sierra Morena to the north. The scenery here is
unusual for this part of the world as it is green and lush with
rich agricultural land on either side of the river.

The river and road diverge after Córdoba with the NIV
taking a more southerly course via Écija to Sevilla. The
environment close to Córdoba is unique. There are numerous
hills that are not very high but not peaked; they are
undulating and their low flat tops appear to roll into each
other and create an unusual scenario. There is nothing else of
interest before Sevilla but one should be aware of the intense
heat here in the summer. The triangle between Sevilla,
Córdoba and Granada is one of the hottest in Europe, indeed
I was told that a few years ago the temperature reached 50
Centigrade in Sevilla, close to 125 Fahrenheit. South of Sevilla
the NIV has not been upgraded as much, perhaps because of
the autopista that runs parallel. The driving can be somewhat
slow, and this is not helped by the bland scenery. If you have
the time Jerez is of interest and there are many bodegas where
the world famous sherry can be tasted. If not, the road
bypasses the town on its way to El Puerto de Santa Maria and
the coast. In the summer it is humid here and little is to be seen
from the road. Cádiz is located at the end of a thin peninsula
and it is a popular resort town for the Spanish. It reminds me
of an English resort, with its long promenade and lack of
presumption. If you go there, the fried seafood shops offer a
delicious selection to be eaten inside or taken away, enhanced
by a glass of cold beer or wine.

Route Planner

REF	TOWN	NAME	PKG	KMs FROM MADRID
NIV/1	Getafe	Los Olivos	G	12.6
NIV/2	Getafe	Los Angeles	VG	14.2

REF	TOWN	NAME	PKG	KMs FROM MADRID
NIV/3	Valdemoro	Maguilar	VG	25
NIV/4	Seseña	El 36	G	36
NIV/5	Ontigola	Tres Jotas	G	55
NIV/6	Ocana	Amigo	G	57
NIV/7	Dos Barrios	Guzmán	G	72
NIV/8	La Guardia	El Hidalgo	G	80
NIV/9	La Guardia	Torres Mancha	G	84.7
NIV/10	Tembleque	La Purísima	G	94
NIV/11	Tembleque	El Queso	VG	102
NIV/12	Madridejos	Santa Ana	G	112
NIV/13	Madridejos	Contreras	G	119
NIV/14	Camunas	Aragon II	G	131
NIV/15	Puerto Lápice	Aprisco	G	134
NIV/16	Villarta de San Juan	Rosita	G	147
NIV/17	Villarta de San Juan	San Antonio	G	147
NIV/18	Villarta de San Juan	La Viña	G	147
NIV/19	Manzanares	Saga	G	171
NIV/20	Manzanares	Saga I	G	171
NIV/21	Manzanares	El Cruce	G	173
NIV/22	Manzanares	Mesón de Sancho	O/S	175
NIV/23	Manzanares	Escobar	O/S	175
NIV/24	Manzanares	Manzanares	VG	176
NIV/25	Villanueva de Franco	Flor de la Mancha	G	185
NIV/26	Valdepeñas	El Hidalgo	VG	194
NIV/27	Valdepeñas	Vista Alegre	G	200
NIV/28	Valdepeñas	Juma II	G	200
NIV/29	Valdepeñas	Tu Casa	G	200
NIV/30	Santa Cruz de Mudela	Encarna	G	217
NIV/31	Santa Cruz de Mudela	Santa Cruz	G	217
NIV/32	Santa Cruz de Mudela	Angel I	G	217.4
NIV/33	Santa Cruz de Mudela	El Puente	G	220
NIV/34	Santa Cruz de Mudela	Las Canteras	G	220
NIV/35	Almuradiel	El Cazador	G	231
NIV/36	Almuradiel	Los Monteros	G	231
NIV/37	Almuradiel	Casa Marcos	G	232
NIV/38	Almuradiel	Victoria	G	232
NIV/39	Almuradiel	Los Podencos	G	232
NIV/40	Venta de Cardenas	Fuente La Tesa	G	244

REF	TOWN	NAME	PKG	KMs FROM MADRID
NIV/41	Santa Elena	El Mesón	G	257
NIV/42	Santa Elena	Casa Celedonio	G	262
NIV/43	La Carolina	Orellana	G	265
NIV/44	La Carolina	Navas de Tolosa	G	266
NIV/45	La Carolina	Gran Parada	G	269
NIV/46	La Carolina	La Perdiz	VG	269
NIV/47	Guarroman	Los Mellizos	G	280
NIV/48	Guarroman	Yuma	G	280
NIV/49	Guarroman	La Mezquita	G	282
NIV/50	Bailén	El Córdobes	G	291
NIV/51	Bailén	Zodiaco	G	294
NIV/52	Bailén	El Paso	G	294
NIV/53	Bailén	La Barra	G	294
NIV/54	Bailén	Los Angeles	G	294
NIV/55	Bailén	Lope de Sosa	VG	295
NIV/56	Andújar	Casa de Postas	G	309
NIV/57	Andújar	El Arco	G	319
NIV/58	Andújar	Del Val	G	321.6
NIV/59	Andújar	Botijo	G	324
NIV/60	Andújar	El Soto	G	325.5
NIV/61	Villa del Rio	Cuatro Caminos	G	348
NIV/62	Villa del Rio	El Sol	G	351
NIV/63	Montoro	Montoro	G	357
NIV/64	El Carpio	El Quini	G	372
NIV/65	El Carpio	Malagueño	G	372
NIV/66	Alcolea	Las Vegas	G	388
NIV/67	Alcolea	La Lancha	G	393
NIV/68	Alcolea	El Yate	G	393
NIV/69	Córdoba	Maríano	E	406
NIV/70	Córdoba	Oasis	VG	406
NIV/71	Aldea Quintana	Miranda	G	424
NIV/72	Aldea Quintana	Sanchez Escribano	G	424
NIV/73	Aldea Quintana	El 90	G	425
NIV/74	La Carlota	Aragones	G	428
NIV/75	La Carlota	El Pilar	G	429
NIV/76	La Carlota	Acero	O/S	433
NIV/77	La Carlota	El Jardín	G	433
NIV/78	Éjica	Astigi	G	450
NIV/79	Éjica	Ciudad del Sol	G	454
NIV/80	Éjica	Santiago	G	455.5
NIV/81	Éjica	Vega Hermanos	G	461
NIV/82	La Luisiana	Casa Eloy	G	469
NIV/83	La Luisiana	Luis y Ana	G	469
NIV/84	La Luisiana	El Volante	G	469
NIV/85	La Campana	Apolo XV	G	482
NIV/86	La Campana	La Cigüeña	G	487
NIV/87	La Campana	Area Los Potros	G	487.7

REF	TOWN	NAME	PKG	KMs FROM MADRID
NIV/88	Carmona	El Chaparral	G	518
NIV/89	Carmona	Venta El Aguila	G	520
NIV/90	Torreblanca	Torreblanca	E	
NIV/91	Sevilla	Monte Carmelo	E	541
NIV/92	Dos Hermanos	Las Macetas	G	558.6
NIV/93	Los Palacios	La Viña Sevillana	G	566
NIV/94	Los Palacios	San Sebastián	O/S	570
NIV/95	Los Palacios	Al Andalus	O/S	571
NIV/96	Los Palacios	La Gran Ruta	O/S	571
NIV/97	Utrera	Mesón El Paisano	G	588
NIV/98	Las Cabezas de San Juan	El Cruce	G	596
NIV/99	El Cuervo	Manolo	G	613
NIV/100	El Cuervo	Andalucia	G	615
NIV/101	Jerez de la Frontera	Aloha	VG	637
NIV/102	Puerto de Santa Maria	El Caballo Blanco	G	658

The Hotels

NIV/1 M*** Los Olivos

Getafe, Madrid

☎ (91) 695.67.00

🅿 G	✕ ✓
🍷 ✗	🛏 ✗
🛏 5,000	🍴 4,000

Madrid: 12.6 km

A modern motel located just off the northbound carriageway of this very busy road. It is called The Olive Trees.

NIV/2 M*** Los Angeles

Getafe, Madrid

☎ (91) 696.38.15

🅿 VG	✕ ✓
🍷 ✓	🛏 ✓
🛏 8,000	🍴 6,700

Madrid: 14.2 km

This, like the Los Olivos, is rated as a three-star motel but in fact it is much grander in every way and there are many more facilities. It is quite difficult to see and, in the mad rush that is usual on this northbound carriageway of the NIV, one can easily drive straight past.

NIV/3 HR*** Maguilar

Valdemoro, Madrid

☎ (91) 895.04.00

P	VG	✗	✓
☕	✗	🛏	✓
🛏	4,028	🚗	2,915
Madrid: 25 km			

Located on the slip road off the northbound carriageway this is more easily accessed from the north, but follow the signs carefully. Going south take the exit just past and then come back down the slip road, however it is not easy to get back on to the southbound side. The hotel cannot be missed as it is quite large, impressive and nice inside.

NIV/4 P** El 36

Seseña, Toledo

☎ (91) 895.70.35

P	G	✗	✓
☕	✗	🛏	✗
🛏	4,500	🚗	2,500
Madrid: 36 km			

This is also only accessed from the northbound carriageway. It is not very originally named. I am not particularly impressed with it and it is rather expensive.

NIV/5 HR** Tres Jotas

Ontigola, Toledo

☎ (925) 91.23.06

P	G	✗	✓
☕	✓	🛏	✗
🛏	3,710	🚗	1,590
Madrid: 55 km			

An impressive modern building that is the first place on the southbound carriageway, it is on my list for future visits. The bar is very nice and there is an open grill for snacks.

NIV/6 HR** Amigo

Ocana, Toledo

☎ (925) 13.02.85

P	G	✗	✓
☕	✗	🛏	✗
🛏	3,000	🚗	1,600
Madrid: 57 km			

Also located on the southbound carriageway this is somewhat more modest than the Tres Jotas. The location could be better as it is next to the Spanish equivalent of an MOT testing centre.

NIV/7 H** Guzmán

Dos Barrios, Toledo

☎ (925) 13.70.25

P	G	✗	✓
☕	✗	🛏	✓
🛏 4,770		🍴 2,650	

Madrid: 72 km

Located on the northbound carriageway this is quite a large hotel and very nice; however it is difficult to access from the southbound side.

NIV/8 HR* El Hidalgo

La Guardia, Toledo

☎ (925) 13.81.50

P	G	✗	✓
☕	✗	🛏	✗
🛏 4,500		🍴 2,500	

Madrid: 80 km

Although on the northbound side, this can be reached from the southbound side easily through the cambio de sentido. It is called The Nobleman and is not too bad, but does not deserve such a name.

NIV/9 P** Torres Mancha

La Guardia, Toledo

☎ (925)

P	G	✗	✓
☕	✗	🛏	✗
🛏 4,000		🍴 2,000	

Madrid: 84.7 km

A rather large new pension that might be considered a little expensive.

NIV/10 HR** La Purísma

Tembleque, Toledo

☎ (925) 14.50.79

P	G	✗	✓
☕	✗	🛏	✗
🛏 2,700		🍴 1,200	

Madrid: 94 km

This is in the town of Tembleque which is now bypassed by the upgraded NIV. Named The Virgin, it is not too grand but actually on the basic side.

NIV/11 M** El Queso

Tembleque, Toledo

☎ (925) 14.50.63

🅿 VG		✗ ✓
☕ ✓		🛏 ✗
🏷 2,756		🛏 2,204
Madrid: 102 km		

Situated on the southbound side but also easily accessed from the north if you follow the signs, it is quite nice and has a large shop. The name means The Cheese.

NIV/12 P** Santa Ana

Madridejos, Toledo

☎ (925) 46.04.76

🅿 G		✗ ✓
☕ ✗		🛏 ✗
🏷 4,000		🛏 ✗
Madrid: 112 km		

Close to the junction of the Toledo Road, this is unusually long in shape and a little expensive.

NIV/13 H** Contreras

Madridejos, Toledo

☎ (925) 46.07.38

🅿 G		✗ ✓
☕ ✗		🛏 ✗
🏷 3,600		🛏 2,880
Madrid: 119 km		

Next to the junction of the Toledo road, this is quite large but not really so good.

NIV/14 Hostal** Aragon II

Camunas, Toledo

☎ (925) 46.00.52

🅿 G		✗ ✓
☕ ✗		🛏 ✗
🏷 1,500		🛏 1,250
Madrid: 131 km		

Just north of the border, between Toledo and La Mancha, this is an isolated position and more easily accessed from the northbound carriageway. I would be surprised if it has a bath/shower in any of the rooms.

NIV/15 HR** Aprisco

Puerto Lápice, Ciudad Real

☎ (926) 57.61.50

🅿 G	✗ ✓
● ✓	↝ ✓
🛏 2,500	🍴 1,250
Madrid: 134 km	

This is an intriguing place, housed in a collection of interesting buildings, one of them thatched. It is in the one part of La Mancha, on this route, that is not totally flat and there is a huge pool as well. Strangely the bill for the restaurant has to be paid separately from that for the room. All in all it is excellent value. Will be located on the northbound side of the new road.

NIV/16 Hostal* Rosita

Villarta de San Juan, Ciudad Real

☎ (926) 64.00.54

🅿 G	✗ ✓
● ✗	↝ ✗
🛏 1,500	🍴 1,000
Madrid: 147 km	

This is the first of three places, all near each other, at the southern end of this small town. It was not possible

in 1991 to ascertain where the new road would go but I would not be surprised if it bypassed the town completely. This is a small basic hostal and I would expect that the rooms do not have a bath/shower.

NIV/17 HR* San Antonio

Villarta de San Juan, Ciudad Real

☎ (926) 64.01.54

🅿 G	✗ ✓
● ✗	↝ ✗
🛏 1,700	🍴 1,000
Madrid: 147 km	

Another rather basic place, though with caged partridges when I visited; again do not expect a bath/shower in the room.

NIV/18 Hostal** La Viña

Villarta de San Juan, Ciudad Real

☎ (926) 64.02.65

🅿 G	✗ ✓
● ✗	↝ ✗
🛏 2,700	🍴 1,200
Madrid: 147 km	

The largest of the three, this is quite nice but I have found that it may be closed for the winter.

NIV/19 Hostal** Saga

Manzanares, Ciudad Real

☎ (926) 61.13.00

🅿 G		✗	✓
☕ ✗		🛏 ✗	
🛏 1,970		✉ 1,190	

Madrid: 171 km

Located on the slip road off the northbound carriageway, just a short distance north of its brother, Saga II, on the other side of the road. This is quite basic and is sure to be noisy.

NIV/20 Hostal** Saga II

Manzanares, Ciudad Real

☎ (926) 61.11.11

🅿 G		✗	✓
☕ ✗		🛏 ✗	
🛏 1,970		✉ 1,190	

Madrid: 171 km

The same applies for this as for its brother, the only difference is that it is on the southbound side of the road.

NIV/21 H*** El Cruce

Manzanares, Ciudad Real

☎ (926) 61.19.00

🅿 G		✗	✓
☕ ✗		🛏 ✗	
🛏 4,500		✉ 4,000	

Madrid: 173 km

Named The Crossroads, this is a delightful hotel that does not appear to be overly priced. It is just by the north exit for Manzanares.

NIV/22 Hostal** Mesón de Sancho

Manzanares, Ciudad Real

☎ (926) 61.10.16

🅿 O/S		✗	✓
☕ ✗		🛏 ✗	
🛏 2,000		✉ 1,200	

Madrid: 175 km

Located in the town, between the NIV and the centre, this is a pleasant hostal and I have stayed here twice. The on-street parking is not a problem. The singles do not have a bath/shower.

NIV/23 P* Escobar

Manzanares, Ciudad Real

☎ (926) 61.20.36

P	O/S	✗	✓
☕	✗	🛏	✗
🍴	1,200	🍴	✗

Madrid: 175 km

Not far from the Mesón de Sancho, this is much smaller and more basic; no rooms have a bath/shower. The *tapas* on display are mouth-watering to look at.

NIV/24 HR** Manzanares

Manzanares, Ciudad Real

☎ (926) 61.00.40

P	VG	✗	✓
☕	✓	🛏	✓
🍴	3,500	🍴	2,300

Madrid: 176 km

Quite a large modern place set in its own attractive grounds, this is often full so it is wise to call ahead. It is just off the southern exit for Manzanares

and across from the Parador Nacional.

NIV/25 Hostal** Flor de la Mancha

Villanueva de Franco, Ciudad Real

☎ (926) 32.32.00

P	G	✗	✓
☕	✗	🛏	✗
🍴	2,800	🍴	1,700

Madrid: 185 km

Located about half way between Manzanares and Valdepeñas this is only accessed from the northbound carriageway. Of medium-size it appears to be popular with truck drivers.

NIV/26 M*** El Hidalgo

Valdepeñas, Ciudad Real

☎ (926) 32.32.50

P	VG	✗	✓
☕	✓	🛏	✓
🍴	7,900	🍴	6,300

Madrid: 194 km

This really lives up to its name. The Nobleman, and as usual with hotels in the Meliá chain it has everything one could want. Although located on the southbound side there is also good access from the north carriageway.

NIV/27 HR** Vista Alegre

Valdepeñas, Ciudad Real

☎ (926) 32.22.04

🅿 G		✗ ✓
☕ ✗		🍴 ✗
🛏 2,300		🛏 1,840
Madrid: 200 km		

Care needs to be taken when approaching here from the north; this, and the Juma II, is on the slip road and they are just past a bridge over the NIV. This is not too bad but likely to be noisy as the traffic will always be speeding by; it's amazing how much noise the trucks make and it always sounds worse at night. Access from the south is much more difficult.

NIV/28 HR** Juma II

Valdepeñas, Ciudad Real

☎ (926) 31.14.40

🅿 VG		✗ ✓
☕ ✗		🍴 ✗
🛏 2,900		🛏 1,800
Madrid: 200 km		

The same locational comments apply here as for the Vista Alegre next door. This is slightly smaller and painted in a very ugly green. It has a nicer brother in Guarroman about 80 km down the road.

NIV/29 H* Tu Casa

Valdepeñas, Ciudad Real

☎ (926) 32.22.00

🅿 G		✗ ✓
☕ ✗		🍴 ✗
🛏 1,700		🛏 700
Madrid: 200 km		

Across from the Vista Alegre and Juma, this is on the slip road off the northbound carriageway and can only be accessed from that direction. It is very small and just past a windmill that is used as a restaurant. The singles will not have a bath/shower.

NIV/30 HR** Encarna

Santa Cruz de Mudela, Ciudad Real

☎ (926) 34.31.07

🅿 G		✗ ✓
☕ ✗		🍴 ✗
🛏 4,000		🛏 2,000
Madrid: 217 km		

This only opened in 1990 and everything is still very new. The restaurant and rooms are in different buildings.

NIV/31 Hostal** Santa Cruz

Santa Cruz de Mudela, Ciudad Real

☎ (926) 34.25.54

🅿 G	✗ ✓
🍽 ✗	🛏 ✗
🛏 1,900	🚪 1,200

Madrid: 217 km

A modern building with an interesting design, close to the southbound carriageway. This is a pleasant hostal and is not over-priced.

NIV/32 Hostal* Angel I

Santa Cruz de Mudela, Ciudad Real

☎ (926) 34.23.66

🅿 G	✗ ✓
🍽 ✗	🛏 ✗
🛏 2,000	🚪 700

Madrid: 217.4 km

Very small and only accessed from the northbound carriageway, this is also rather basic and the singles do not have a bath/shower.

NIV/33 Hostal** El Puente

Santa Cruz de Mudela, Ciudad Real

☎ (926) 34.23.48

🅿 G	✗ ✓
🍽 ✗	🛏 ✗
🛏 2,800	🚪 1,500

Madrid: 220 km

Named The Bridge, this is on the northbound side but can be reached easily from the other side as well. It is quite large and not at all bad.

NIV/34 HR** Las Canteras

Santa Cruz de Mudela, Ciudad Real

☎ (926) 33.91.39

🅿 G	✗ ✓
🍽 ✗	🛏 ✗
🛏 3,200	🚪 1,100

Madrid: 220 km

On the southbound side, but easily accessed via the cambio de sentido from the other carriageway, this is a reasonably sized place. From the disparity of the prices I would assume that the singles do not have a bath/shower.

NIV/35 HR* El Cazador

Almuradiel, Ciudad Real

☎ (926) 33.90.75

🅿 G		✗	✓
☕	✗	⚲	✗
🛏 2,120		⚬ 1,378	

Madrid: 231 km

Named The Hunter, this is one of a string of places here. It looks nicer than it is, and the entrance is unusually at the side and not through the bar.

NIV/36 HR* Los Monteros

Almuradiel, Ciudad Real

☎ (926) 33.90.32

🅿 G		✗	✓
☕	✗	⚲	✗
🛏 2,000		⚬ 1,000	

Madrid: 231 km

Another place with a hunting connection: it is called The Huntsmen.

NIV/37 P** Casa Marcos

Almuradiel, Ciudad Real

☎ (926) 33.90.34

🅿 G		✗	✓
☕	✗	⚲	✗
🛏 2,500		⚬ 1,500	

Madrid: 232 km

On the west side of the road, this is quite pleasant and has a terrace.

NIV/38 F Victoria

Almuradiel, Ciudad Real

☎ (926) 33.90.13

🅿 G		✗	✓
☕	✗	⚲	✗
🛏 1,500		⚬ 750	

Madrid: 232 km

Just past the Casa Marcos this is rather a large plain building. I do not understand the relevance of the Arabic advertising outside.

NIV/39 H*** Los Podencos

Almuradiel, Ciudad Real

☎ (926) 33.90.00

🅿 VG	✕ ✓
🍷 ✓	🛏 ✓
🛎 4,730	🚪 2,860
Madrid: 232 km	

Yet again a hunting connection in this small town. Called The Hounds, this is a large hotel set back quite a way from the road, behind a service station. There are many facilities here including a sauna: I have often thought that would be a good way to relax after a long day's drive.

NIV/40 Hostal* Fuente La Tesa

Venta de Cardenas, Ciudad Real

☎ (926) 33.91.00

🅿 G	✕ ✓
🍷 ✗	🛏 ✗
🛎 2,500	🚪 ✗
Madrid: 244 km	

This is just on the border between La Mancha and Andalucia. The location is very strange. The NIV is a dual carriageway here and this hostal is set between the roads; as a consequence it will be noisy.

NIV/41 HR** El Meson

Santa Elena, Jaén

☎ (953) 62.31.00

🅿 G	✕ ✓
🍷 ✗	🛏 ✗
🛎 3,600	🚪 1,900
Madrid: 257 km	

This is very nice, but it is not easy to find. Take the Santa Elena exit, continue through the town to the other end, and this is at the end of the street. If you are continuing north it is close to the entrance to the northbound carriageway of the NIV. It is a nice place and has an open fire in the bar.

NIV/42 P** Casa Celedonio

Santa Elena, Jaén

☎ (953) 62.31.19

🅿 G	✕ ✓
🍷 ✗	🛏 ✗
🛎 2,500	🚪 1,000
Madrid: 262 km	

In late 1990 there were extensive roadworks here and it is not clear where the pension will end up in relation to the improved NIV. It has much character with many stuffed heads of animals in the bar/restaurant, but also a little basic. The toilets downstairs are of the stand-up variety, one of my pet hates, and the singles do not have a bath/shower.

NIV/44 Hostal* Navas de Tolosa

La Carolina, Jaén

☎ (953) 66.06.27

🅿 G		✗	✓
☕ ✗		✂	✗
🛏 2,200		🛏 1,100	

Madrid: 266 km

In an isolated location north of the town, this is quite small and a little basic. I would expect the singles are without a bath/shower.

NIV/45 HR* Gran Parada

La Carolina, Jaén

☎ (953) 66.02.75

🅿 G		✗	✓
☕ ✗		✂	✗
🛏 2,400		🛏 1,500	

Madrid: 269 km

Set back from the road and almost hidden behind other buildings and a restaurant. Consequently it will be quieter. All things considered, this is not too bad.

NIV/43 HR** Orellana

La Carolina, Jaén

☎ (953) 66.03.04

🅿 G		✗	✓
☕ ✗		✂	✗
🛏 3,400		🛏 2,300	

Madrid: 265 km

Although there were extensive roadworks round here at the end of 1990 it appears that this will be on the southbound carriageway. It is rather nice and the surrounding area is pretty; there is also a small *plaza de toros* across the road. It is some distance north of the town in an isolated position.

NIV/46 H**** La Perdiz

La Carolina, Jaén

☎ (953) 66.03.00

🅿 VG		✗	✓
☕ ✓		✂	✓
🛏 6,300		🛏 5,000	

Madrid: 269 km

This is an extremely attractive hotel with nice gardens and a classic decor. From its slightly elevated position there are views to the mountains in the south-east. It is impossible to miss this hotel as it is advertised for miles before you get there.

NIV/47 Hostal* Los Mellizos

Guarroman, Jaén

☏ (953) 61.51.59

🅿 G	✗ ✓
🍷 ✗	🛏 ✗
🍴 2,000	🍽 1,000
Madrid: 280 km	

The smallest and most basic of the places in this town. It is just across from the Yuma, and not that nice.

NIV/49 Hostal* La Mezquita

Guarroman, Jaén

☏ (953) 61.51.82

🅿 G	✗ ✓
🍷 ✗	🛏 ✗
🍴 2,000	🍽 1,000
Madrid: 282 km	

This has a pleasant atmosphere and the rooms, although a little basic and without a bath/shower, are acceptable.

NIV/48 HR** Yuma

Guarroman, Jaén

☏ (953) 61.50.36

🅿 G	✗ ✓
🍷 ✗	🛏 ✗
🍴 3,395	🍽 2,600
Madrid: 280 km	

Much nicer than its brother in Manzanares this has some style, only spoilt by the service station immediately outside.

NIV/50 HR** El Córdobes

Bailén, Jaén

☏ (953) 15.86.33

🅿 G	✗ ✓
🍷 ✗	🛏 ✗
🍴 Not known	🍽 Not known
Madrid: 291 km	

I first saw this place at Easter 1990 when it was being built; however by 1991 it still had not been completed and only the bar was open. It remains to be seen if the hotel part will be completed.

NIV/51 H** Zodiaco

Bailén, Jaén

☎ (953) 67.10.58

🅿 E		✕ ✓
🍽 ✗		🛏 ✗
🛌 3,475		🍴 2,600
Madrid: 294 km		

There is a cluster of hotels etc in Bailén and this is the first. It is rather nice and has some style although the location close to the junction with the Linares road could be better.

NIV/52 HR* El Paso

Bailén, Jaén

☎ (953) 67.10.50

🅿 G		✕ ✓
🍽 ✗		🛏 ✗
🛌 1,265		🍴 765
Madrid: 294 km		

This is small, basic, with a bad location but cheap.

NIV/53 H* La Barra

Bailén, Jaén

☎ (953) 67.11.00

🅿 G		✕ ✓
🍽 ✗		🛏 ✗
🛌 2,491		🍴 1,484
Madrid: 294 km		

Set back some distance from the road this has a strange architectural mix, one half ornate the other bland. It might well be a little down-market.

NIV/54 Hostal* Los Angeles

Bailén, Jaén

☎ (953) 67.17.69

🅿 G		✕ ✓
🍽 ✗		🛏 ✗
🛌 3,000		🍴 1,500
Madrid: 294 km		

Just past the La Barra this is much closer to the road and is rather plain and ordinary.

NIV/55 M*** Don Lope de Sosa

Bailén, Jaén

☏ (953) 67.00.62

🅿 VG		✗ ✓
☕ ✓		🛏 ✗
🛏 4,648		🛏 3,696

Madrid: 295 km

Located just before the junction with the N323, Jaén/Granada road, this is a very nice motel. I have not stayed here, but I did stop in the bar for a while and I was surprised how expensive the drinks were.

NIV/56 P* Casa de Postas

Andújar, Jaén

☏ ✗

🅿 G		✗ ✓
☕ ✗		🛏 ✗
🛏 2,000		🛏 1,000

Madrid: 309 km

This is some distance before Andújar and it is very small, basic and close to the new road. Surprisingly it really does not have a telephone.

NIV/57 Hostal* El Arco

Andújar, Jaén

☏ (953) 50.30.14

🅿 G		✗ ✓
☕ ✗		🛏 ✗
🛏 3,000		🛏 1,500

Madrid: 319 km

I think that this will end up on the Sevilla-bound side of the road; it is very much a run-of-the-mill hostal.

NIV/58 H** Del Val

Andújar, Jaén

☏ (953) 50.09.50

🅿 G		✗ ✓
☕ ✓		🛏 ✓
🛏 3,600		🛏 2,800

Madrid: 321.6 km

Not far off the eastern exit for Andújar, and towards the town, this is rather a nice hotel with many facilities. It also has the advantage of being quieter.

NIV/59 Hostal* Botijo

Andújar, Jaén

📞 (953) 50.10.93

🅿 G		✗	✓
☕ ✗		🛏 ✗	
🛏 1,850		🛏 900	

Madrid: 324 km

Located on a busy corner, this hostal is a little basic and will be noisy. Do not expect a bath/shower in the single rooms.

NIV/60 H* El Soto

Andújar, Jaén

📞 (953) 50.11.27

🅿 G		✗	✓
☕ ✗		🛏 ✗	
🛏 2,800		🛏 1,700	

Madrid: 325.5 km

This is set back from the road and, from the outside, it looks nice, I was going to stay here one night, but the rooms are not that good so I settled for the Del Val.

NIV/61 Hostal* Cuatro Caminos

Villa del Rio, Córdoba

📞 (957) 17.61.60

🅿 G		✗	✓
☕ ✗		🛏 ✗	
🛏 2,600		🛏 1,300	

Madrid: 348 km

At the eastern end of this small town, well off the NIV, it is small and a little basic.

NIV/62 Hostal* El Sol

Villa del Rio, Córdoba

📞 (957) 17.62.91

🅿 G		✗	✓
☕ ✗		🛏 ✗	
🛏 2,600		🛏 1,300	

Madrid: 351 km

At the opposite end of town than the Cuatro Caminos, this is a little larger but not very grand.

NIV/63 Hostal** Montoro

Montoro, Córdoba

☎ (957) 16.07.92

🅿 E		✗	✓
🍴 ✗		🛏 ✗	
🛏 2,400		🛏 1,150	
Madrid: 357 km			

Although the location is not that
good, I rather like this hostal as it has
some style. Private garages are
available for 750 a night extra.

NIV/64 HR* El Quini

El Carpio, Córdoba

☎ (957) 18.01.14

🅿 G		✗	✓
🍴 ✗		🛏 ✗	
🛏 1,500		🛏 ✗	
Madrid: 372 km			

This is a small town and it is reflected
in these two places. They are both
small, plain, a little run down and
very close to the road.

NIV/65 CH Malagueño

El Carpio, Córdoba

☎ (957) 18.03.11

🅿 G		✗	✓
🍴 ✗		🛏 ✗	
🛏 1,200		🛏 600	
Madrid: 372 km			

See NIV/64

NIV/67 Hostal** La Lancha

Alcolea, Córdoba

☎ (957) 32.01.37

🅿 G		✗	✓
🍴 ✗		🛏 ✗	
🛏 2,700		🛏 1,700	
Madrid: 393 km			

This is on the northbound side of the
road and directly opposite the El
Yate. The building is a little smaller
but otherwise there is not much
between them.

NIV/66 HR* Las Vegas

Alcolea, Córdoba

☎ (957) 32.03.80

🅿 G	✕ ✓
☕ ✗	🛏 ✗
🍴 2,385	🛏 1,590
Madrid: 388 km	

This is not at all bad and appears to be good value.

NIV/69 HR** Maríano

Córdoba, Córdoba

☎ (957) 29.41.66

🅿 E	✕ ✓
☕ ✗	🛏 ✗
🍴 3,074	🛏 1,980
Madrid: 406 km	

This is on the old NIV just outside the centre of the town; the new road now completely bypasses Córdoba. It is suitable for those motorists who wish to stay overnight and visit the marvellous cathedral mosque.

NIV/68 Hostal** El Yate

Alcolea, Córdoba

☎ (957) 32.08.08

🅿 G	✕ ✓
☕ ✗	🛏 ✗
🍴 2,600	🛏 1,400
Madrid: 393 km	

A large impressive building with tiny children's playground outside. There is little to choose between this and its neighbour La Lancha.

NIV/70 H* Oasis

Córdoba, Córdoba

☎ (957) 29.83.11

🅿 VG	✕ ✓
☕ ✗	🛏 ✓
🍴 4,500	🛏 3,200
Madrid: 406 km	

A little past the Maríano and the same comments apply. This is much nicer, and although the parking is not as good, there is a pool.

NIV/71 CH Miranda

Aldea Quintana, Córdoba

☎ (957) 30.60.03

🅿 G	✗ ✓
☕ ✗	🛠 ✗
🛏 1,700	🍴 850

Madrid: 424 km

It is small, oddly shaped, and close to the Sanchez Escribano.

NIV/72 Hostal* Sanchez Escribano

Aldea Quintana, Córdoba

☎ (957) 30.60.09

🅿 G	✗ ✓
☕ ✗	🛠 ✗
🛏 2,500	🍴 1,800

Madrid: 424 km

Quite a large place, in an isolated position, not far from the junction with the N331 Córdoba/Málaga road.

NIV/73 CH El 90

Aldea Quintana, Córdoba

☎ (957) 30.61.13

🅿 G	✗ ✓
☕ ✓	🛠 ✓
🛏 1,600	🍴 1,000

Madrid: 425 km

This is very small, and appears to be a bit basic.

NIV/75 H** El Pilar

La Carlota, Córdoba

☎ (957) 30.01.67

🅿 G	✗ ✓
☕ ✓	🛠 ✓
🛏 2,900	🍴 2,140

Madrid: 429 km

A modern hotel that is very spread out; it is on the north side of the road and has a pool.

NIV/74 Hostal** Aragones

La Carlota, Córdoba

☎ (957) 30.01.95

🅿 G		✕ ✓
☕ ✗		🛏 ✗
🛏 2,500		🍴 1,300
Madrid: 428 km		

I quite like this place; it is an imposing building in an isolated rural position. The bar and restaurant are large, and chickens run around the car park.

NIV/77 P* El Jardin

La Carlota, Códoba

☎ (957) 30.01.05

🅿 G		✕ ✓
☕ ✗		🛏 ✗
🛏 2,000		🍴 1,000
Madrid: 433 km		

An interesting pension, the restaurant has a collection of paintings that are modern in style and often erotic in nature. I have stayed here and it is more than adequate.

NIV/76 Hostal* Acero

La Carlota, Córdoba

☎ (957) 30.00.77

🅿 O/S		✕ ✓
☕ ✗		🛏 ✗
🛏 2,500		🍴 1,500
Madrid: 433 km		

It is just before the El Jardín, plain and clean.

NIV/78 Hostal** Astigi

Éjica, Sevilla

☎ (95) 483.01.62

🅿 G		✕ ✓
☕ ✗		🛏 ✗
🛏 4,600		🍴 3,500
Madrid: 450 km		

Positioned before the town towards the entrance to the autovia. It is on a hill and a little hidden behind a service station. There is also a disco and a two-fork restaurant.

78, 79 and 80 are off the Autovia

NIV/79 H** Ciudad del Sol

Éjica, Sevilla

☏ (95) 483.03.00

🅿 G	✗	✓
🍷 ✓	🍴	✗
🛏 4,558		🚪 1,908
Madrid: 454 km		

Located close to the centre of town, with many facilities, it is appropriately called the City of the Sun.

NIV/80 HR** Santiago

Éjica, Sevilla

☏ (95) 483.00.04

🅿 G	✗	✓
🍷 ✗	🍴	✗
🛏 2,950		🚪 1,295
Madrid: 455.5 km		

Well hidden behind a service station, it is very old-fashioned and contains many antiques.

NIV/81 HYR* Vega Hermanos

Éjica, Sevilla

☏ (95) 483.03.00

🅿 G	✗	✓
🍷 ✗	🍴	✗
🛏 2,438		🚪 1,500
Madrid: 461 km		

This has a small terrace and a disco, but the new road has cut much closer to the building.

NIV/82 CH Casa Eloy (NIV/82)

La Luisiana, Sevilla

☏ (95) 483.60.40

🅿 G	✗	✓
🍷 ✗	🍴	✗
🛏 2,000		🚪 1,000
Madrid: 469 km		

Right in the middle of this small town, it is basically just a bar with rooms above.

NIV/83 HR* Luis y Ana

La Luisiana, Sevilla

📞 (95) 483.61.56

🅿 G	✕ ✓
🛏 ✗	🛎 ✗
🍴 3,300	🚪 2,000

Madrid: 469 km

It is quite nice, and set back well off the road; rooms without a bath/shower are 1,600 amd 2,700 respectively.

NIV/84 HR* El Volante

La Luisiana, Sevilla

📞 (95) 483.60.42

🅿 G	✕ ✓
🛏 ✗	🛎 ✗
🍴 1,850	🚪 950

Madrid: 469 km

Small and appears to be frequented by truckers.

NIV/85 Hostal* Apolo XV

La Campana, Sevilla

📞 (95) 474.10.02

🅿 G	✕ ✓
🛏 ✗	🛎 ✗
🍴 3,000	🚪 2,000

Madrid: 482 km

It is in an isolated position, on the south – Córdoba-bound – side of the road with a large bar and medium-size restaurant.

NIV/86 Hostal* La Cigüeña

La Campana, Sevilla

📞 (95) 474.12.50

🅿 G	✕ ✓
🛏 ✗	🛎 ✓
🍴 2,800	🚪 1,200

Madrid: 487 km

The new road has cut very close to this friendly place and, as a consequence, it is only accessible from the Sevilla-bound carriageway. It is in an isolated position, has a pool, and is called The Stork.

NIV/87 Hostal* Area Los Potros

La Campana, Sevilla

☎ (95) 483.73.02)

🅿 G		✗ ✓
🍵 ✗		🛏 ✗
🏨 3,000		🍴 1,500
Madrid: 487.7 km		

A new place on the south – Córdoba-bound – side of the autovia, with a service station next door.

NIV/89 CH Venta El Aguila

Carmona, Sevilla

☎ (95) 414.00.14

🅿 G		✗ ✓
🍵 ✗		🛏 ✗
🏨 1,700		🍴 850
Madrid: 520 km		

Small and on the south – Córdoba-bound – carriageway.

NIV/88 HR* El Chaparral

Carmona, Sevilla

☎ (95) 415.05.25

🅿 G		✗ ✓
🍵 ✗		🛏 ✗
🏨 3,500		🍴 2,500
Madrid: 518 km		

On the north – Sevilla-bound side – of the autovia, this is small and in a remote location. There are two other places in this small chain: the Gran Rutas at Los Palacios and Paradas.

NIV/90 HR* Torreblanca

Torreblanca, Sevilla

☎ (95) 451.53.68

🅿 E		✗ ✓
🍵 ✗		🛏 ✗
🏨 3,500		🍴 2,500
Sevilla: 6 km		

Torreblanca is not the most glamorous suburb of Sevilla by any means but this place is quiet, clean and has a variety of different types of rooms at varying prices. A single without a bath/shower is as little as 1,200. The garage is in a yard across the plaza and only costs 400. On the Sevilla to Málaga/Granada road there are two local buses that only take about 20 minutes to town. The local bars also have good cheap meals that are far less expensive than in town.

NIV/91 HR*** Monte Carmelo

Turia, 9, Sevilla

☏ (95) 427.90.00

🅿 E		✗	✗
☕ ✗		⚑ ✗	
🛏 7,000		🚪 4,500	
Madrid: 541 km			

Across the river from the busy tourist side of the city, this is a pleasant discreet place in a quiet area. The parking is an extra 800 a night.

NIV/92 HR* Las Macetas

Dos Hermanos, Sevilla

☏ (95) 472.15.48

🅿 G		✗	✓
☕ ✗		⚑ ✗	
🛏 2,200		🚪 1,500	
Madrid: 558.6 km			

Located a short distance outside Sevilla this is interesting, and called The Flowerpots. There were chickens and a peacock wandering around outside the day I visited.

NIV/93 Hostal* La Viña Sevillana

Los Palacios, Sevilla

☏ (95) 489.00.36

🅿 G		✗	✓
☕ ✗		⚑ ✗	
🛏 2,500		🚪 1,500	
Madrid: 566 km			

Just north of Los Palacios, this is called The Sevillian Wine. It is likely to be noisy.

NIV/94 H** San Sebastián

Los Palacios, Sevilla

☏ (95) 486.58.55

🅿 O/S		✗	✓
☕ ✓		⚑ ✗	
🛏 4,000		🚪 3,500	
Madrid: 570 km			

On a slip road as you enter Los Palacios, this hotel is very nice, if a little small: certainly the best of the bunch here. The on-street parking is better also.

NIV/95 H* Al Andalus

Los Palacios, Sevilla

📞 (95) 489.00.24

🅿 O/S	✕ ✓
🍴 ✗	⛽ ✗
🛏 5,000	🛏 3,000
Madrid: 571 km	

This is small, close to the street, and might be somewhat expensive.

NIV/96 HR* La Gran Ruta

Los Palacios, Sevilla

📞 (95) 486.56.91

🅿 O/S	✕ ✓
🍴 ✗	⛽ ✗
🛏 2,000	🛏 1,000
Madrid: 571 km	

There are others in this chain in the Provincia de Sevilla. This one is very basic and the parking is bad.

NIV/97 Hostal** Mesón El Paisano

Utrera, Sevilla

📞 (95) 415.08.18

🅿 G	✕ ✓
🍴 ✗	⛽ ✗
🛏 4,500	🛏 2,500
Madrid: 588 km	

This is a mystery to me; the tarjeta does not show a town and no telephone number either. It is quite large, in an isolated location and strangely it did not appear in any official guide until 1991.

NIV/98 Hostal** El Cruce

Las Cabezas de San Juan, Sevilla

📞 (95) 486.84.95

🅿 G	✕ ✓
🍴 ✗	⛽ ✗
🛏 5,000	🛏 2,500
Madrid: 596 km	

Suitably named The Crossroads, the accommodation is in a separate building to the oddly shaped bar. For me it is a little on the expensive side.

NIV/99 HR* Manolo

El Cuervo, Sevilla

📞 (95) 487.91.12

🅿 G	✗ ✓
☕ ✗	🛏 ✗
🛎 3,500	🍴 1,750
Madrid: 613 km	

An interesting large place just to the north of town. Considering that all rooms have air-conditioning and TV it is reasonably priced.

NIV/100 HR* Andalucia

El Cuervo, Sevilla

📞 (95) 487.91.74

🅿 G	✗ ✓
☕ ✗	🛏 ✗
🛎 2,500	🍴 1,250
Madrid: 615 km	

Old-fashioned and a little basic, this is not too bad.

NIV/101 M** Aloha

Jerez de la Frontera, Cádiz

📞 (956) 30.25.00

🅿 VG	✗ ✓
☕ ✓	🛏 ✓
🛎 6,200	🍴 4,900
Madrid: 637 km	

Situated on the road round Jerez, not far from the centre of town, this is a genuine motel with a pub and pool.

NIV/102 H**** El Caballo Blanco

Puerto de Santa Maria, Cádiz

📞 (956) 86.37.45

🅿 G	✗ ✓
☕ ✓	🛏 ✓
🛎 13,200	🍴 10,500
Madrid: 658 km	

A typical Meliá hotel where there is everything one would want; this is close to the beaches as well. It is called The White Horse.

1 The Route

With a total length of only 400 km (250 miles) this is the second shortest of the six routes from Madrid; also there are no other options on this journey. The first 32 km are to autovia standard and the scenery is of no particular interest until the mountains of the Sierra de Gredos appear to the north. This area is very pretty and extremely popular with Madrileños and, as a result, there can be huge traffic jams on Sunday evenings as everyone returns to Madrid. To a lesser extent the same applies in the other direction on Friday evenings; public holidays are also a problem.

Talavera de la Reina is the first large town on the route and a new road, to autovia standard, now bypasses what used to be a real bottleneck. Talavera is famous for two things: ceramics and the death of the famous matador, Joselito. It is not at all uncommon to see ceramics on sale by the sides of many roads in Spain but, although bright and pretty, generally they are not of the highest quality. Talavera has its share of these, but also there are many quality workshops where skilled craftsmen can be seen producing beautiful works of art. These goods are not cheap, even here, and they can be seen in many shops throughout Spain: you can identify them as the name of the town is written on them. The other claim to fame that this city has is that on 16 May 1920 Joselito, considered by many to be one of the most famous matadors ever, was killed in the plaza de toros by a bull named Bailador, the Dancer. Not far past Talavera is Oropesa where there is an impressive castle that was built in 1366. Today, after being restored, it is a hotel and part of the Parador Nacional chain.

About half way to Badajoz the scenery changes dramatically and at Romangordo there is a large lake; this is surprising to

see here, and the local hotel calls itself the Beach of
Extremadura. The NV then begins to climb steeply up a small
mountain range to a height of 839 metres and then descends,
less sharply, through mainly uninteresting scenery to Trujillo
where the castle dominates the skyline. The scenery is not
much better between Trujillo and Mérida, where there are
famous Roman ruins. Between Mérida and Badajoz it becomes
much more agricultural and there are many roadside stalls
selling produce. This can seem amazingly cheap by UK
standards – for example, 11lbs of tomatoes were advertised for
only 50 pence. This is an extremely hot area and it is not
uncommon for the temperature to reach over 115 Fahrenheit,
even in the early evening.

The border with Portugal is only 6 km from Badajoz and the
road then continues through to Lisbon. Elvas, the first town in
Portugal, has a magnificent aqueduct and is also a place to
stock up on cheap goods. Alcohol, in particular, is much
cheaper here than in Spain and there is an amazing selection,
from beer to Acorn liqueurs.

If you are continuing through to Lisbon a word of warning:
after Elvas there are very few places to buy food, drink or
petrol for nearly 112 km (70 miles). As this can be such a hot
area, be prepared and carry your own supply of liquids
preferably in a cooler. This is especially important for children
and also in the unfortunate event of a breakdown.

Route Planner

REF	TOWN	NAME	PKG	KMs FROM MADRID
NV/1	Navalcarnero	Las Vegas	G	25.6
NV/2	Navalcarnero	El Labrador	G	36.8
NV/3	Valmojado	La Cañada	G	43
NV/4	Quismondo	Enrique Esteban	G	67.2
NV/5	Santa Olalla	Recio	G	80
NV/6	El Casar de Escalona	Hogar Transportista	G	88.3
NV/7	Torralba de Oropesa	El Cortijo	G	146
NV/8	Oropesa	La Plata	G	149
NV/9	Lagartera	El Huesped Sevillana	G	149
NV/10	Lagartera	Antonio	G	150
NV/11	Lagartera	Mesón de Lagartera	G	150
NV/12	Herreruela de Oropesa	Coimbra	G	154.3

NV/13	Herreruela de Oropesa	Los Castanos	G	154.3
NV/14	Navalmoral de la Mata	La Bamba	G	179
NV/15	Navalmoral de la Mata	Moya	G	180.8
NV/16	Navalmoral de la Mata	Brasilia	G	181
NV/17	Navalmoral de la Mata	La Parrilla	G	182
NV/18	Navalmoral de la Mata	Las Naciones	G	189
NV/19	Almaraz	Portugal	G	194.5
NV/20	Almaraz	Zorita	G	195
NV/21	Almaraz	Alcon	G	196
NV/22	Romangordo	La Playa Estremadura	G	202
NV/23	Romangordo	Moya	G	203
NV/24	Casas de Miravete	Torre Eiffel	G	210
NV/25	?	Ventilla El Camiones	G	216.5
NV/26	Jaraicejo	Oporto	G	226
NV/27	Jaraicejo	Mont Blanc	G	226
NV/28	Torrecilas de la Tiesa	El Cruce	G	240
NV/29	Trujillo	Peru	G	251
NV/30	Trujillo	La Estación	G	252
NV/31	Trujillo	Las Cigüeñas	G	253
NV/32	Miajadas	La Perla	G	290
NV/33	Miajadas	Valenciano	G	290
NV/34	Miajadas	El Paso	O/S	290
NV/35	Miajadas	Triana	G	290
NV/36	Miajadas	Sur	G	292
NV/37	Miajadas	La Torre	G	293
NV/38	Trujillanos	California	G	332
NV/39	Mérida	Lomas	VG	338
NV/40	Mérida	Zeus	G	341
NV/41	Mérida	Puente	G	341
NV/42	Lobon	*No name*	G	370
NV/43	Talavera la Real	Complejo Mayca	G	386
NV/44	Badajoz	Rio	G	401
NV/45	Badajoz	Lisboa	G	401

The Hotels

NV/1 HR** Las Vegas

Navalcarnero, Madrid

☎ (91) 811.04.00

🅿 G	✗	✓
☕ ✗	🛏	✓
🛏 3,975	⛵	✗

Madrid: 25.6 km

An unusually designed building where each room has a secluded balcony. It is isolated and more easily accessed from the westbound carriageway.

NV/2 H** Gran Hotel El Labrador

Navalcarnero, Madrid

☎ (91) 813.93.06

🅿 G	✗	✓
☕ ✓	🛏	✓
🛏 4,400	⛵ 3,700	

Madrid: 36.8 km

Named The Farmer, this is a lovely hotel in an isolated location.

NV/3 HR** La Cañada

Valmojado, Toledo

☎ (91) 817.05.75

🅿 G	✗	✓
☕ ✗	🛏	✗
🛏 2,500	⛵ 1,600	

Madrid: 43 km

This is in a prominent position in the small town of Valmojado and looks a little better from the outside than it actually is inside.

NV/4 CH Enrique Esteban

Quismondo, Toledo

☎ (925) 79.02.38

🅿 G	✗	✓
☕ ✗	🛏	✗
🛏 2,500	⛵ 1,000	

Madrid: 67.2 km

Very small and basic, this is also noisy as it is close to the road.

NV/5 H** Recio

Santa Olalla, Toledo

📞 (925) 79.72.09

🅿 G	✖ ✓
🍴 ✓	🛏 ✓
🛌 3,950	🍴 2,675
Madrid: 80 km	

A large hotel that is well kept and has all modern facilities.

NV/6 CH Hogar del Transportista

El Casar de Escalona, Toledo

📞 (925) 86.30.03

🅿 G	✖ ✓
🍴 ✗	🛏 ✗
🛌 1,600	🍴 900
Madrid: 88.3 km	

A very small CH where the restaurant was crowded with lorry drivers, thus justifying its name – the Home of Transporters.

NV/7 P* El Cortijo

Torralba de Oropesa, Toledo

📞 (925) 43.10.00

🅿 G	✖ ✓
🍴 ✗	🛏 ✗
🛌 1,400	🍴 700
Madrid: 146 km	

Called The Farmhouse (perhaps that is why there is a concrete pig on the terrace), this is out-of-the-way and basic.

NV/8 Hostal* La Plata

Oropesa, Toledo

📞 (925) 43.00.67

🅿 G	✖ ✓
🍴 ✗	🛏 ✗
🛌 2,800	🍴 1,000
Madrid: 149 km	

Again, this is a small place and it has very good views of the castle at the back. The single rooms do not have a bath/shower.

NV/9 Hostal* El Huésped del Sevillana

Lagartera, Toledo

☎ (925) 43.02.40

🅿 G	✗ ✓
☕ ✗	🧺 ✗
🛏 2,500	🍽 1,500

Madrid: 149 km

This hostal, called the Guest of the Sevillian, is small but pleasant and has views across to the sierra in the distance.

NV/11 P* Mesón de Lagartera

Lagartera, Toledo

☎ (925) 43.08.49

🅿 G	✗ ✓
☕ ✗	🧺 ✗
🛏 1,600	🍽 900

Madrid: 150 km

The Inn of Lagartera is a very small place that is located on the main road and is likely to be noisy.

NV/10 Hostal** Antonio

Lagartera, Toledo

☎ (925) 43.04.26

🅿 G	✗ ✓
☕ ✗	🧺 ✗
🛏 4,000	🍽 2,000

Madrid: 150 km

A nice clean hostal set a little back from the main road. The rooms are air-conditioned and there is satellite TV in the bar.

NV/12 Hostal* Coimbra

Herreruela de Oropesa, Toledo

☎ (925) 43.50.19

🅿 G	✗ ✓
☕ ✗	🧺 ✓
🛏 2,000	🍽 1,500

Madrid: 154.3 km

This place is very unusual: besides being a hostal it doubles as a *piscina municipal* for this small town. I have only ever seen one other place like it and, coincidentally, it is on this route also. It attracted me so much that I stopped travelling at about four in the afternoon; it was well over 100 Fahrenheit and the pool was just too tempting, especially combined with the prices. Although the rooms are basic, without bath or toilet, some have air-conditioners which is a bonus. For a room, a meal with a bottle of wine and several drinks at the bar the bill came to just £13.

NV/13 Hostal* Los Castanos

Herreruela de Oropesa, Toledo

📞 (925) 43.51.94

🅿 G		✗	✓
🍷	✗	💤	✗
🛏 2,000		🛏 1,000	

Madrid: 154.3 km

Called The Chestnut Trees, this is small and like the Coimbra across the road only accessed from the *cambio de sentido* – change of lanes – from either direction.

NV/14 Hostal** La Bamba

Navalmoral de la Mata, Cáceres

📞 (927) 53.08.50

🅿 G		✗	✓
🍷	✗	💤	✗
🛏 2,200		🛏 1,400	

Madrid: 179 km

A reasonably large hostal that unfortunately is not in a very nice location.

NV/15 H* Moya

Navalmoral de la Mata, Cáceres

📞 (927) 53.05.00

🅿 G		✗	✓
🍷	✗	💤	✗
🛏 2,500		🛏 1,500	

Madrid: 180.8 km

A large hotel situated on a busy junction with a service station outside the front door. As it is also by the busy road it is not the best of locations. It has a brother, a motel, just 23 km further down the road.

NV/16 HR* Brasilia

Navalmoral de la Mata, Cáceres

📞 (927) 53.07.50

🅿 G		✗	✓
🍷	✗	💤	✓
🛏 4,750		🛏 2,970	

Madrid: 181 km

Attractively designed, this has a nice restaurant and pool but is close to the main road.

NV/17 Hostal** La Parrilla

Navalmoral de la Mata, Cáceres

☎ (927) 53.00.00

🅿 G	✗	✓
☕ ✗	🌱	✗
🛏 4.500	🛏 2,950	

Madrid: 182 km

This has a nicer location than the others as it is just outside the town. All rooms have air-conditioning and it advertises that it has fitted carpets.

NV/18 H* Las Naciones

Navalmoral de la Mata, Cáceres

☎ (927) 53.13.36

🅿 G	✗	✓
☕ ✓	🌱	✓
🛏 2,700	🛏 1,600	

Madrid: 189 km

Located in an isolated position, this is rather a modern hotel that has a disco and piano bar.

NV/19 Hostal* Portugal

Almaraz

☎ (927) 54.40.70

🅿 G	✗	✓
☕ ✗	🌱	✗
🛏 3,000	🛏 ✗	

Madrid: 194.5 km

On the outside this looks a little bland but inside it has a nice bar and lounge area.

NV/20 Hostal* Zorita

Almaraz, Cáceres

☎ (927) 54.44.13

🅿 G	✗	✓
☕ ✗	🌱	✗
🛏 2,000	🛏 1,000	

Madrid: 195 km

This is just past the previous hostal and is smaller and not quite as nice. They do have a friendly Boxer dog though.

NV/21 P** Alcon

Almaraz, Cáceres

☎ (927) 54.40.98

🅿 G	✗ ✓
🍷 ✗	🛏 ✗
🛏 2,500	🍴 ✗

Madrid: 196 km

The hotel is set back a little from the road, behind the attractive bar/restaurant.

NV/23 H* Moya

Romangordo, Cáceres

☎ (927) 54.41.98

🅿 G	✗ ✓
🍷 ✗	🛏 ✗
🛏 2,500	🍴 1,500

Madrid: 203 km

Located in the same environment as the previous hostal, this is next to a service station and is quite small.

NV/22 Hostal** La Playa de Extremadura

Romangordo, Cáceres

☎ (927) 54.41.39

🅿 G	✗ ✓
🍷 ✗	🛏 ✗
🛏 2,800	🍴 1,500

Madrid: 202 km

To anyone familiar with landlocked Extremadura this name, The Beach of Extremadura, is a contradiction in terms. However this is located overlooking a wide river/lake and indeed has a beach, of sorts. The area is very pretty and is just before a small mountain range. It would appear that the hostal has seen better times.

NV/24 Hostal* Torre Eiffel

Casas de Miravete, Cáceres

☎ (927) 54.01.96

🅿 G	✗ ✓
🍷 ✗	🛏 ✗
🛏 2,500	🍴 2,000

Madrid: 210 km

Located in a scenic position half way up a small mountain range this is inexplicably named The Eiffel Tower.

NV/25 Ventilla El Camiones

Cáceres

🅿 G		✘	✓
🍷 ✘		⚡	✘
🛏 2,500		🍴 2,000	

Madrid: 216.5 km

This is in the middle of nowhere right at the summit of the mountain range. They do not have a business card and it is not in any official listings, therefore I could not get any more information on this place.

NV/26 HR* Oporto

Jaraicejo, Cáceres

☎ (927) 33.60.03

🅿 G		✘	✓
🍷 ✘		⚡	✘
🛏 2,500		🍴 2,000	

Madrid: 226 km

This is a not unattractive hostal and has a variety of local produce for sale.

NV/27 HR* Mont Blanc

Jaraicejo, Cáceres

☎ (927) 33.61.90

🅿 G		✘	✓
🍷 ✘		⚡	✘
🛏 1,900		🍴 1,000	

Madrid: 226 km

Another place with a strange name; this is located just across from the Oporto, but is a little bigger.

NV/28 HR* El Cruce

Torrecillas de la Tiesa, Cáceres

☎ (927) 33.84.29

🅿 G		✘	✓
🍷 ✘		⚡	✘
🛏 2,700		🍴 1,700	

Madrid: 240 km

Located in a very isolated position this is nice and clean.

NV/29 Hostal** Peru

Trujillo, Cáceres

☎ (927) 32.07.45

🅿 G		✘	✓
🍷 ✘		⚡	✘
🛏 3,500		🍴 2,000	

Madrid: 251 km

A large impressive hostal that is located just a short distance before Trujillo. There is plenty of parking and they have a disco so it might be noisy at weekends.

grand with all rooms having air-conditioning. The name means The Storks, birds that nest on large buildings all around this region.

NV/30 HR* La Estación

Trujillo, Cáceres

📞 (927) 32.12.53

🅿 G		✖ ✓
🍷 ✗		🛏 ✗
🛏 3,050		🍴 1,480
Madrid: 252 km		

This is strangely shaped and, as the name implies, is part of a service station. There is a well stocked shop between the bar and restaurant.

NV/31 H** Las Cigüeñas

Trujillo, Cáceres

📞 (927) 32.12.50

🅿 G		✖ ✓
🍷 ✗		🛏 ✗
🛏 6,890		🍴 3,710
Madrid: 253 km		

The photograph does not do this hotel justice; due to its shape, the trees and the road it was not possible to get a better one. It is very large and

NV/32 Hostal* La Perla

Miajadas, Cáceres

📞 (927) 34.72.89

🅿 G		✖ ✓
🍷 ✓		🛏 ✗
🛏 2,000		🍴 1,000
Madrid: 290 km		

The name of this hostal translates easily to The Pearl. It is located on a corner and shaped like a piece of cheese. There is an outside terrace and, unusually, a piano bar in the cafeteria.

NV/33 P* Valenciano

Miajadas, Cáceres

📞 (927) 34.73.45

🅿 G		✖ ✓
🍷 ✗		🛏 ✗
🛏 2,500		🍴 1,500
Madrid: 290 km		

A small pension just past the La Perla, it advertises itself as having a good restaurant.

Slightly larger and more isolated than the previous places in this town. It has an outside terrace and a very small children's playground.

NV/34 Hostal* El Paso

Miajadas, Cáceres

☏ (927) 34.76.71

🅿 O/S		✗ ✓
☕ ✗		⚘ ✗
🛏 2,000		🛏 1,200
Madrid: 290 km		

Located in the main street of this town, this is small but looks quite nice.

NV/35 Hostal** Triana

Miajadas, Cáceres

☏ (927) 34.80.10

🅿 G		✗ ✓
☕ ✗		⚘ ✗
🛏 3,400		🛏 2,000
Madrid: 290 km		

This appears nicer than the El Paso and is air-conditioned.

NV/36 HR* Sur 35

Miajadas, Cáceres

☏ (927) 34.77.08

🅿 G		✗ ✓
☕ ✗		⚘ ✗
🛏 2,500		🛏 1,500
Madrid: 292 km		

NV/39 H**** Lomas

Mérida, Badajoz

☏ (924) 31.10.11

🅿 VG		✗ ✓
☕ ✓		⚘ ✓
🛏 9,550		🛏 6,300
Madrid: 338 km		

A very large and elegant four-star hotel where all rooms are air-conditioned and have colour TV and minibar. There is also a pool, solarium, barbecue, pub and a disco; in other words this has everything you would want from a hotel.

NV/37 H* La Torre

Miajadas, Cáceres

☎ (927) 34.78.55

🅿 G	✗ ✓
🍴 ✗	💤 ✗
🛏 3,000	🛏 2,000

Madrid: 293 km

There is no mistaking why this attractive ivy covered hotel is called The Tower. It has an outside terrace and the restaurant is in a separate building. A room for three is 4,000.

NV/38 Hostal* California

Trujillanos, Cáceres

☎ (927) 31.62.10

🅿 G	✗ ✓
🍴 ✗	💤 ✗
🛏 4,000	🛏 2,000

Madrid: 332 km

An isolated clean modern hostal.

NV/40 H** Zeus

Mérida, Badajoz

☎ (924) 31.83.00

🅿 G	✗ ✓
🍴 ✗	💤 ✗
🛏 4,500	🛏 2,800

Madrid: 341 km

Although not in a pleasant location, this is a very nice hotel that is just across from the *plaza de toros*. They had a lovely English sheepdog when I visited.

NV/41 H* Puente

Mérida, Badajoz

☎ (924) 31.11.13)

🅿 G	✗ ✓
🍴 ✗	💤 ✗
🛏 2,800	🛏 1,500

Madrid: 341 km

Smaller than the others close by and the parking is not so good. There is a statue outside and it is also near the *plaza de toros*.

NV/42 P* No name

Lobon, Badajoz

☎ (924) 45.14.67

🅿 G	✗ ✓
☕ ✗	🍴 ✗
🛏 2,000	🛏 1,500

Madrid: 370 km

A very small plain pension.

NV/43 HR* Complejo Mayca

Talavera la Real, Badajoz

☎ (924) 44.01.17

🅿 G	✗ ✓
☕ ✓	🍴 ✓
🛏 2,800	🛏 1,800

Madrid: 386 km

Complejo means complex in Spanish and that is what this certainly is. It doubles as a *piscina municipal*, see NV/12, and this one has water-slides as well. There is an outside bar and also a disco. From the outside this does not look very nice.

NV/44 H*** Rio

Avenida Díaz Ambrona, s/n Badajoz

☎ (924) 23.76.00

🅿 G	✗ ✓
☕ ✓	🍴 ✓
🛏 5,500	🛏 4,300

Madrid: 401 km

A large hotel just outside the centre of town, near the road to Portugal.

NV/45 H*** Lisboa

Avenida de Elvas, 13, Badajoz

☎ (924) 23.82.00

🅿 G	✗ ✓
☕ ✗	🍴 ✗
🛏 5,830	🛏 4,664

Madrid: 401 km

Just across from the Hotel Rio, this is much larger and also close to the road to Portugal.

8 NVI MADRID–LUGO–LA CORUÑA

The Route

This is a long route, approximately 590 km (about 370 miles),
and there are no cities that make natural breakpoints. In this
instance it is the natural geography on the route, hills, plains
and mountains that make their own divisions.

There is also an alternative for the first part of the journey,
the A6 autopista toll road; however as is common with these
motorways it runs parallel with the NVI for much of its route.
From the centre of Madrid follow the A6 signposts and, after a
short distance, it becomes a dual carriageway of autovia
standard. For the initial 44 km the A6 and the NVI are the
same road. They separate just before the town of Guadarrama
and from there the A6 becomes a toll road.

The first hotel on the NVI is the Miravalle (Valleyview),
from where there is a fine view of the huge cross in the valley
of El Escorial. This and the monastery/palace built by Philip II
attract many people every year. After the town of Guadarrama
the road climbs up the Sierra de Guadarrama, on the way
there are dramatic views back down a wide valley towards
Madrid, to a height of 1511 metres, over 4,500 feet. The
scenery here is very pretty as the road winds down into the
small resort town of San Rafael and, on the way, enters the
Provincia de Segovia. At 64.5 km the land has become far more
agricultural and, at the head of this small valley, close to 72 km,
the view ahead is of rolling hills followed by an unbroken plain.

This is the first of three consecutive plains, each on a lower
elevation than the previous one, and they last with very few
geographical features all the way to Astorga, about 240 km (150
miles) away. This is very much an agricultural area and there are
few distractions; every now and again there is a small town set

back from the road with the inevitable church dominating the skyline, occasionally a castle breaks the monotony.

The first plain lasts until 96 km, and apart from a place where three roads, the autopista, old NVI and new NVI run parallel – at close to 80 km – and a large piscina municipal at 82 km, there is very little of interest.

The second plain is much larger, about 116 km, and enters the Provincia de Avila after only two km. Medina del Campo in the Provincia de Valladolid is the first interesting town; just before the centre there is an interesting military complex, and it was in La Mota castle that Isabella the Catholic – the conqueror of the last Muslim kingdom in Spain at Granada – died in 1504. By Rueda it is apparent from the vineyards that wine is an important product: the local speciality is known as Vino de Toro. The scenery changes for a while as the road crosses the River Duero at Tordesillas. Here in 1494 Spain and Portugal signed the treaty dividing the New World between them, a decision that left Portugal with only Brazil in Latin America. At Mota del Marques there are impressive ruins of another castle and, around 212 km, the NVI drops down on to another plain.

This plain, the third and last, stretches all the way to Astorga and although the scenery changes for short distances it is not very interesting. Around 225 km the road enters the Provincia de Zamora; if you are travelling through this area during August beware – it is the fiesta season and the hotels are usually fully booked. There are a few trees near 259 km and a river near 270 km, after which the area becomes a little more undulating. Between 273 and 293 km there are caves that appear to be lived in, similar to the famous ones in the Provincia de Granada, although these are somewhat smaller. In Astorga there are signs advertising Mantecado: this is only the second place in Spain where I have seen this, the other being Estepa – in the Provincia de Sevilla – which is dominated by the product. Mantecado is like a thick crumbly biscuit, the flavour of which can be identified by the colour of the bright silver paper wrappings. It is especially popular at Christmas-time.

Shortly after Astorga the scenery changes abruptly, and dramatically the road climbs through pretty countryside to a height of 1,225 metres until by 344 km there are mountains in the background. After 366 km the road begins to descend through the hills and some tunnels, into a wide valley that is surrounded by hills and mountains. There is a large distance between hotels here; the first hotel in this valley is nearly 50 km from the previous one. Before the NVI leaves this valley, through a tunnel at 406.5 km, it climbs a little and passes through another wine producing area. Once through the tunnel the scenery changes again into a much smaller, more rural valley that is particularly scenic. At 410/411 km there is an interesting example of local architecture: a long house – on a bend – with a wooden balcony running the length of the first floor. There is a bridge across the valley and then, around 424 km, the road enters Galicia and the Provincia de Lugo. This area is very hilly, mountainous and rather attractive and stays that way for about 55 km, after which the road begins to descend. Just before Lugo the country becomes much flatter and very agricultural; this continues past Lugo where it becomes even more rural and farming is predominant.

About 40 km from La Coruña the NVI begins to wind slowly down to the coast and until it reaches the outer suburbs of the city, the scenery is quite pleasant.

Route Planner

REF	TOWN	NAME	PKG	KMs FROM MADRID
NVI/1	Guadarrama	Miravalle	G	44
NVI/2	Guadarrama	Piquio	O/S	48
NVI/3	Guadarrama	Valladolid	O/S	48.5
NVI/4	Guadarrama	San Francisco Asis	G	51.5
NVI/5	Tablada	Casa Tere	G	54
NVI/6	San Rafael	Avenida	O/S	61.5
NVI/7	San Rafael	Lucia	G	61.5
NVI/8	Navas de San Antonio	El Corzo	G	75.8
NVI/9	Ituero y Lama	Montesol	G	79.5
NVI/10	Villacastin	El Peñon	G	82
NVI/11	Villacastin	El Pilar	G	84
NVI/12	Villacastin	Tejadilla	G	84
NVI/13	Villacastin	Beunos Aires	G	84
NVI/14	Sanchidrian	Eva	G	103
NVI/15	Ataquines	Los Arcos	G	141
NVI/16	Medina del Campo	San Roque	G	157
NVI/17	Rueda	Arena	G	172
NVI/18	Tordesillas	Juana 1 de Castilla	G	178
NVI/19	Tordesillas	Juan Manuel	E	182
NVI/20	Tordesillas	Juarez	G	183

REF	TOWN	NAME	PKG	KMs FROM MADRID
NVI/21	Mota del Marques	Botafumeiro	G	203
NVI/22	Villadefrades	Galicia	G	216
NVI/23	Villalpando	Athlanta	G	235
NVI/24	Villalpando	La Granja	G	236
NVI/25	Villalpando	Riesgo	G	237
NVI/26	Villalpando	Miluchy	G	237
NVI/27	San Esteban del Molar	Alvarez	G	250
NVI/28	Benavente	Arenas	G	261
NVI/29	Benavente	Alameda	G	262
NVI/30	Pobladura del Valle	Las Nieves	G	278
NVI/31	Valcavado del Paramo	Los Angeles	G	292
NVI/32	La Bañeza	Vermar	G	300.5
NVI/33	Toral de Fondo	Galicia	G	309
NVI/34	Celada	La Paz	G	322
NVI/35	Astorga	Fuentes	O/S	326
NVI/36	Astorga	De Pradorrey	VG	329
NVI/37	Pradorrey	Astorga	G	330
NVI/38	Almazcara	Los Rosales	G	379
NVI/39	Narayola	Nuevo Lugar	G	395
NVI/40	Carracedelo	Las Palmeras	G	396
NVI/41	Villafranca del Bierzo	Stop	O/S	406.5
NVI/42	Villafranca del Bierzo	El Cruce	G	406.5
NVI/43	Trabadelo	Nova Ruta	G	414
NVI/44	La Portela	Valcarce	G	418
NVI/45	Piedrafita del Cebrero	Rebollal	O/S	432.5
NVI/46	Los Nogales	Fonfria	G	447
NVI/47	Los Nogales	Muiño	G	448
NVI/48	Becerrar	Riviera	G	
NVI/49	Veiga de Anzuelos	Prados	G	482
NVI/50	Corgo	San Cristobal	E	488
NVI/51	Conturiz	Torre de Nuñez	G	496
NVI/52	Rabade	San Vicente	G	516
NVI/53	Parga	Casa Santiago	G	535.5
NVI/54	Guitiriz	As Pontes	G	539.6
NVI/55	Guitiriz	Casa Pepe	O/S	541.5
NVI/56	Villoriz-Aranga	Alimac	G	553.8
NVI/57	Guisamo	Varela	G	581

The Hotels

NV/1 H*** Miravalle

Guadarrama, Madrid

📞 (91) 850.03.00

🅿 G		✗	✓
🍽 ✗		🛏 ✗	
🛎 4,240		🍴 3,180	

Madrid: 44 km

I have not seen too many three-star hostals and this one is very nice. It is located on the junction of the El Escorial road, just before the town of Guadarrama, and is the first hotel after leaving the autovia.

NVI/3 HR* Valladolid

Guadarrama, Madrid

📞 (91) 854.04.11

🅿 O/S		✗	✓
🍽 ✗		🛏 ✗	
🛎 2,600		🍴 ✗	

Madrid: 48.5 km

A nice place in this pleasant town. It could be a little noisy and the parking is not good.

NVI/2 Hostal** Piquio

Guadarrama, Madrid

📞 (91) 854.12.54

🅿 O/S		✗	✗
🍽 ✗		🛏 ✗	
🛎 3,600		🍴 ✗	

Madrid: 48 km

A nice clean smart hostal that is likely to be noisy, as it is located on a junction in the centre of town. The parking here is very bad.

NVI/4 HR** San Francisco de Asis

Guadarrama, Madrid

📞 (91) 854.14.54

🅿 G		✗	✓
🍽 ✓		🛏 ✓	
🛎 3,500		🍴 ✗	

Madrid: 51.5 km

A nice hostal with lovely views back down the long wide valley towards Madrid. There is a dance hall so it might get a little noisy at weekends.

NVI/5 HR* Casa Tere (NVI/5)

Tablada, Madrid

☎ (91) 854.14.62

🅿 G		✕	✓
☕	✗	🍴	✗
🛏 2,000		🛁	✗

Madrid: 54 km

A pretty hostal with a nice outside terrace and attractive views. The rooms do not have bath/showers.

NVI/8 Hostal* El Corzo

Navas de San Antonio, Segovia

☎ (911) 19.30.25

🅿 G		✕	✓
☕	✗	🍴	✗
🛏 2,800		🛁	✗

Madrid: 75.8 km

Called The Roe Deer, this is an unusally designed small hostal.

NVI/6 Hostal** Avenida

San Rafael, Segovia

☎ (911) 17.10.11

🅿 G		✕	✓
☕	✗	🍴	✗
🛏 2,400		🛁 1,200	

Madrid: 61.5 km

A slightly old-fashioned place on the main street of this resort town.

NVI/7 H* Lucia

San Rafael, Segovia

☎ (911) 17.10.02

🅿 G	✗	✓
🍷 ✗	🛏 ✗	
🛏 4,250	🚐 ✗	

Madrid: 61.5 km

A small hotel, next to a service station, that is also close to the junction of the Segovia road, I think that this is a little expensive.

NVI/9 Hostal** Montesol

Ituero y Lama, Segovia

☎ (911) 10.70.23

🅿 G	✗	✓
🍷 ✗	🛏 ✗	
🛏 2,800	🚐 ✗	

Madrid: 79.5 km

A very pleasant hotel in an isolated position, with attractive views.

NVI/10 Hostal* El Peñon

Villacastin, Segovia

☎ (911) 10.70.62

🅿 G	✗	✓
🍷 ✗	🛏 ✗	
🛏 2,400	🚐 1,300	

Madrid: 82 km

A very strange and unusual hostal. It has the worst bars I have ever seen in Spain, so bad there was hardly a drink to be seen.

NVI/11 H* El Pilar

Villacastin, Segovia

☎ (911) 10.70.50

🅿 G	✗	✓
🍷 ✗	🛏 ✗	
🛏 2,500	🚐 ✗	

Madrid: 84 km

Villacastin is dominated by a very large old church. This hotel has a slighty old-fashioned atmosphere and is larger than the other places in this town.

NVI/12 Hostal* Tejadilla

Villacastín, Segovia

☎ (911) 10.74.80

🅿 G		✗	✓
☕ ✗		🛁	✗
🛏 2,000		🚪	✗

Madrid: 84 km

Small and pleasant, this is close to the church.

NVI/13 Hostal* Buenos Aires

Villacastín, Segovia

☎ (911) 10.70.95

🅿 G		✗	✓
☕ ✗		🛁	✗
🛏 2,800		🚪 1,300	

Madrid: 84 km

A small place where the singles do not have bath/showers. A double without bath is 2,300. It has lovely views of the old church.

NVI/14 Hostal* Eva

Sanchidrián, Avila

☎ (918) 31.80.43

🅿 G		✗	✓
☕ ✗		🛁	✗
🛏 2,500		🚪	✗

Madrid: 103 km

A rather large hostal on the edge of town with an outside terrace. It is across the road from a very small *plaza de toros*.

NVI/15 Hostal** Los Arcos

Ataquines, Valladolid

☎ (983) 81.53.50

🅿 G		✗	✓
☕ ✗		🛁	✗
🛏 4,000		🚪 2,000	

Madrid: 141 km

This is quite new, very clean and has a large bar. When the new roadworks are finished it will be on the Madrid-bound carriageway.

NVI/16 HR** San Roque

Medina del Campo, Valladolid

📞 (983) 80. 06.02

🅿 G	✗ ✓
🍽 ✓	🛏 ✗
🛏 3,000	🛏 2,300
Madrid: 157 km	

A very large modern hostal-residencia on the outskirts of town that has two restaurants, one seating 600 people especially for weddings and communions. By definition this could get noisy at weekends; it will also be accessed more easily from the Madrid-bound side of the road.

NVI/18 Hostal** Juana I de Castilla

Tordesillas, Valladolid

📞 (983) 77.03.51

🅿 G	✗ ✓
🍽 ✗	🛏 ✓
🛏 3,800	🛏 2,500
Madrid: 178 km	

Located just before the town, this is a nice medium-sized place with a large pool and tennis courts.

NVI/17 Hostal** Arena

Rueda, Valladolid

📞 (983) 86. 81.13

🅿 G	✗ ✓
🍽 ✗	🛏 ✗
🛏 2,700	🛏 1,700
Madrid: 172 km	

This has attractive wooden panelling and is slightly set back from the main road through this interesting town.

NVI/19 Hostal** Juan Manuel

Tordesillas, Valladolid

📞 (983) 77.09.11

🅿 E	✗ ✓
🍽 ✗	🛏 ✗
🛏 3,000	🛏 2,000
Madrid: 182 km	

A large pleasant place in the centre of town. Private parking facilities are an extra 400 a night.

NVI/20 Hostal* Juarez

Tordesillas, Valladolid

☎ (983) 77.01.28

P G		✗	✓
☕ ✗		⚬	✗
🛏 3,500		🍴 2,000	
Madrid: 183 km			

A small hostal that could be noisy. The location is not very nice.

NVI/21 Hostal** Botafumeiro

Mota del Marques, Valladolid

☎ (983) 78.01.99

P G		✗	✓
☕ ✗		⚬	✗
🛏 4,000		🍴 2,000	
Madrid: 203 km			

A fairly large modern-style hostel that has lovely views of the castle at the back.

NVI/22 HR* Galicia

Villadefrades, Valladolid

☎ (983) 71.72.08

P G		✗	✓
☕ ✗		⚬	✗
🛏 2,000		🍴 1,000	
Madrid: 216 km			

A medium-sized hostal that advertises itself as open for 24 hours a day.

NVI/23 Hostal* Athlanta

Villalpando, Zamora

☎ (988) 66.00.10

P G		✗	✓
☕ ✗		⚬	✗
🛏 3,000		🍴 1,500	
Madrid: 235 km			

Located just before the town, this is not big. There is a car repair shop next door.

NVI/24 Hostal* La Granja

Villalpando, Zamora

☎ (988) 66.00.39

🅿 G	✗ ✓
🍴 ✗	🛏 ✗
🛏 2,000	🍴 1,000

Madrid: 236 km

Called The Farm, this is small and nice inside but, being close to the road, is likely to be noisy.

NVI/25 Hostal* Riesgo

Villalpando, Zamora

☎ (988) 66.02.03

🅿 G	✗ ✓
🍴 ✗	🛏 ✗
🛏 2,500	🍴 ✗

Madrid: 237 km

Named Hotel Danger, this is not at all bad, but is on a fast corner and is noisy.

NVI/26 Hostal* Miluchy

Villalpando, Zamora

☎ (988) 66.00.53

🅿 G	✗ ✓
🍴 ✗	🛏 ✗
🛏 2,000	🍴 1,000

Madrid: 237 km

The rooms here are rather basic and small with no bath/shower; however it is cheap, clean and there is a small shop as well. It is just across from the Riesgo and also noisy, as the trucks take the bend at speed.

NVI/27 Hostal* Alvarez

San Esteban del Molar, Zamora

☎ (988) 66.53.63

🅿 G	✗ ✓
🍴 ✗	🛏 ✗
🛏 4,000	🍴 2,000

Madrid: 250 km

Rather small, and located just before the town.

NVI/28 H* Arenas

Benavente, Zamora

☎ (988) 63.03.34

🅿 G		✗	✓
🍽 ✗		�\~ ✗	
🛏 4,000		🍴 2,500	

Madrid: 261 km

A very strange shaped hotel, again located just before the town.

NVI/29 Hostal** Alameda

Benavente, Zamora

☎ (988) 63.38.47

🅿 G		✗	✓
🍽 ✗		�\~ ✗	
🛏 3,000		🍴 1,700	

Madrid: 262 km

Another oddly shaped building, but the interior is rather nice.

NVI/30 Hostal* Las Nieves

Pobladura del Valle, Zamora

☎ (988) 65.02.39

🅿 G		✗	✓
🍽 ✗		🛠\~ ✗	
🛏 2,500		🍴 2,000	

Madrid: 278 km

Named The Snows, this is rather small and appears to be expensive.

NVI/31 HR** Los Angeles

Valcavado del Paramo, León

☎ (987) 66.62.05

🅿 G		✗	✓
🍽 ✗		🛠\~ ✗	
🛏 3,500		🍴 2,000	

Madrid: 292 km

This is in a very isolated position and appears to be quite pleasant.

NVI/32 HR** Vermar

La Bañeza, León

☏ (987) 64.18.12

🅿 G	✗	✓
🍷 ✗	🛏 ✗	
🛏 3,600	🍴 2,000	

Madrid: 300.5 km

A large isolated place that is somewhat plain inside.

NVI/33 HR* Galicai

Toral de Fondo, León

☏ (987) 63.20.80

🅿 G	✗	✓
🍷 ✗	🛏 ✗	
🛏 2,500	🍴 1,500	

Madrid: 309 km

For a hostal-residencia this seems to be a little on the small side; it is also somewhat isolated.

NVI/36 M*** De Pradorrey

Astorga, León

☏ (987) 61.57.29

🅿 VG	✗	✓
🍷 ✓	🛏 ✗	
🛏 8,000	🍴 4,700	

Madrid: 329 km

This is one of those magnificent hotels that appear out of nowhere every once in a while. It is not far north of Astorga, in an isolated location. The bar is in a medieval tower with the decor following the same theme. Surprisingly there is no pool.

NVI/34 HR** La Paz

Celada, León

☏ (987) 61.52.77

🅿 G	✗	✓
🍷 ✗	🛏 ✗	
🛏 3,800	🍴 2,700	

Madrid: 322 km

Clean and modern in a fairly good location.

NVI/35 CH Fuentes

Astorga, León

📞 (987) 61.55.72

🅿 O/S		✗	✓
🍷 ✗		🛏 ✗	
🛏 2,400		✉ 1,200	

Madrid: 326 km

Not much more than a bar and, being close to the street, I would be surprised if it is not noisy. The parking is not good.

NVI/37 H** Astorga

Pradorrey, León

📞 (987) 61.75.75

🅿 G		✗	✓
🍷 ✗		🛏 ✗	
🛏 3,500		✉ 2,500	

Madrid: 330 km

A very nice hotel in modern style. The only drawback is that it suffers in comparison to the splendid motel next door (De Pradorrey).

NVI/38 Hostal** Los Rosales

Almazcara, León

📞 (987) 46.71.67

🅿 G		✗	✓
🍷 ✗		🛏 ✗	
🛏 3,300		✉ 2,500	

Madrid: 379 km

This is quite a large hostal located in a valley surrounded by mountains. It is a long way from the previous hotel.

NVI/39 H** Nuevo Lugar

Narayola, León

📞 (987) 45.00.11

🅿 G		✗	✓
🍷 ✓		🛏 ✗	
🛏 3,500		✉ 2,000	

Madrid: 395 km

A large nice hotel in an open environment.

NVI/40 HR** Las Palmeras

Carracedelo, León

☎ (987) 56.25.05

🅿 G	✗ ✓
☕ ✓	🛏 ✗
🛏 3,000	⛽ 1,500
Madrid: 396 km	

A large place with nice views, called the Palm Trees. It looks like a stopping place for coaches.

NVI/42 Hostal* El Cruce

Villafranca del Bierzo, León

☎ (987) 54.01.85

🅿 G	✗ ✓
☕ ✗	🛏 ✗
🛏 2,800	⛽ 1,800
Madrid: 406.5 km	

Set in a rural environment, just before a tunnel, this is a much larger than the Fonda across the road and has a very pleasant atmosphere. It is called The Crossroads.

NVI/41 F Stop

Villafranca del Bierzo, León

☎ (987)

🅿 O/S	✗ ✓
☕ ✗	🛏 ✗
🛏 1,200	⛽ 600
Madrid: 406.5 km	

Located just before a tunnel, this is rather small and basic.

NVI/43 Hostal** Nova Ruta

Trabadelo, León

☎ (987) 54.30.81

🅿 G	✗ ✓
☕ ✗	🛏 ✗
🛏 3,500	⛽ 1,800
Madrid: 414 km	

Located in a very pretty valley, this is a small hostal with a river running directly behind it.

NVI/44 HR** Valcarce

La Portela, León

☎ (987) 54.30.98

🅿 G		✗ ✓
☕ ✓		🛏 ✗
🛎 3,500		🍴 1,800
Madrid: 418 km		

Larger than the previous hostal, and set in the same environment. A little spoilt by the proximity of a service station.

NVI/45 Hostal** Rebollal

Piedrafita del Cebrero, Lugo

☎ (982) 36.90.15

🅿 O/S		✗ ✓
☕ ✗		🛏 ✗
🛎 2,200		🍴 1,100
Madrid: 432.5 km		

A small pleasant place in the town, with no parking facilities.

NVI/46 Hostal** Fonfria

Los Nogales, Lugo

☎ (982) 36.00.41

🅿 G		✗ ✓
☕ ✓		🛏 ✗
🛎 2,800		🍴 1,500
Madrid: 447 km		

Very nice with pretty views.

NVI/47 Hostal** Muiño

Los Nogales, Lugo

☎ (982) 36.07.62

🅿 G		✗ ✓
☕ ✗		🛏 ✗
🛎 3,000		🍴 1,500
Madrid: 448 km		

A hostal with the same outlook as the previous one, but slightly smaller.

NVI/48 Hostal** Riviera

Becerra, Lugo

☎ (982) 36.01.85

🅿 G	✗ ✓
🍴 ✗	🛏 ✗
🛏 3,500	🛁 1,500
Madrid:	

A medium-size place that has nice views but is rather run down. The singles do not have a bath/shower.

NVI/49 Hostal** Prados

Veiga de Anzuelos, Lugo

☎ (982) 30.01.09

🅿 G	✗ ✓
🍴 ✗	🛏 ✗
🛏 3,000	🛁 1,000
Madrid: 482 km	

Not in a particularly nice location, across from a large dairy. The singles do not have a bath/shower.

NVI/50 M* San Cristobal

Corgo, Lugo

☎ (982) 22.37.25

🅿 E	✗ ✓
🍴 ✓	🛏 ✗
🛏 3,800	🛁 3,300
Madrid: 488 km	

A motel complex that is set back off the road immediately behind a service station. It advertises that it has a chimney (fireplace) typical of the area.

NVI/51 Hostal* Torre de Nuñez

Conturiz, Lugo

☎ (982) 22.72.13

🅿 G	✗ ✓
🍴 ✓	🛏 ✗
🛏 3,600	🛁 2,330
Madrid: 496 km	

A large distinctive-shaped hostal. The towers at either end indicate how it got its name. There are very pretty views to the rear.

NVI/52 HR* San Vicente

Rabade, Lugo

☎ (982) 39.05.11

🅿 G	✕ ✓
🍴 ✓	🛏 ✗
🛏 3,250	🍽 1,900

Madrid: 516 km

This modern-style place is quite nice and located in the town.

NVI/53 P** Casa Santiago

Parga, Lugo

☎ (982) 37.04.88

🅿 G	✕ ✓
🍴 ✗	🛏 ✗
🛏 2,000	🍽 1,000

Madrid: 535.5 km

In an isolated country position, this is a small pension. As the rooms appear to be set back from the road, they could well be quiet.

NVI/54 H* As Pontes

Guitiriz, Lugo

☎ (982) 37.01.83

🅿 G	✕ ✓
🍴 ✓	🛏 ✓
🛏 2,335	🍽 1,550

Madrid: 539.6 km

An interesting place that has a gift shop, pub, cafeteria, service station and pool. It is not over priced and is nice and clean inside.

NVI/56 Hostal* Alimac

Villoriz-Aranga, La Coruña

☎ (981) 79.31.31

🅿 G	✕ ✓
🍴 ✗	🛏 ✗
🛏 2,400	🍽 1,200

Madrid: 553.8 km

Set back from the road, in an isolated rural position with a friendly atmosphere.

NVI/57 Apartamentos Varela

Guisamo, La Coruña

☏ (981) 79.51.57

🅿 G		✗ ✓
🍷 ✗		🍴 ✗
🛏 7,000		🛏 ✗

Madrid: 581 km

Located just before La Coruña, this has only apartments. Nice views to the hills behind it.

NVI/55 P* Casa Pepe

Guitiriz, Lugo

☏ (982) 37.01.05

🅿 O/S		✗ ✓
🍷 ✗		🍴 ✗
🛏 1,500		🛏 800

Madrid: 541.5 km

Basically this is just rooms over a bar. It is small and located at the northern end of this agricultural town.

G   A   L   E   R   I   A   S

9 A68/NI/N232 BILBAO–LOGROÑO–ZARAGOZA

The Route

Although the whole of this journey can be completed on the A68 autopista this would be an expensive way of doing it. In any event this runs parallel with the N232 from the junction of the A68/A1/NI roads and all the hotels are found on the N232. It is the route via the N232 that will be detailed here.

For the initial part of the trip take the A68 from Bilbao. As motorways go this is quite attractive but the only hotels are found at the Area de Servicio Altube after 36 km: there is a motel on the south side and a hotel on the north. Leave the A68 at its exit with the NI, then take the NI north for a short distance and join the N232 heading towards Haro, Logroño and Zaragoza.

The N232 is a very strange road in that it originates in two different places, 130 km (80 miles) apart, which are separated by a mountain range. The main part, as already described, starts at the junction with the NI. The other branch begins just south of the Puerto de Escudo at over 3,000 feet, on the N623 Santander to Burgos road. It then winds over a high plateau and down through a beautiful gorge, and once out of the mountains there is a long flat stretch to the NI. For several miles, towards the dramatic scenery of the Pancorbo Ravine, it and the NI are synonymous. Then the N232 branches off eastwards, entering the Province of La Rioja, and joining with the main N232 just east of Haro.

From the NI to Logroño the scenery is very pleasant, with hills all around and mountains in the distance. As this is the important wine producing area of La Rioja there are vineyards everywhere, and there are many outlets where wine can be bought directly from the Bodegas. After Logroño the country becomes flatter and less pretty but by Ausejo – an interesting place in its own right – it climbs a little again. This does not last for very long and for the rest of the journey it is mainly agricultural and flat with mountains in the distance to both the north and south. For the last 30 km into Zaragoza the N232 has been improved and it becomes a dual carriageway.

It is not possible on this route to ascertain exactly the distances between hotels. This is because the measurements, both on the roadside and as shown on hotel *tarjetas*, vary between the different starting points of the N232. This is complicated by the fact that after Tudela, where the N121 joins from Pamplona, some of the distances are measured off that route.

Route Planner

REF	TOWN	NAME	PKG
A68/1	Murgia	Altube	VG
A68/2	Murgia	Altube	G
N232/3	Haro	El Portal de la Rioja	G
N232/4	Haro	Iturrimurri	G
N232/5	Logroño	Murrieta	E
N232/6	Recajo	Pablo	G
N232/7	Agoncillo	El Molino	G
N232/8	Agoncillo	Chusmi	G
N232/9	Ausejo	Maite	G
N232/10	Calahorra	Chef Nino	E
N232/11	Rincon de Soto	Area Santamaria	G
N232/12	Alfaro	Palacios	G
N232/13	Ribaforada	Sancho de Fuerte	G
N232/14	Figueruelas	Belgis	G
N232/15	Pinseque	Los Faroles	G
N232/16	Zaragoza	El Aguila	VG

G   A   L   E   R   I   A   S

The Hotels

A68/1 M** Altube

Murgia, Alava

☎ (945) 43.01.50

🅿 VG	✗	✓
☕ ✓	🍴	✗
🛏 4,770	⇌ 3,920	
Bilbao: 35 km		

Located off the Zaragoza-bound carriageway at the Area de Servicio Altube, this has 20 rooms. Everything is at motorway prices.

N232/3 H* El Portal de la Rioja

Haro, La Rioja

☎ (941) 31.14.80

🅿 G	✗	✓
☕ ✗	🍴	✗
🛏 3,500	⇌ 1,750	

Named The Doorway of La Rioja, this is a very unusual five-sided building situated on a hill, with wide-ranging views over La Rioja. It is a short distance before Haro. There is a wine

museum adjacent to the hotel. It appears to be popular, as on the occasions I have tried to stay here it has been fully booked.

A68/2 H* Altube

Murgia, Alava

☎ (945) 43.01.73

🅿 G	✗	✓
☕ ✓	🍴	✗
🛏 4,770	⇌ 3,920	
Bilbao: 35 km		

Like its counterpart the Motel Altube, this is located at the Area de Servicio Altube but on the north-bound carriageway.

N232/5 H*** Murrieta

Logroño, La Rioja

☎ (941) 22.41.50

🅿 E	✗	✓
☕ ✓	🍴	✗
🛏 6,300	⇌ 4,500	

This city centre hotel has private parking, a whisky bar and is air-conditioned.

N232/4 H** Iturrimurri

Haro, La Rioja

📞 (941) 31.12.13

🅿 G	✗ ✓
🛏 ✗	🍴 ✓
🏨 5,500	🍽 3,000

A very nice hotel but unfortunately it does not have a location to match. It has a brother at Ciordia, Navarra, on the NI between San Sebastián and Vitoria.

N232/6 CH Pablo

Recajo, La Rioja

📞 (941) 43.11.57

🅿 G	✗ ✓
🛏 ✗	🍴 ✗
🏨 1,800	🍽 ✗

This guesthouse is just a bar with rooms above. The location is not very nice; it is across from the train station.

N232/7 Hostal* El Molino

Agoncillo, La Rioja

📞 (941) 43.13.16

🅿 G	✗ ✓
🛏 ✗	🍴 ✗
🏨 2,756	🍽 1,060

This is quite a large place but the location is not great, the N232 is on one side and the motorway on the other. It is clean and well kept, but the singles are small and do not have a bath/shower. The bar is open all night.

N232/8 Hostal* Chusmi

Agoncillo, La Rioja

📞 (941) 43.10.13

🅿 G	✗ ✓
🛏 ✗	🍴 ✗
🏨 1,400	🍽 ✗

The parking is good but, again, it is likely to be noisy as it is close to the road.

N232/9 H* Maite

Ausejo, La Rioja

☎ (941) 43.00.00

🅿 G	✗ ✓
☕ ✗	🍴 ✓
🛏 3,500	🍽 2,000

A pleasant hotel with views to the distant hills, and an inviting pool. People I know who have stayed here highly recommend it. The old part of this town is very interesting.

N232/10 H** Chef Nino

Basconia, s/n Calahorra, La Rioja

☎ (941) 13.20.29

🅿 E	✗ ✓
☕ ✗	🍴 ✗
🛏 5,000	🍽 3,000

A nice hotel in a quiet central part of town. Private parking is 500 a day extra.

N232/11 P* Area Santamaria

Rincon de Soto, La Rioja

☎ (941) 16.01.52

🅿 G	✗ ✓
☕ ✗	🍴 ✗
🛏 1,800	🍽 900

A small place with a bright and airy restaurant.

N232/12 H** Palacios

Alfaro, La Rioja

☎ (941) 18.01.00

🅿 G	✗ ✓
☕ ✓	🍴 ✓
🛏 4,575	🍽 3,250

A very large hotel with all facilities. Located in a busy position directly across from the *plaza de toros* and close to local wine and food outlets.

N232/13 H*** Sancho de Fuerte

Ribaforada, Navarra

☏ (948) 86.41.58

🅿 G	✗	✓
🍷 ✓	🛏	✓
🛏 6,000	🍴 4,500	

A very large and impressive hotel located just past Tudela, on the way to Zaragoza, in an isolated position. There is a large pool in a garden.

N232/15 HR** Los Faroles

Pinseque, Zaragoza

☏ (976) 61.71.56

🅿 G	✗	✓
🍷 ✓	🛏	✗
🛏 2,500	🍴 1,250	

Named The Lanterns, this is squeezed between the railway and the road. It is only accessed from the Zaragoza-bound carriageway and could be noisy, especially in the front-facing rooms.

N232/14 HR* Belgis

Figueruelas, Zaragoza

☏ (976) 61.08.42

🅿 G	✗	✓
🍷 ✗	🛏	✗
🛏 2,400	🍴 1,200	

This hostal-residencia is nothing special and is only accessed from the Zaragoza-bound carriageway.

N232/16 H*** El Aguila

Zaragoza

☏ (976) 77.03.14

🅿 VG	✗	✓
🍷 ✓	🛏	✗
🛏 5,500	🍴 3,000	

Called The Eagle, this is a very nice hotel that is set well back from the road, but only accessible to cars going away from Zaragoza.

10 N321/N331 MÁLAGA–CÓRDOBA

The Route

This is a route of about 187 km (nearly 117 miles). The initial section of 30 km on the N321, from Málaga to the Puerto de las Pedrizas, is by far the most difficult. After passing through the suburbs of Málaga, and past the La Rosaleda football stadium, the road begins to climb. Although it is in the process of being upgraded the terrain is not helpful and there is even a series of tunnels. Being single carriageway, as late as spring 1991, it is rather slow as there are always trucks or buses around and it is difficult to overtake. An odd feature are the brightly coloured steamrollers that are perched on the side of the road; these also appear on other roads and I have not been able to get a satisfactory reason as to why they are there. It is a relief to reach the Puerto, at a height of well over 780 metres (2,000 feet), as much of the traffic continues on the N321 towards Granada.

The N331 is also single carriageway, and for a short distance it crosses a plateau with pretty views before it winds steeply down into the valley towards Antequera. The town is bypassed as the road briefly joins the new autovia before turning off northwards towards Córdoba 118 km away. For the first 18 km it passes through a fertile agricultural valley and enters the Provincia de Córdoba at El Tejar, after which it climbs very steeply through a pine covered ravine where an old castle is visible in the distance at Benameji.

The vista is then one of undulating hills and it is much more open; past Lucena there are any number of furniture shops and the reason then becomes obvious – furniture factories.

Montilla, a little further on, is very famous for its Fino sherry: this is a very popular drink in Andalucia, particularly the dry variety, and is often served direct from the barrel.

Between the town and the Pensión Alfar, on the east side of the road, there is an interesting shop that makes its own barrels, of all sizes. This Toneleria also sells wrought-iron products, Fino glasses and Fino itself. It is worth a visit if only to see an art that is almost extinct in the UK.

There is not much of interest on the rest of the trip except for the very strange rolling flat-topped undulating hills between Fernán-Nuñez and Córdoba. These are unique to this area and described more fully in Chapter 6, the NIV.

Route Planner

REF	TOWN	NAME	PKG	KMs FROM CÓRDOBA
N321/1	Puerto de las Pedrizas	Las Pedrizas	G	157
N321/2	Antequera	La Yerda	G	152
N321/3	Antequera	La Sierra	G	151
N331/4	El Tejar	Carmona	G	100
N331/5	El Tejar	Reina	G	100
N331/6	Lucena	Las Palomas	G	75
N331/7	Lucena	Los Santos	G	68
N331/8	Aguilar	Las Vinas	G	51
N331/9	Aguilar	La Luna	G	50
N331/10	Aguilar	Patachula	O/S	50
N331/11	Aguilar	Ruta del Sol	G	49
N331/12	Montilla	Don Gonzalo	G	39
N331/13	Montilla	Alfar	G	36
N331/14	Montemayor	Castillo Montemayor	G	33
N331/15	Montemayor	El Cary	G	33
N331/16	Montemayor	El Artista	G	32
N331/17	Fernán-Nuñez	Las Caballas	G	29
N331/18	Fernán-Nuñez	El Quini	G	29

G   A   L   E   R   I   A   S

The Hotels

N321/1 HR** Las Pedrizas

Puerto de las Pedrizas, Málaga

☎ (952) 75.12.50

🅿 G	✗ ✓
🛎 ✗	🛏 ✗
🛏 4,600	🍴 2,500

Cordóba: 157 km

A nice place in an isolated position, located just before the road splits for Sevilla/Córdoba and Granada. About 30 km from Málaga.

N331/4 P* Carmona

El Tejar, Córdoba

☎ (957) 53.01.69

🅿 G	✗ ✓
🛎 ✗	🛏 ✗
🛏 1,800	🍴 900

Cordóba: 100 km

Modern, plain, and just to the west of the road – just inside the province of Córdoba.

N331/5 P* Reina

El Tejar, Córdoba

☎ (957) 53.01.87

🅿 G	✗ ✓
🛎 ✗	🛏 ✗
🛏 2,000	🍴 1,000

Cordóba: 100 km

Just across the road from the Carmona and a little smaller, it has local produce for sale.

N331/2 Hostal** La Yerda

Antequera, Málaga

☎ (952) 84.22.87

🅿 G	✗ ✓
🛎 ✗	🛏 ✗
🛏 2,375	🍴 1,450

Cordóba: 152 km

Rather small, but there are attractive mountain views to the south. It is quite a way before the interesting town of Antequera.

N331/3 H*** La Sierra

Antequera, Málaga

☎ (952) 84.54.10

🅿 G	✗ ✓
🛎 ✗	🛏 ✗
🛏 6,500	🍴 4,000

CORDÓBA: 151 km

Located just one km past the La Yerda, with similar views, this is a particularly delightful hotel that seems a little out of place in this isolated position.

N331/6 P** Las Palomas

Lucena, Córdoba

☏ (957) 50.29.79

P G		✗	✓
☞ ✗		⚐ ✗	
☳ 3,000		⊨ 1,500	

Cordóba: 75 km

Modern and clean, it is about 75 km from Córdoba.

N331/7 H** Los Santos

Lucena, Córdoba

☏ (957) 50.05.54

P G		✗	✓
☞ ✗		⚐ ✓	
☳ 3,000		⊨ 2,000	

Cordóba: 68 km

Rather larger than the other places here, this is quite nice and pleasant.

N331/8 HR* Las Vinas

Aguilar, Córdoba

☏ (957) 66.08.97

P G		✗	✓
☞ ✗		⚐ ✗	
☳ 1,750		⊨ 950	

Cordóba: 51 km

Located on a busy crossroads, just outside a petrol station. Modern and clean.

N331/9 Hostal* La Luna

Aguilar, Córdoba

☏ (957) 66.01.48

P G		✗	✓
☞ ✗		⚐ ✗	
☳ 1,500		⊨ 900	

Cordóba: 50 km

Small but with a strange frontage. The outside has been covered over to create a car park and it makes for an unusual effect. It is named The Moon.

N331/10 P* Patachula

Aguilar, Córdoba

☏ (957) 66.08.51

P O/S		✗	✓
☞ ✗		⚐ ✗	
☳ 1,750		⊨ 950	

Cordóba: 50 km

Very small and immediately across from the La Luna. Parking is on the street and not good.

N331/11 Hostal* Ruta del Sol

Aguilar, Córdoba

☏ (957) 66.09.54

P G		✗	✓
☞ ✗		⚐ ✗	
☳ 2,600		⊨ 1,300	

Cordóba: 49 km

Just outside Aguilar, to the north, it is therefore a little quieter. The name means the Route of the Sun.

N331/12 H*** Don Gonzalo

Montilla, Córdoba

☏ (957) 65.06.58

P G		✗	✓
☞ ✗		⚐ ✗	
☳ 5,000		⊨ 3,300	

Cordóba: 39 km

Very nice and has many facilities. I was surprised that the room I was shown, although large, did not have a TV.

N331/13 P* Alfar

Montilla, Córdoba

☎ (957) 65.11.20

P	G	✗	✓
☕	✗	⚟	✗
🛏 2,500		⚟ 1,500	

Cordóba: 36 km

Just north of Montilla this is a very new place and good value. It has a two-fork restaurant, with a large open fireplace, and the Menu del Dia is 650. Although there is TV in the bar and restaurant there is also a small TV lounge on the first floor.

N331/14 H** Castillo de Montemayor

Montemayor, Córdoba

☎ (957) 38.42.53

P	G	✗	✓
☕	✗	⚟	✗
🛏 4,800		⚟ 2,200	

Cordóba: 33 km

Large and nice, with views to the impressive castle – hence its name, the Montemayor Castle.

N331/15 P* El Cary

Montemayor, Córdoba

☎ (957) 38.41.98

P	G	✗	✓
☕	✗	⚟	✗
🛏 2,400		⚟ 1,200	

Cordóba: 33 km

Across the road from the much larger Castillo, this has local produce on sale.

N331/16 P** El Artista

Montemayor, Córdoba

☎ (957) 38.42.36

P	G	✗	✓
☕	✗	⚟	✗
🛏 2,500		⚟ 1,500	

Cordóba: 32 km

In between the sizes of the other two here, it also has local produce. The name translates as The Artist.

N331/17 P* Las Caballas

Fernán-Nuñez, Córdoba

☎ (957) 38.03.61

P	G	✗	✓
☕	✗	⚟	✗
🛏 1,400		⚟ 700	

Cordóba: 29 km

Located over a bar, on a busy part of the road. Small and modern.

N331/18 F El Quini

Avenida Juan Carlos 1, 19, Fernán-Nuñez, Córdoba

☎ (957) 38.01.85

P	G	✗	✓
☕	✗	⚟	✗
🛏 1,000		⚟ 500	

Cordóba: 29 km

A small place over a bar, rated as a Fonda. One of the cheapest places I have seen in Spain; there are many more, not as nice, which are costlier.

GALERIAS

11 N321/N331/N334
MÁLAGA–SEVILLA

The Route

This is a journey of about 219 km (nearly 136 miles). The initial section of 30 km on the N321, from Málaga to the Puerto de las Pedrizas, is by far the most difficult. After passing through the suburbs of Málaga, and past the La Rosaleda football stadium, the road begins to climb. Although it is in the process of being upgraded, the terrain is not helpful and there is even a series of tunnels. Being single carriageway, as late as the spring of 1991, it is rather slow as there are always trucks or buses around and it is difficult to overtake. An odd feature are the brightly coloured steamrollers that are perched on the side of the road; these also appear on other roads and I have not been able to get a satisfactory reason as to why they are there. It is a relief to reach the Puerto, at a height of well over 780 metres (2,000 feet), as much of the traffic continues on the N321 towards Granada.

The N331 is also single carriageway, and for a short distance it crosses a plateau with pretty views before it winds steeply down into the valley towards Antequera. The town is bypassed and the road then joins the N334, a new fast autovia that never appears to have much traffic: the driving is easy and fast all the way to Sevilla. However there is almost nothing of any interest to see, apart from the occasional small town and the predominant church tower.

The exception is Estepa. Although it is now bypassed by the new road, it is an interesting place to spend a half hour or so.

Its claim to fame is Mantecado. To non-Spaniards this will not mean anything, but in Spain it is very popular especially at Christmas time. Mantecado is rather like a thick biscuit but generally much crumblier in texture. It comes in a variety of flavours with each piece wrapped in colourful shiny foil paper.

In Estepa there are dozens of places making it and, of course, free samples can be had. A small box (not particularly cheap) makes an original gift.

I have only seen one other town in Spain that makes this, and that is over 800 km (500 miles) away.

Route Planner

REF	TOWN	NAME	PKG	KMs FROM SEVILLA
N321/1				
N321/2	See Chapter 10 for these three hotels.			
N321/3				
N334/4	Mollina	Molino de Saydo	G	146
N334/5	Fuente de Piedra	Tropical	G	136.5
N334/6	Fuente de Piedra	La Laguna	G	135
N334/7	Lora de Estepa	El Algarrobo	G	118
N334/8	Lora de Estepa	El Puntal del Sur	G	117
N334/9	Aguadulce	Rio Blanco	G	96
N334/10	Paradas	La Gran Ruta	G	51
N334/11	Paradas	Nueva Andalucia	G	50.3
N334/12	Arahal	Los Dos Naranjos	G	42.4
N334/13	Mairena del Alcor	Hispalis 3	G	28.8
N334/14	Alcalá de Guadaira	Sanabria	G	12

The Hotels

N321/1, N331 2 & 3—These are the same as in Chapter 10.

N334/4 H** Molino de Saydo

Mollina, Málaga

📞 (952) 74.04.75

🅿 G	✗ ✓
🛏 ✗	🛁 ✓
🛏 6,000	🍴 4,000
Sevilla: 146 km	

This hotel is now on a side road as the new autovia bypasses it. Take the

Mollina exit: 2 km up the road, it is a long low place and has a pool.

N334/5 P* Tropical

Fuente de Piedra, Málaga

📞 (952) 73.52.18

🅿 G	✗ ✓
🛏 ✗	🛁 ✗
🛏 5,000	🍴 2,500
Sevilla: 136.5 km	

Again, this has been bypassed by the new road. Take the Fuente de Piedra exit to the old road and then turn left, back towards Málaga.

N334/6 P** La Laguna

Fuente de Piedra, Málaga

📞 (952) 73.52.92

🅿 G		✗	✓
🍴	✗	🛏	✗
🛏 3,000		🛏 2,000	

Sevilla: 135 km

Follow the same directions as for the Tropical. This is close to the junction with the old road.

N334/7 P** El Algarrobo

Lora de Estepa, Sevilla

📞 (95) 482.00.80

🅿 G		✗	✓
🍴	✗	🛏	✗
🛏 2,500		🛏 1,000	

Sevilla: 118 km

On the slip road for the Casariche exit off the autovia. It is quite small and basic, called The Locust Tree.

N334/8 HR* El Puntal del Sur

Lora de Estepa, Sevilla

📞 (95) 482.01.68

🅿 G		✗	✓
🍴	✗	🛏	✗
🛏 4,000		🛏 2,500	

Sevilla: 17 km

Located just a short distance past the El Algarrobo, on the same exit, this is somewhat nicer.

N334/9 Hostal** Rio Blanco

Aguadulce, Sevilla

📞 (95) 481.61.69

🅿 G		✗	✓
🍴	✗	🛏	✗
🛏 2,800		🛏 1,600	

Sevilla: 96 km

Located just off the autovia, to the south of the exit. A medium-size place that is being expanded.

N334/10 HR* La Gran Ruta

Paradas, Sevilla

☎ (95) 484.91.44

🅿 G	✗ ✓
☕ ✗	🛏 ✗
🛏 3,200	🚪 1,700
Sevilla: 51 km	

This place, more easily accessed from the Málaga-bound carriageway, is very close to the road and likely to be noisy.

N334/12 HR* Los Dos Naranjos

Arahal, Sevilla

☎ (95) 484.08.01

🅿 G	✗ ✓
☕ ✗	🛏 ✗
🛏 2,400	🚪 1,200
Sevilla: 42.4 km	

A medium-size place that is more easily accessed from the Málaga-bound carriageway.

N334/11 HR* Nueva Andalucia

Paradas, Sevilla

☎ (95) 484.92.65

🅿 G	✗ ✓
☕ ✗	🛏 ✗
🛏 3,000	🚪 1,500
Sevilla: 50.3 km	

Unmistakable because of its Andalucian colours (green and white) it's usually somewhat busy, as it is by a junction.

N334/13 Hostal* Hispalis 3

Mairena del Alcor, Sevilla

☎ (95) 474.29.43

🅿 G	✗ ✓
☕ ✗	🛏 ✗
🛏 2,500	🚪 1,500
Sevilla: 28.8 km	

This is on the Sevilla-bound carriageway and has a run-of-the-mill bar and restaurant. The rooms are in a newer block.

N334/14 P* Sanabria

Alcalá de Guadaira, Sevilla

☎ (95) 561.08.41

🅿 G	✗ ✓
☕ ✗	⤳ ✗
🛏 1,800	🍴 800

Sevilla: 12 km

Small and noisy, on the north side of
the road in an industrial area.

G   A   L   E   R   I   A   S

12 N321/N342 MÁLAGA–GRANADA

The Route

The total distance of this route is about 129 km (approx 85 miles). The initial section of 30 km on the N321, from Málaga to the Puerto de las Pedrizas, is by far the most difficult. After passing through the suburbs of Málaga, and past the La Rosaleda football stadium, the road begins to climb. Although it is in the process of being upgraded the terrain is not helpful and there is even a series of tunnels. Being single carriageway, as late as the spring of 1991, it is rather slow as there are always trucks or buses around and it is difficult to overtake. An odd feature are the brightly coloured steamrollers that are perched on the side of the road; these also appear on the other roads and I have not been able to get a satisfactory reason as to why they are there.

It is a relief to reach the Puerto, at a height of well over 780 metres (2,000 feet). There the N331 branches off towards Córdoba/Sevilla, and the N321 continues across a wide plateau towards Estacíon de Salinas where it joins the N342. Here it is an autovia and, after descending a little and passing the isolated Riofrio hotel, it now bypasses the old town of Loja. There are six hotels of various sizes here as well as a small water park, and the town itself is quite interesting. The rest of the journey is rather dull although there are mountains in the background, both to the north and south. The one compensation is that the driving is easy and fast. Once past the airport at Chauchina, which is also close to the Federico Garcia Lorca museum, there are just bland suburbs, but Santa Fé is historically interesting as it is where Isabella and Ferdinand had their military camp whilst preparing the Christian reconquest of Granada: they eventually entered the city on 2nd January 1492.

Route Planner

REF	TOWN	NAME	PKG	KMs ON N342
N321/1	See Chapter 10 for this hotel.			
N342/2	Salinas	El Cortijo	G	
N342/3	Riofrio	Riofrio	G	
(The next six hotels are located off the new autovia in the town of Loja)				
N342/4	Loja	El Taxi	G	338
N342/5	Loja	Lopez	G	338
N342/6	Loja	El Sol	G	338
N342/7	Loja	Las Terrazas	G	338
N342/8	Loja	El Mirador	E	337
N342/9	Loja	Del Manzanil	G	335
N342/10	Moralena	Paraiso	G	315
(The next three pensions are located next to each other, on the north side of the N342 close to the airport)				
N342/11	Chauchina	Marinetto	G	300
N342/12	Chauchina	Las Vegas	G	300
N342/13	Chauchina	El Gruce	G	300
N342/14	Santa Fé	Rosada	G	295
N342/15	Santa Fé	Apolo	G	294
N342/16	Santa Fé	Santa Fé	G	293
N342/17	Granada	Sol Alcano	VG	289

G   A   L   E   R   I   A   S

The Hotels

N321/1

This is the same as in Chapter 10.

N342/3 HR** Riofrio

Riofrio, Granada

📞 (958) 32.10.66

🅿 G		✗	✓
☕ ✓		🍴	✗
🛏 2,000		🛏 1,500	

In an isolated location just a little before Loja, it is unmistakable because of the large fish signposts.

N342/2 Hostal* El Cortijo

Salinas, Málaga

📞

🅿 G		✗	✓
☕ ✗		🍴	✗
🛏 2,000		🛏 1,300	

Named The Farmhouse, this is small and isolated, up on the plateau.

Note: The next six hotels are located off the autovia in the town of Loja:

N342/4 HR* El Taxi

Loja, Granada

📞 (958) 32.00.46

🅿 G		✗	✓
☕ ✗		🍴	✗
🛏 2,400		🛏 1,200	

Km on N342: 338

Slightly larger than the hotels immediately around and, as is common, it has local produce for sale. The car parking facilities are good.

N342/5 P* Lopez

Loja, Granada

📞 (958) 32.00.49

🅿 G		✗	✓
☕ ✗		🍴	✗
🛏 1,600		🛏 800	

Km on N342: 338

Small and on the other side of the road from El Taxi.

N342/6 P* El Sol

Loja, Granada

☎ (958) 32.11.93

🅿 G		✗ ✓
☕ ✗		🛏 ✗
🛏 1,650		🍴 850

Km on N342: 338

This is also small, and a little past the Lopez.

N342/7 HR* Las Terrazas

Loja, Granada

☎ (958) 32.07.56

🅿 G		✗ ✓
☕ ✗		🛏 ✗
🛏 2,500		🍴 1,250

Km on N342: 338

Nicer than the others ahead of it and, as the name implies, there are terraces overlooking the town. It is located on a bend as well as a hill.

N342/8 HR** El Mirador

Loja, Granada

☎ (958) 32.00.42

🅿 E		✗ ✓
☕ ✗		🛏 ✗
🛏 2,800		🍴 1,700

Km on N342: 337

This is large, has a private garage and attractive views over the old town.

N342/9 H** Del Manzanil

Loja, Granada

☎ (958) 32.18.50

🅿 G		✗ ✓
☕ ✓		🛏 ✗
🛏 3,850		🍴 2,500

Km on N342: 335

The largest, and either the first or last place on the N342 in Loja, depending upon your direction of entry. There is a small duck pond outside and a car wash next door.

N342/10 H* Paraiso

Moralena, Granada

☎ (958) 46.00.40

🅿 G	✕ ✓
☕ ✗	🍴 ✗
🛏 3,500	🚪 1,500

Km on N342: 315

This is only accessible from the Málaga-bound side of the autovia. It is nice, painted brilliant white, and very isolated but does not quite live up to its name, Paradise.

> Note: The next three pensions are located close to each other, on the north side of the N342, across from the airport:

N342/11 P* Marinetto

Chauchina, Granada

☎ (958) 44.60.52

🅿 G	✕ ✓
☕ ✗	🍴 ✗
🛏 2,200	🚪 1,500

N342/12 P* Las Vegas

Chauchina, Granada

☎ (958) 44.62.77

🅿 G	✕ ✓
☕ ✗	🍴 ✗
🛏 3,000	🚪 2,000

N342/13 P* El Cruce

Chauchina, Granada

☎ (958) 44.60.02

🅿 G	✕ ✓
☕ ✗	🍴 ✗
🛏 2,000	🚪 1,000

> These three are all quite similar somewhat nondescript but clean stopping places with small bedrooms.

N342/14 HR* Rosada

Santa Fé, Granada

☎ (958) 44.03.85

🅿 G	✗	✗
☕ ✗	🛏	✗
🛏 3,300		🚪 1,000

Km on N342: 295

Of medium-size and on the north side of the road it is only accessible from a slip road. It is about the only place I have seen without a bar.

N342/16 HR** Santa Fé

Santa Fé, Granada

☎ (958) 44.03.70

🅿 G	✗	✓
☕ ✗	🛏	✓
🛏 4,000		🚪 2,500

Km on N342: 293

The nicest place on this stretch. It is only accessible from the north side and has a pool.

N342/15 CH* Apolo

Santa Fé, Granada

☎ (958) 44.03.83

🅿 G	✗	✓
☕ ✗	🛏	✗
🛏 1,600		🚪 1,000

Km on N342: 294

A small place that, again, is only accessible from the north side slip road.

N342/17 H*** Sol Alcano

Granada

☎ (958) 28.30.50

🅿 VG	✗	✓
☕ ✓	🛏	✓
🛏 6,700		🚪 4,800

Km on N342: 289

This is large, very nice and although located off the Málaga-bound carriageway is easily entered from the other direction.

13 N323 BAILÉN–GRANADA–MOTRIL

The Route

This is quite a mixture of a route. From the junction of the NIV at Bailén to Jaén the single carriageway road crosses an open plain where, apart from the mountains to the south, the dominant feature on the fields full of olive (*aceituna*) trees. Not far north of Jaén, on the western side of the road, there is a new prison after which the N323 bypasses the city where the old castle, now a hotel and part of the Parador Nacional chain, is the most dominant feature. The scenery then begins to change, slowly at first, and then more dramatically as the road begins to climb through a series of rather tight valley/gorges. These are not unattractive but the driving can be very tedious if, as is usual, one gets stuck behind slow-moving trucks. This lasts for about 30 km until the scenery begins to open out a little and by Iznalloz, 400 km from Madrid, the road crosses a high plateau with jagged mountain peaks in the distance. The only sight of interest between here and Granada is a large reservoir, which is rarely full even in winter but where there are some picnic grounds.

A short distance from the city, weather permitting, there is a dramatic and beautiful sight: directly in front of you is the long wall of the Sierra Nevada mountains where the highest peaks are snow-covered even in the heat of the summer *el verano*. In the winter *invierno*, and even as late as April, it is completely snow-covered.

Granada itself is a driver's nightmare at any time of the day, let alone rush hours, and there have been many occasions when it has taken over 1½ hours to get through the town. In fact, as late as 1990, it has taken me as long to get from Jaén to Motril as from Madrid to Jaén. Be alert if you choose to drive in the city. It is not unknown for people on mopeds to draw up beside the car and smash a window to grab anything on show. Always keep cameras and handbags underneath the seats well out of sight. By 1992 all this will have changed as extensive road works are being undertaken that will bypass the city. Unfortunately, at the time of publication, it is not possible to predict where this new road will begin or end. It does appear that it will continue about 10 km past Granada. If this is so, it is very good news indeed as the road will come out close to the Suspiro de Moro, the Sigh of the Moor. This is so called because it is said that when Boabdil, the last Moorish ruler of Granada – and also in Spain – was evicted he looked back at the city from this point and cried. It is reported that his mother's response was to tell him to stop crying like a woman for something he could not defend as a man.

For approximately the next 15 km the N323 passes over a high plateau with the peaks of the Sierra Nevada to the east. Then for the next 20 km, as the road descends to the Mediterranean, the surrounding scenery is particularly stunning. Until 1990 this was a tortuous road, winding around the mountains and then doubling back on itself. There was even, at Izbor, a single lane tunnel that did not have traffic lights controlling the flow at either end. All this has now changed and road improvements will shorten the journey from Granada to Motril by 20 km over a total distance of 70 km. By Velez de Benaudalla the road has levelled out and, close to the Mediterranean, roadside traders sell fruit.

Route Planner

REF	TOWN	NAME	PKG	KMs FROM MADRID
N323/1	Las Infantas	Juleca	G	320
N323/2	La Guardia	La Yuca	G	340
N323/3	La Guardia	Mistral	G	346
N323/4	Carchel	El Oasis	G	362
N323/5	Campillo de Arenas	Santa Lucia	G	366
N323/6	Campillo de Arenas	Puerta de Arenas	G	367
N323/7	Campillo de Arenas	Frontera	G	375
N323/8	Iznalloz	La Nava	G	400
N323/9	Iznalloz	El 402	G	402

(The next two places have been bypassed by the new road; however they are not far from the centre of town and offer a change from the city)

N323/10	Granada	Los Rosales	VG	428
N323/11	Granada	Sierra Nevada	VG	428

REF	TOWN	NAME	PKG	KMs ON N342
N323/12	Granada	Atenas	E	432
N323/13	Armilla	Los Galones	G	436
N323/14	Armilla	Los Llanos	G	440
N323/15	Otura	Boabdil	G	444
N323/16	Padul	El Cruce	G	454
N323/17	Dúrcal	Carmen	G	458
N323/18	Velez de Benaudalla	La Brasa	G	486

The Hotels

N323/1 P** Juleca

Las Infantas, Jaén

☎ (953) 26.56.06

🅿 G		✕ ✓
☕ ✗		🍴 ✓
🛏 3,000		🛏 1,500
Madrid: 320 km		

Located just south of the village of Las Infantas, in an isolated position half way between Bailén and Jaén, this is a clean and neat pension. The restaurant and bar is in another building and, as it is popular with travelling businessmen, it is best to call ahead. There is a farm right behind it so the eggs *huevos* should be fresh.

N323/2 HR*** La Yuca

La Guardia, Jaén

☎ (953) 22.19.50

🅿 G		✕ ✓
☕ ✗		🍴 ✗
🛏 4.134		🛏 2,703
Madrid: 340 km		

Located a few km past Jaén on the junction of the Baeza/Ubeda and Granada roads, this is a very pleasant place surrounded by trees.

N323/3 H** Mistral

La Guardia, Jaén

☎ (953) 25.13.04

🅿 G		✕ ✓
☕ ✗		🍴 ✗
🛏 3,900		🛏 2,900
Madrid: 346 km		

Rather modern in style with views back towards Jaén, this is a reasonable hotel but, to my mind, a little expensive. All the rooms are air-conditioned and at weekends there is a barbeque on the patio.

N323/4 H* El Oasis

Carchel, Jaén

☎ (953) 30.20.83

🅿 G		✕ ✓
☕ ✗		🍴 ✗
🛏 2,700		🛏 1,600
Madrid: 362 km		

Located in an isolated interesting position, this is a shade old-fashioned. Parking facilities on both sides of the road.

N323/5 Santa Lucia

Campillo de Arenas, Jaén

☎ (953) 30.90.31

P G	✗ ✓
☕ ✗	⛵ ✓
🛏 2,600	🍴 1,300

Madrid: 366 km

Set further back from the road than most other places this is neat, clean and quite nice. It is not expensive given that it has a pool.

N323/6 Puerta de Arenas

Campillo de Arenas, Jaén

☎ (953) 30.92.03

P G	✗ ✓
☕ ✗	⛵ ✗
🛏 1,600	🍴 1,000

Madrid: 367 km

Small and rather basic. It is located next to a very large rock that has a hole in the middle through which the road passes.

N323/7 Frontera

Campillo de Arenas, Jaén

☎ (953) 30.94.00

P G	✗ ✓
☕ ✗	⛵ ✗
🛏 2,275	🍴 1,430

Madrid: 375 km

A very nice modern place that is only spoilt by its location immediately behind a large service station.

N323/8 Hostal* La Nava

Iznalloz, Granada

☎ (958) 37.02.98

P G	✗ ✓
☕ ✗	⛵ ✗
🛏 2,200	🍴 850

Madrid: 400 km

In an isolated location with attractive views to the sierra, this is a large hostal where the singles do not have a bath/shower.

N323/9 Hostal* El 402

Iznalloz, Granada

☎ (958) 15.06.07

🅿 G		✗	✓
🛏 ✗		🛫 ✗	
🛏 2,200		🛏 1,200	

Madrid: 402 km

Again this is in an isolated position with good views to the mountains. It is not that large, and does not have an original name.

N323/10 HR* Los Rosales

Granada, Granada

☎ (958) 15.06.07

🅿 VG		✗	✓
🛏 ✗		🛫 ✗	
🛏 2,800		🛏 1,800	

Madrid: 428 km

During 1990/91 there were extensive roadworks in Granada that will eventually clear up what has been a bottleneck of immense proportions. The new road will run around the town and this and the next hotel will be bypassed, leaving them much quieter. It is in an attractive old style building and has a friendly atmosphere. Being only a short taxi ride from the centre it is an ideal place to leave the car while exploring the city.

N323/11 M** Sierra Nevada

Granada

☎ (958) 20.00.61

🅿 VG		✗	✓
🛏 ✗		🛫	✓
🛏 4,200		🛏 2,600	

Madrid: 428 km

In location this is the same as Los Rosales but in every other respect totally different. It is a mixture of camping and hotel set in very large grounds with many facilities, including two pools.

N323/12 HR** Atenas

Gran Via de Colón, Granada

☎ (958) 27.87.50

🅿 E		✗	✗
🛏 ✗		🛫 ✗	
🛏 2,950		🛏 2,200	

Madrid: 434 km

This is somewhat of a rarity, an inexpensive city central hotel with private parking facilities. It is on a very busy and noisy street close to the cathedral. The garage is an extra 1,000 a day.

N323/13 HR** Los Galones

Armilla, Granada

☎ (958) 57.09.47

🅿 G	✖ ✓
🛎 ✗	🛏 ✓
🍴 4,500	🛏 3,000

Madrid: 436 km

Just to the south of the city this will be bypassed by the new road and that will make it much more peaceful. The swimming pool is small and in the front gardens.

N323/14 HR* Los Llanos

Armilla, Granada

☎ (958) 59.70.01

🅿 G	✖ ✓
🛎 ✗	🛏 ✗
🍴 2,500	🛏 1,500

Madrid: 440 km

One more place that will be bypassed but even then the location will not be too good. It does though have an interesting restaurant with a *Horno de Asar* (open brick oven).

N323/15 Hostal* Boabdil

Otura, Granada

☎ (958) 55.52.27

🅿 G	✖ ✓
🛎 ✗	🛏 ✗
🍴 2,000	🛏 1,000

Madrid: 444 km

Named after the last Muslim ruler of Granada and also the last in Spain, this hostal is quite small and has views to the Sierra Nevada from the front. It is somewhat spoilt by the proximity of a service station. Although some distance south of Granada there were extensive roadworks going on in 1991 and it was not apparent whether this will be bypassed.

N323/16 P** El Cruce

Padul, Granada

☎ ✗

🅿 G	✖ ✓
🛎 ✗	🛏 ✗
🍴 2,500	🛏 1,500

Madrid: 458 km

Located on a plateau this is rather basic but as some improvements were being made it might soon get a little better.

N323/17 M* Carmen

Dúrcal, Granada

☎	✗		
🅿 G		✗	✓
☕	✗	🛏	✗
🛏 2,500		🛏	✗

Madrid: 458 km

Set back from the road this advertises itself as a motel, but it is not. However it is very nice indeed being bright, modern and clean.

N323/18 HR* La Brasa

Velez de Benaudella, Granada

☎ (958) 65.82.51			
🅿 G		✗	✓
☕	✗	🛏	✗
🛏 2,300		🛏 1,500	

Madrid: 486 km

Situated at the base of the Sierra de Lújar this is the last hotel before the coast. Rather plain and a little basic.

G A L E R I A S

14 N340 CÁDIZ–ALGECIRAS/MOTRIL–ALMERÍA–MURCIA

The Route

The N340 is the longest road in Spain. It begins in Cádiz on the south western (Atlantic) coast and first proceeds southward to Algeciras before turning northward and following the Mediterranean coast for most of its length all the way to Barcelona. This is a distance of approximately 1,200 km (750 miles).

For the purposes of this guide I shall be excluding those parts of the road that fall into the following categories:

One, resort areas on the coast where there is an abundance of hotels. The largest of these areas area is between San Roque just north of Gibraltar, and Motril in the Provincia de Granada. This is the most popular part of the Costa del Sol and takes in such cities as Marbella, Fuengirola, Torremolinos, Málaga and Nerja.

The second category is when the N340 has an autopista or autovia running parallel to it: this takes in the sections between Murcia and Alicante (autovia) and Valencia to Barcelona (autopista). The latter section also passes through coastal towns where there are many hotels.

The last category is the section between Alicante and Valencia, where the N340 runs inland across a peninsula. As the A7 autopista and the N332 take the coastal route passing such resorts as Gandia, Denia and Benidorm, the majority of the traffic will take this route.

Of the sections covered, the first is the 115 km stretch between Cádiz and Los Barrios, just south of San Roque. For the first 70 km or so this is not very interesting: the road runs parallel to the coast but is inland and away from the sea. At Tarifa, the southernmost tip of Spain, the road meets the sea by the Straits of Gibraltar and there is a flurry of expensive hotels. This area is very popular with people who like watersports, as the almost perpetual winds are ideal for sailing and windsurfing. After Tarifa the road begins to climb a little and there is a viewpoint and cafe that offer spectacular views across the straits to Africa, only 13 km (eight miles) away. The N340 when winds down into the less than impressive town of Algeciras, and then around the bay to Los Barrios.

The next section of the N340 that is detailed is between Motril and Murcia, a distance of 328 km (about 200 miles). Between Motril and Adra is one of the last unspoilt sections of the Costa del Sol; the mountains and sea are never far apart. The road passes beaches of all kinds and sleepy small towns and villages; it is sad to think that, not so long ago, places like Torremolinos were like this. From Adra to Aguadulce the N340 cuts straight across a peninsula towards the city of Almería, and only the mountains to the north stop it being very boring. The predominant sight in this area are the plastic coverings over the fields; these act as greenhouses and allow three or four crops a year to be grown. The road turns north after Almería and after a short distance enters a very strange area which is basically a desert and consists of nothing but yellow/grey scrubland. The only thing of interest are the mini-Hollywoods: although now just tourist attractions they were the locations for many western movies in the late 1960s and early 1970s.

After turning towards the coast at Mojacar, a traditional village that is now a tourist resort, the road heads north again, away from the coastal mountains towards Huercal-Overa. After Huercal it becomes much flatter, Puerto-Lumbreras is full of shops selling local ceramics and Lorca is an historic city surrounded by hills. Shortly after Lorca the orange and lemon trees begin to appear and continue almost non-stop to Valencia and beyond.

Just before the centre of Murcia there is a bypass around the city. This continues into an autovia that goes directly to Alicante.

Route Planner

REF	TOWN	NAME	PKG	KMs FROM CADIZ
N340/1	Chiclana de la Frontera	La Marisma	G	4.5
N340/2	Conil	Avenida	G	18
N340/3	Conil	Las Cumbres	G	18
N340/4	Conil	El Canario	G	20
N340/5	Vejer de la Frontera	Los Arcos	G	39
N340/6	Vejer de la Frontera	Lele	G	39
N340/7	Tarifa	Ponderosa	G	76.5
N340/8	Tarifa	Ensenada	G	76.5
N340/9	Tarifa	Oasis	G	76.5
N340/10	Tarifa	Balcon de España	G	78
N340/11	Tarifa	Hurricane	VG	78
N340/12	Tarifa	La Cordoniz	G	79
N340/13	Tarifa	Dos Mares	VG	79.5
N340/14	Tarifa	Mesón de Sancho	G	94
N340/15	Algeciras	El Buen Gusto	G	109
N340/16	Algeciras	Blumen	G	109
N340/17	Los Barrios	Guadacorte	VG	115
N340/18	Torrenueva	Los Balandros	G	336
N340/19	Torrenueva	Sacratif	O/S	337
N340/20	Calahonda	El Ancla	O/S	344
N340/21	Calahonda	Miguel	O/S	344
N340/22	Castell de Ferro	Iberico	G	351
N340/23	Castell de Ferro	Paredes	G	352
N340/24	Castell de Ferro	Costa del Sol	G	353
N340/25	La Mamola	Onteniente	G	362.5
N340/26	El Pozuelo	Wuppertal 2	G	374
N340/27	El Pozuelo	Beatrix	G	374.5
N340/28	El Pozuelo	Wuppertal 1 & 2	O/S	374.5
N340/29	Adra	Delfin	O/S	388
N340/30	Adra	Abdera	VG	389
N340/31	El Ejido	Margo	G	
N340/32	Santa Maria del Aguila	Amelia	G	411.5
N340/33	La Redonda	El Edén	E	415
N340/34	Aguadulce	Lola	O/S	429
N340/35	Enix	Playaluz	VG	436
N340/36	Almeria	Soylmar	G	438.5
N340/37	Tabernas	Retamares	G	475
N340/38	Tabernas	La Molina	G	476
N340/39	Sorbas	Sorbas	G	496
N340/40	Los Gallardos	Anita	G	511
N340/41	Los Gallardos	La Rueda	G	520

REF	TOWN	NAME	PKG	KMs FROM CADIZ
N340/42	Vera	Regio	O/S	532
N340/43	Vera	Isabel	O/S	532
N340/44	Real de Vera	La Brasa	G	533
N340/45	El Real de Antas	Argar	G	533.5
N340/46	El Real de Antas	Mi Casa	G	536
N340/47	El Real de Antas	Venta Rodrigo	G	536
N340/48	La Ballabona	Ballabona	G	543
N340/49	Huercal-Overa	Overa	G	548
N340/50	Huercal-Overa	Andalucia	G	550.5
N340/51	Huercal-Overa	Avenida	G	555
N340/52	La Atalaya	Atalaya	G	556.6
N340/53	Puerto-Lumbreras	Granados	O/S	576
N340/54	Puerto-Lumbreras	Salas	G	577
N340/55	Puerto-Lumbreras	Los Rosales	G	577
N340/56	Puerto-Lumbreras	Artero	G	577.5
N340/57	Puerto-Lumbreras	Riscal	G	577.5
N340/58	Puerto-Lumbreras	Morillas	G	579
N340/59	La Hoya	Navarro	E	
N340/60	La Hoya	La Hoya	E	606.3
N340/61	Totana	Los Camioneros	G	615
N340/62	Alhama de Murcia	Tanger	E	
N340/63	Sangonera La Seca	La Pinada	G	644.7
N340/64	Sangonera La Seca	De La Paz	VG	647
N340/65	Sangonera La Seca	Pérez y Navarro	E	650

The Hotels

N340/1 HR La Marisma**

Chiclana de la Frontera, Cádiz

☎ (956) 53.09.94

🅿 G		✗	✓
🍴 ✗		🛥	✗
🛏 4,000		🚪	✗

CÁDIZ: 4.5 km

A very pleasant hostal with nice gardens, just outside Cádiz.

N340/2 P* Avenida

Conil, Cádiz

☎ (956)

🅿 G		✗	✓
🍴 ✗		🛥	✗
🛏 3,500		🚪	✗

Cádiz: 18 km

A small pension. To my mind, rather expensive.

N340/3 HR* Las Cumbres

Chiclana de la Frontera, Cádiz

☎ (956) 44.55.14

🅿 G		✗ ✓
☕ ✓		🛏 ✓
🍴 4,200		🛌 ✗

Cádiz: 18 km

Nice, with all modern facilities but not in a particularly pleasant location.

N340/5 HR* Los Arcos

Vejer de la Frontera, Cádiz

☎ (956) 45.01.08

🅿 G		✗ ✓
☕ ✗		🛏 ✗
🍴 3,500		🛌 ✗

Cádiz: 39 km

The first of two places next to each other; they are both nice and this one is a little smaller.

N340/4 CH* El Canario

Conil, Cádiz

☎ (956) 44.55.76

🅿 G		✗ ✓
☕ ✗		🛏 ✗
🍴 4,000		🛌 2,500

Cádiz: 20 km

Basically just a bar and as such rather expensive.

N340/6 H** Lele

Vejer de la Frontera, Cádiz

☎ (956) 45.02.86

🅿 G		✗ ✓
☕ ✗		🛏 ✗
🍴 6,000		🛌 3,000

Cádiz: 39 km

This is larger than its close neighbour and is quite impressive.

N340/7 Hostal** Ponderosa

Tarifa, Cádiz

☎ (956) 64.33.30

🅿 G		✗	✓
☕ ✗		🧺 ✗	
🛏 4,000		🛏 ✗	
Cádiz: 76.5 km			

A pleasant hostal with views to the beach.

N340/8 H** Ensenada

Tarifa, Cádiz

☎ (956) 64.36.37

🅿 G		✗	✓
☕ ✗		🧺 ✓	
🛏 8,000		🛏 6,000	
Cádiz: 76.5 km			

A three-sided hotel where the rooms open on to a small plaza, it is only 100 yards from the sea.

N340/9 Hostal** Oasis

Tarifa, Cádiz

☎ (956) 68.50.65

🅿 G		✗	✓
☕ ✗		🧺 ✗	
🛏 6,000		🛏 ✗	
Cádiz: 76.5 km			

Another nice place with sea views that is close to the beach. All rooms have a terrace.

N340/10 H*** Balcon de España

Tarifa, Cádiz

☎ (956) 68.43.26

🅿 G		✗	✓
☕ ✓		🧺 ✓	
🛏 14,000		🛏 ✗	
Cádiz: 78 km			

A beautiful hotel that has attractive gardens, a pool and tennis courts. It is also close to the beach and has nice views. The pricing is different here; it is based on half-board for three people.

N340/11 H** Hurricane

Tarifa, Cádiz

☎ (956) 68.49.19

P VG	✗ ✓
🛏 ✗	🍴 ✗
🛏 8,000	🍴 5,000

Cádiz: 78 km

Not far off the road on the sea side, but very difficult to see because of the luxurious gardens. The prices vary according to the season and the view; an extra bed is 2,400 or 3,000 at Easter.

N340/12 H* La Cordoniz

Tarifa, Cádiz

☎ (956) 68.47.44

P G	✗ ✓
🛏 ✗	🍴 ✗
🛏 6,500	🍴 5,200

Cádiz: 79 km

This is called The Quail. The prices include breakfast but there are no sea views.

N340/13 H** Dos Mares

Tarifa, Cádiz

☎ (956) 68.40.35

P VG	✗ ✓
🛏 ✓	🍴 ✓
🛏 9,000	🍴 ✗

Cádiz: 79.5 km

The name, Two Seas, speaks for itself. This is a lovely place located on the beach and has horseriding, tennis, a surf centre and a beach bar. Rooms without a sea view are 8,000.

N340/14 H** Mesón de Sancho

Tarifa, Cádiz

☎ (956) 68.49.00

P G	✗ ✓
🛏 ✓	🍴 ✓
🛏 5,750	🍴 4,600

Cádiz: 94 km

Another nice hotel that has buildings on both sides of the road. This has mountain instead of sea views, and there is a small *plaza de toros*.

N340/15 Hostal* El Buen Gusto

Algeciras, Cádiz

☎ (956) 66.10.61

🅿 G	✕ ✓
☕ ✗	🍴 ✗
🛏 3,000	🛏 1,500

Cádiz: 109 km

A little outside the town, small and noisy. Called The Good Taste, it is accessible only from the west bound Algeciras carriageway.

N340/16 HR* Blumen

Algeciras, Cádiz

☎ (956) 63.16.75

🅿 G	✕ ✓
☕ ✗	🍴 ✗
🛏 3,600	🛏 1,900

Cádiz: 109 km

A medium-size place that is accessed from the westbound carriageway, and likely to be noisy.

N340/17 HR*** Guadacorte

Los Barrios, Cádiz

☎ (956) 67.75.00

🅿 VG	✕ ✓
☕ ✓	🍴 ✓
🛏 9,180	🛏 6,325

Cádiz: 115 km

A large impressive hotel-residencia that has all the expected facilities. It is also close to Gibraltar. Due to its location it cannot easily be photographed and this one does not do it justice.

N340/18 Hostal** Los Balandros

Torrenueva, Granada

☎ (958) 83.57.40

🅿 G	✕ ✓
☕ ✗	🍴 ✗
🛏 4,500	🛏 3,500

Cádiz: 336 km

A very pleasant new hostal that is located just outside town. This is close to the sea and is called The Sloops.

This hotel is split between two buildings and is close to the sea in this delightful small resort. It has an excellent restaurant which I thoroughly recommend.

N340/19 H* Sacratif

Torrenueva, Granada

☎ (958) 65.50.11

🅿 O/S	✗ ✓
🍴 ✗	⚘ ✗
🛏 4,500	🛌 2,850
Cádiz: 337 km	

Located on the main road through Torrenueva this has a slightly old-fashioned atmosphere. It is not far from the beach. The price includes breakfast.

N340/20 H* El Ancla

Calahonda, Granada

☎ (958) 62.33.36

🅿 O/S	✗ ✓
🍴 ✗	⚘ ✗
🛏 7,200	🛌 4,200
Cádiz: 344 km	

N340/21 Hostal* Miguel

Calahonda, Granada

☎ (958) 62.30.42

🅿 O/S	✗ ✓
🍴 ✗	⚘ ✗
🛏 2,650	🛌 ✗
Cádiz: 344 km	

A very basic hostal which has no parking facilities and will be noisy.

N340/22 Hostal* Iberico

Castell de Ferro, Granada

☎ (958) 64.60.80

🅿 G	✗ ✓
🍴 ✓	⚘ ✗
🛏 3,500	🛌 2,300
Cádiz: 351 km	

Located just outside this small town it is close to beautiful beaches. There are mountain views at the back.

N340/23 H* Paredes

Castell de Ferro, Granada

📞 (958) 64.61.59

🅿 G		✗	✓
☕ ✗		🛏	✓
🛏 7,200		🛏 3,600	

Cádiz: 352 km

This hotel has limited parking. Although close to the road the rooms are set back in a quadrangle and open on to a small pool. It is also very close to the beach.

N340/25 P* Onteniente

La Mamola, Granada

📞 (958) 82.96.58

🅿 G		✗	✓
☕ ✗		🛏	✗
🛏 2,000		🛏 1,000	

Cádiz: 362.5 km

Close to the sea this is a small place that might be noisy.

N340/24 Hostal* Costa del Sol

Castell de Ferro, Granada

📞 (958) 64.60.54

🅿 G		✗	✓
☕ ✗		🛏	✗
🛏 3,000		🛏 1,500	

Cádiz: 353 km

Located in the small plaza of this town which is typical of what the Costa del Sol used to be like before the mass influx of tourists. The restaurant has delightful views of the fishing boats on the beach. Parking here is somewhat restricted.

N340/26 Hostal** Wuppertal 2

El Pozuelo, Granada

📞 (958) 82.91.38

🅿 G		✗	✓
☕ ✗		🛏	✗
🛏 3,000		🛏 1,500	

Cádiz: 374 km

A rather large place with some sea views, it might be connected to the much smaller Wuppertal 1 & 2 down the road.

N340/27 H* Beatrix

El Pozuelo, Granada

📞 (958) 82.90.40

🅿 G	✗ ✓
🍷 ✗	🛏 ✗
🛏 4,000	🍴 2,500

Cádiz: 374.5 km

Not very large, but modern, this hotel has a dining room that is close to the sea.

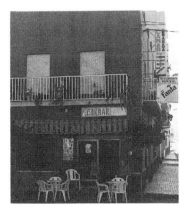

N340/28 P* Wuppertal 1 & 2

El Pozuelo, Granada

📞 (958) 82.91.66

🅿 O/S	✗ ✓
🍷 ✗	🛏 ✗
🛏 2,000	🍴 1,000

Cádiz: 374.5 km

A very small pension, close to the road and beach, that seems to have a connection, in name at least, with the Wuppertal 1 down the road.

N340/29 HR* Delfin

Adra, Almería

📞 (951) 40.00.50

🅿 O/S	✗ ✓
🍷 ✗	🛏 ✗
🛏 3,000	🍴 1,500

Cádiz: 388 km

Named the Dolphin this place is located on the one-way system through Adra in the direction of Motril/Málaga. It has a bright cheerful atmosphere.

N340/31 HR* Margo

El Ejido, Almería

📞 (951) 48.10.56

🅿 G	✗ ✓
🍷 ✗	🛏 ✗
🛏 2,000	🍴 1,400

Cádiz:

This is likely to be noisy as it is located in the town on the slip road, on the Almería-bound side.

N340/30 Hostal** Abdera
Adra, Almería
📞 (951) 40.01.00

🅿 VG		✗ ✓
☕ ✗		🛠 ✗
🛏 3,600		🚪 1,750

Cádiz: 389 km

In complete contrast to the Delfín this is a very old-fashioned hostal. The parking is inside around the patio and there is an unusual U-shaped bar. It may not have the most modern facilities but, for me, makes up for that with a certain charm.

N340/33 M** El Edén
La Redonda, Almería
📞 (951) 48.37.36

🅿 E		✗ ✓
☕ ✓		🛠 ✗
🛏 5,000		🚪 3,000

Cádiz: 415 km

This very nice motel is unfortunately not in such a nice location. Each room appears to have its own private garage and there is a lily pond outside the front door.

N340/32 H** Amelia
Santa Maria del Aguila, Almería
📞 (951) 48.16.51

🅿 G		✗ ✓
☕ ✗		🛠 ✗
🛏 4,000		🚪 2,500

Cádiz: 411.5 km

A very nice modern hotel that is located just 50 yards to the north off the N340.

N340/34 CH Lola
Aguadulce, Almería
📞 (951) 34.06.94

🅿 O/S		✗ ✗
☕ ✗		🛠 ✗
🛏 2,000		🚪 ✗

Cádiz: 429 km

A strange place that has beds only. It is very small, on a busy part of the road, and the family live in what was intended to be the garage.

N340/35 H*** Playaluz

Enix, Almería

📞 (951) 34.05.04

🅿 VG		✕ ✓
🛏 ✓		🍴 ✓
🛏 12,000		🛌 9,000

Cádiz: 436 km

A very beautiful hotel next to the sea, with pretty views to Almería. It has everything you might want, including an indoor and outdoor pool, and there is what amounts to a semi-private beach.

N340/36 H*** Solymar

Almería, Almería

📞 (951) 23.46.22

🅿 G		✕ ✓
🛏 ✗		🍴 ✗
🛏 9,800		🛌 5,800

Cádiz: 438.5 km

A very nice hotel, named Sun and Sea, that overlooks the harbour and Moorish castle and is just to the west of the city. It appears to have an international emphasis.

N340/37 Hostal* Retamares

Tabernas, Almería

📞 (951) 36.50.23

🅿 G		✕ ✓
🛏 ✗		🍴 ✗
🛏 1,400		🛌 700

Cádiz: 475 km

An interesting hostal in the middle of the desert environment. There is a large *Horno de Asado* (open brick oven) in the restaurant and many hams hanging from the ceiling. I doubt if the singles, maybe even the doubles, have a bath/shower.

N340/38 Hostal* La Molina

Tabernas, Almería

📞 (951) 36.51.66

🅿 G		✕ ✓
🛏 ✗		🍴 ✗
🛏 3,000		🛌 1,500

Cádiz: 476 km

A fairly large hostal just past the Retamares, but I do not think it is as interesting.

N340/39 HR** Sorbas

Sorbas, Almería

☎ (951) 36.41.60

P G	✗ ✓
☕ ✗	✗
🛏 3,200	🛏 2,000

Cádiz: 496 km

On a bend in the road and above a disco this could well be noisy. All information on this modern place is available from the bar across the road.

N340/40 P* Anita

Los Gallardos, Almería

☎ (951) 45.90.22

P G	✗ ✓
☕ ✗	✗
🛏 1,500	🛏 800

Cádiz: 511 km

A very small interesting pension with nice views. I would suspect that the singles do not have a bath/shower.

N340/41 Hostal* La Rueda

Los Gallardos, Almería

☎ (951) 46.91.07

P G	✗ ✓
☕ ✗	✗
🛏 2,000	✗

Cádiz: 520 km

This hostal, called The Wheel, is very well kept, neat, and with an open fire; travelling through here in the summer it is hard to imagine that it will ever be used. There are also good views.

N340/42 Hostal* Regio

Vera, Almería

☎ (951) 45.09.89

P O/S	✗ ✓
☕ ✗	✗
🛏 3,200	🛏 1,950

Cádiz: 532 km

A hostal with a traditional style called The Royal. Being close to the road it might be noisy.

N340/43 Hostal* Isabel

Vera, Almería

☎ (951) 45.07.25

🅿 O/S	✗ ✓
☕ ✗	🛏 ✗
🛌 3,000	🍴 1,800

Cádiz: 532 km

Located just across from the Regio this is again close to the road and has a modern style.

N340/44 Hostal* La Brasa

Real de Vera, Almería

☎ (951) 45.07.53

🅿 G	✗ ✓
☕ ✗	🛏 ✗
🛌 2,000	🍴 ✗

Cádiz: 533 km

A small nice hostal located in a reasonably isolated position just north of Vera.

N340/45 H** Argar

El Real de Antas, Almería

☎ (951) 45.14.01

🅿 G	✗ ✓
☕ ✓	🛏 ✓
🛌 4,950	🍴 3,300

Cádiz: 533.5 km

A very nice large hotel that has a pool with an open air bar. If it had been a little later in the evening I would have stayed here.

N340/46 HR* Mi Casa

El Real de Antas, Almería

☎ (951) 45.30.48

🅿 G	✗ ✓
☕ ✗	🛏 ✗
🛌 1,500	🍴 800

Cádiz: 536 km

Called My House, this is a new hostal-residencía that has a pleasant restaurant.

N340/47 F Venta Rodrigo

El Real de Antas, Almería

📞 (951) 45.30.08

🅿 G		✗ ✓
☕ ✗		⚑ ✗
🛏 2,800		🚪 ✗

Cádiz: 536 km

A small unimpressive Fonda that I consider to be rather expensive.

N340/48 M* Ballabona

La Ballabona, Almería

📞 (951) 47.12.19

🅿 G		✗ ✓
☕ ✗		⚑ ✗
🛏 4,500		🚪 2,000

Cádiz: 543 km

A very new modern place that calls itself a motel although in reality it is not. The location is very isolated.

N340/49 Hostal* Overa

Hurcal-Overa, Almería

📞 (951) 47.08.79

🅿 G		✗ ✓
☕ ✗		⚑ ✗
🛏 3,000		🚪 1,500

Cádiz: 548 km

I quite like the style of this hostal: it is on the large side and has interesting views.

N340/51 Hostal* Avenida

Huercal-Overa, Almería

📞 (951) 47.04.15

🅿 G		✗ ✓
☕ ✓		⚑ ✗
🛏 3,000		🚪 1,500

Cádiz: 555 km

A very nice-looking hostal just to the north of town. The bar and cafeteria are particularly pleasant but the toilets, strangely, were in a dreadful state.

N340/50 Hostal* Andalucia

Huercal-Overa, Almería

☎ (951) 47.05.37

🅿 G	✗	✓
🍴 ✗		⛽ ✗
🛏 3,000		🍽 1,500

Cádiz: 550.5 km

Located in an isolated position on a hill with surrounding views.

N340/52 Hostal* Atalaya

La Atalaya, Almería

☎ (951) 47.08.89

🅿 G	✗	✓
🍴 ✗		⛽ ✗
🛏 2,600		🍽 1,300

Cádiz: 556.6 km

This is fairly small but much more pleasant on the inside than it looks from the road.

N340/53 Hostal* Granados

Puerto-Lumbreras, Murcia

☎ (968) 40.23.48

🅿 O/S	✗	✗
🍴 ✗		⛽ ✗
🛏 1,800		🍽 ✗

Cádiz: 576 km

Located at the southern end of town close to the junction of the Granada road, this is a small hostal and all enquiries are made in the shop below.

N340/54 H** Salas

Puerto-Lumbreras, Murcia

☎ (968) 40.21.00

🅿 G	✗	✓
🍴 ✓		⛽ ✗
🛏 4,000		🍽 2,000

Cádiz: 577 km

A very nice large hotel that has a restaurant capable of seating 400 people. However, as with all places here, it is close to the road and might be noisy.

N340/55 Hostal* Los Rosales

Puerto-Lumbreras, Murcia

☎ (951) 40.20.00

🅿 G	✗	✓
🍴 ✗		⛽ ✗
🛏 2,800		🍽 1,500

Cádiz: 577 km

Directly across the road from the Salas this is smaller and shaped like a piece of cheese. It has an outside terrace.

N340/56 Hostal* Artero

Puerto-Lumbreras, Murcia

☎ (968) 40.22.82

🅿 G		✗ ✓
☕ ✓		🛏 ✗
🛏 2,700		🛏 1,325

Cádiz: 577.5 km

A typical small hostal that is just down the street from the Salas.

N340/58 Hostal** Morillas

Puerto-Lumbreras, Murcia

☎ (968) 40.21.59

🅿 G		✗ ✓
☕ ✗		🛏 ✗
🛏 3,800		🛏 2,100

Cádiz: 579 km

Located at the northern end of town directly opposite the Parador Nacional, this is small but pleasant.

N340/57 H** Riscal

Puerto-Lumbreras, Murcia

☎ (968) 40.20.50

🅿 G		✗ ✓
☕ ✓		🛏 ✗
🛏 3.950		🛏 2.700

Cádiz: 577.5 km

This appears to be on the organised bus tour route as the restaurant can seat 600 people.

N340/59 F Navarro

La Hoya, Murcia

☎ (968) 46.96.00

🅿 E		✗ ✓
☕ ✗		🛏 ✗
🛏 2,500		🛏 1,500

Cádiz:

A small Fonda where private garage facilities are free.

N340/60 H* La Hoya

La Hoya, Murcia

☎ (968) 46.27.05

🅿 E	✗ ✓
☕ ✓	🛏 ✓
🛏 4,000	🛏 3,000
Cádiz: 606.3 km	

The flags that cover the outside of this hotel do not make it very attractive but indicate that the people here are multilingual. A set meal is 750 pesetas.

N340/61 Hostal* Los Camioneros

Totana, Murcia

☎ (968) 42.10.37

🅿 G	✗ ✓
☕ ✗	🛏 ✗
🛏 3,000	🛏 1,500
Cádiz: 615 km	

A medium-size place that lives up to its name, The Lorrydrivers. There are pleasant views to the distant mountains.

N340/62 Hostal* Tanger

Alhama de Murcia, Murcia

☎ (968) 63.06.99

🅿 E	✗ ✓
☕ ✗	🛏 ✗
🛏 2,300	🛏 1,200
Cádiz:	

Small and, being on the main road through town, likely to be noisy.

N340/63 H* La Pinada

Sangonera La Seca, Murcia

☎ (968) 80.71.82

🅿 G	✗ ✓
☕ ✗	🛏 ✗
🛏 3,600	🛏 1,800
Cádiz: 644.7 km	

An isolated medium-size place that was very busy the lunchtime I was there.

N340/64 H De La Paz**

Sangonera La Seca, Murcia

☎ (968) 80.13.37

P VG		✗ ✓
☕ ✓		🛏 ✓
🛏 6,000		🍽 4,000
Cádiz: 647 km		

A very nice hotel well back from the road, 10 kms from Murcia and with many bullfighting mementos.

N340/65 Hostal* Pérez y Navarro

Sangonera La Seca, Murcia

☎ (968)

P E		✗ ✓
☕ ✗		🛏 ✗
🛏 3,500		🍽 1,500
Cádiz: 650 km		

Quite a small hostal that might be noisy; the private garage facilities appear to be free.

G   A   L   E   R   I   A   S

15 N431 SEVILLA–HUELVA

The Route

There are two clear options on this route: the A49 autovia and the N431. Considering that the distance is only around 90 km (56 miles) there is not going to be that much difference in the journey time.

The A49 is of course faster but, as usual on such a road, it only gives a glimpse of the places being passed. The only judgement that can be made is that it passes through an agricultural area. By taking the N431 much more can be seen as it goes through the small towns on the route.

One of the first, Espartinas, is the birthplace of the most famous active matador, Espartaco. The town that makes this particular route most interesting is Niebla; this has an ancient wall all around it and appears out of nowhere. The last few miles into Heulva are bland indeed as the road passes an industrial area just outside the town.

Route Planner

REF	TOWN	NAME	PKG	KMs FROM SEVILLA
N431/1	La Palma del Condado	Garle	G	47
N431/2	La Palma del Condado	La Viña	VG	47
N431/3	Niebla	Casadores	O/S	58.5
N431/4	Huelva	La Higuerita	G	77
N431/5	Huelva	Santa Ursula	G	99

The Hotels

N341/1 HR* Garle

La Palma del Condado, Huelva

☎ (955) 40.07.50

🅿 G	✗ ✓
🍷 ✗	🛏 ✗
🛏 3,000	✉ 1,400

Sevilla: 47 km

Located close to the road, this is rather plain but has a large restaurant.

N341/2 HR** La Viña

La Palma del Condado, Huelva

☎ (955) 40.02.73

🅿 VG	✗ ✓
🍷 ✗	🛏 ✓
🛏 3,000	✉ 1,500

Sevilla: 47 km

I rather like this place: it is not all that far from Seville. The pool is set in the gardens, and it had the prescience to advertise itself as a place to stay during Expo'92. For those who want a relaxing place this is it.

N341/3 P* Casadores

Niebla, Huelva

☎ (955) 36.30.71

🅿 O/S	✗ ✗
🍷 ✗	🛏 ✗
🛏 1,400	✉ ✗

Sevilla: 58.5 km

A very small pension that can easily be missed. It is a very typical Andalucian house with birdcages on the walls. The rooms though do not have a bath/shower. It is just across from the walls that surround this old town.

N341/4 H** La Higuerita

Huelva, Huelva

☎ (955) 35.65.05

🅿 O/S	✗ ✓
🍷 ✗	🛏 ✗
🛏 3,200	✉ 2,000

Sevilla: 77 km

A very nice hotel but, because of its location in a heavily industrialised area, I cannot think of anybody except for those with business in the area staying here.

N341/5 HR Santa Ursula**

Huelva, Huelva

📞 (955) 25.52.42

🅿 G	✖ ✔
☕ ✖	〰 ✔
🛏 6,000	🛏 4,500

Sevilla: 99 km

Located just a short distance outside
Huelva on the road to Portugal, this is
a nice place. Every room has a colour
TV and there is a beautiful pool set in
the gardens, with the restaurant and
a bar near the deep end.

G A L E R I A S

16 N432 CÓRDOBA-GRANADA

The Route

This is a scenic route of 166 km (about 104 miles), but for some stretches the road is not that good at all. The first part has those strange rolling hills that are distinctive to the area close to Córdoba. After, and until Baena, there are mountains to the south and hills in the north. The road improves for a few km past Baena where Alcaudete and its castle are visible miles away in the distance. As you go through Alcaudete there is on the right a perfect example of an old communal laundry building. These are still used by the old people in small villages but here it is just a reminder of a more traditional life.

The scenery changes quickly after Alcaudete. There are much larger mountains straight ahead while all around the hills become larger with small towns and villages clinging to the sides.

The next sight is particularly stunning. What appears to be a huge castle sits on top of a large hill with a typical whitewashed village protecting the approaches. The town is Alcalá la Real and the 'castle' should be investigated, if at all possible. The drive up to the top is quite dramatic but the view once there is even more so. From a height of around 900 metres (3,000 feet) it puts all the surrounding scenery into perspective and the small towns and villages, agricultural valleys and mountains merge to form a living landscape peculiar to this part of Andalucia. Another surprise is that the castle is not only just that: it is in fact the ruins of an ancient city and, what is more, is in the process of complete restoration. This creates rather a strange effect; for example in the very old church with no windows and a dirt floor a new wooden roof has been installed. The contrast between old and new is remarkable.

Although entrance is supposed to be free you are more than likely to be met by an old man with an official-looking hat who for a suitable contribution will be happy to escort you around.

The next section of the road, after Alcalá, becomes more difficult and the climb up to the Puerto Lope is extremely winding. From there the road twists slowly down the other side of the mountain to the valley. Pinos Puente is the first town and Granada is an easy 16 km drive away.

Route Planner

REF	TOWN	NAME	PKG	KMs FROM CORDOBA
N432/1	Santa Cruz	La Bartola	G	25
N432/2	Santa Cruz	Hidalgo	G	25
N432/3	Castro del Rio	Postas La Parada	G	42
N432/4	Las Palmeiras	Las Palmeiras	G	
N432/5	Alcaudete	Hidalgo	O/S	87
N432/6	Alcaudete	Esparrueda	G	87
N432/7	Alcalá la Real	Fuente Granada	G	114
N432/8	Pinos Puente	Montserrat	G	150

The Hotels

N432/2 Hostal** Hidalgo

Santa Cruz, Córdoba

☎ (957) 37.80.97

🅿 G		✗ ✓
🍴 ✗		🛏 ✗
🛏 3,000		✉ 2,000

Córdoba: 25 km

A modern hostal called The Nobleman. It has a very strange shaped bar.

N432/1 Hostal* La Bartola

Santa Cruz, Córdoba

☎ (957) 37.80.58

🅿 G		✗ ✓
🍴 ✗		🛏 ✗
🛏 1,800		✉ 900

Córdoba: 25 km

A nice clean hostal with a large restaurant.

N432/3 P* Postas La Parada

Castro del Rio, Córdoba

☏ (957) 37.04.74

🅿 G	✗ ✓
☕ ✗	🛏 ✗
🛏 1,200	🚪 800

Córdoba: 42 km

In an isolated position just south of the town, it is next to a service station and is clean but a shade old-fashioned.

N432/4 Las Palmeiras

Las Palmeiras, Córdoba

☏

🅿 G	✗ ✓
☕ ✗	🛏 ✗
🛏 2,000	🚪 1,000

Córdoba:

Very isolated and easy to miss, it has no phone or business card, but many stuffed boars' heads etc around the walls.

N432/5 P** Hidalgo

Alcaudete, Jaén

☏ (953) 56.10.78

🅿 O/S	✗ ✓
☕ ✗	🛏 ✗
🛏 2,400	🚪 1,400

Córdoba: 87 km

It is in the centre of town and does not have parking facilities, but advertises that it has a fine restaurant.

N432/7 H* Fuente Granada

Alcalá la Real, Jaén

☏ (953) 58.06.12

🅿 G	✗ ✓
☕ ✗	🛏 ✗
🛏 3,250	🚪 1,750

Córdoba: 114 km

Quite a nice place just to the south of Alcalá, it has very good views back to the ancient town on top of the hill.

N432/6 P** Esparrueda

Alcaudete, Jaén

☎ (953) 56.10.14

🅿 G		✕	✓
☕	✗	🛆	✗
🛏 2,400		⛉	1,200

Córdoba: 87 km

This is just a short distance off the Córdoba/Granada highway on the road towards Jaén. It is delightful, modern and clean with good service. The set meal in the restaurant is about 690 including wine, and parking is in the service station next door. For value it is one of the best places I have stayed in.

N432/8 HR* Montserrat

Pinos Puente, Granada

☎ (958) 45.03.58

🅿 G		✕	✓
☕	✗	🛆	✓
🛏 3,500		⛉	1,500

Córdoba: 150 km

Set back a little off the road this has good private parking and a pool. It is only 13 km from Granada and could prove a nice place to stay. It appears that many of the rooms are at the back and therefore quiet.

G   A   L   E   R   I   A   S

17 N620 BURGOS– VALLADOLID– SALAMANCA

The Route

This is without doubt the least interesting route in the guide. Between Burgos and Valladolid the road is quite good but there is nothing at all to see. It goes through the outskirts of Valladolid and shortly afterwards in Simancas there is a castle to the south of the road. The countryside here is in parts as flat as that of La Mancha and arable farms predominate. The small town of Alaejos is of interest because it has two large churches that strangely have very similar spires. The road bypasses Salamanca and then continues on towards Portugal.
I understand that the scenery is much more pleasant on that part of the route.

Route Planner

REF	TOWN	NAME	PKG	KMs FROM BURGOS
N620/1	Buniel	Area El Serrano	G	14
N620/2	Estepar	León	G	20
N620/3	Villodrigo	Sandino	G	41
N620/4	Villodrigo	Suco	G	42
N620/5	Quintana del Puente	La Vasca	G	53.3
N620/6	Quintana del Puente	Suco	G	54
N620/7	Torquemada	Las Lagunas	E	60
N620/8	Castillo de Magaz	Europa Centro	E	77
N620/9	Dueñas	La Casona	G	97
N620/10	Dueñas	Las Piramides	E	98.5
N620/11		Paco	G	117
N620/12		Chema Desnor	G	119
N620/13	Valladolid	Feria	G	131
N620/14	Simancas	Los Pinochos	VG	138
N620/15	Simancas	La Barca	G	138.6
N620/16	Simancas	Simancas	G	138.6

N620/17 Geria	La Colina	G	138.8
N620/18 Tordesillas	El Montico	VG	145
N620/19 Tordesillas	La Luna	G	158
N620/20 Siete Iglesias Trabancos	La Doba	G	180
N620/21	Marcos	G	181
N620/22 Cañizal	Galicia	G	183
N620/23 ?	?	G	218
N620/24 Pedrosillo El Ralo	Carolina	G	225
N620/25 Pedrosillo El Ralo	Sol	G	225
N620/26 Pedrosillo El Ralo	Portal de la Armuña	G	225
N620/27 Castellano de Moriscos	Mesón Castellano	G	231

The Hotels

N620/1 Hostal* Area El Serrano

Buniel, Burgos

✆ (947) 41.20.04

🅿 G		✗ ✓
🍴 ✗		🛏 ✗
🛏 4,000		🍴 2,000

Burgos: 14 km

A large modern hostal in an isolated location. It is set back well off the road and is still very new.

N620/2 Hostal* León

Estepar, Burgos

✆ (947) 41.10.00

🅿 G		✗ ✓
🍴 ✗		🛏 ✗
🛏 3,000		🍴 2,000

Burgos: 20 km

This is not so old but it has not worn very well. There is a *supermercado* (supermarket) close by.

G A L E R I A S

N620/3 P* Sandino

Villodrigo, Palencia

☎ (947) 16.12.73

🅿 G	✗ ✓
☕ ✗	🍴 ✗
🛏 1,300	🛏 1,000

Burgos: 41 km

A last resort: it is very bad besides being close to a service station and garage.

N620/4 HR* Suco

Villodrigo, Palencia

☎ (947) 16.60.16

🅿 G	✗ ✓
☕ ✗	🍴 ✗
🛏 3,300	🛏 2,200

Burgos: 42 km

The least impressive place in a chain of hotels within this area. Nevertheless it is not that bad and reasonably priced.

N620/5 Hostal** La Vasca

Quintana del Puente, Palencia

☎ (988) 79.31.17

🅿 G	✗ ✓
☕ ✗	🍴 ✗
🛏 2,800	🛏 1,100

Burgos: 53.3 km

Although it is on the northbound side slip road it can be accessed from the other side via the junction at 56 km. It is very pleasant inside.

N620/6 M* Suco

Quintana del Puente, Palencia

☎ (988) 79.31.06

🅿 G	✗ ✓
☕ ✗	🍴 ✓
🛏 3,500	🛏 2,500

Burgos: 54 km

Located close to a junction this is related to the earlier Suco, but it is a much more modern building and is nice inside. The parking facilities are controlled here.

N620/7 H** Las Lagunas

Torquemada, Palencia

☎ (988) 80.04.06

₽ E	✗ ✓
🛏 ✓	🍴 ✗
🛏 4,000	🛏 3,000

Burgos: 60 km

Named The Lagoons this is a large modern new hotel that can only be accessed from the southbound carriageway. It is in an open isolated position.

N620/9 Hostal* La Casona

Dueñas, Palencia

☎ (988) 798.01.53

₽ G	✗ ✓
🛏 ✗	🍴 ✗
🛏 4,800	🛏 3,500

Burgos: 97 km

In an isolated position this is not as grand as the prices might indicate. A double without bath/shower is 3,500.

N620/10 M* Las Piramides

Dueñas, Palencia

☎ (988) 78.01.77

₽ E	✗ ✓
🛏 ✗	🍴 ✗
🛏 4,500	🛏 ✗

Burgos: 98.5 km

N620/8 H**** Europa Centro

Castillo de Magaz, Palencia

☎ (988) 78.40.00

₽ E	✗ ✓
🛏 ✓	🍴 ✓
🛏 8,000	🛏 6,000

Burgos:

This, arguably the grandest hotel on the route, is set about 1.3 km off the road to the west and cannot be missed. It has a wide range of facilities and belongs to the same chain as the Sucos.

It is not difficult to see why this is called The Pyramids: the style speaks for itself. Accessed from the northbound side there are only doubles: the price includes a private garage, without which a room is only 3,500.

N620/11 Hostal* Paco

📞 (983) 34.20.34

🅿 G	✗	✓
☕ ✗		🍴 ✗
🛏 2,500		🛏 1,500

Burgos: 117 km

Quite large, pleasant and in an isolated position, this is only accessed from the northbound side.

N620/12 Hotel* Chema Desnor

✗ 📞 (983) 34.31.38

🅿 G	✗	✓
☕ ✗		🍴 ✗
🛏 4,000		🛏 ✗

Burgos: 119 km

On the southbound side, this is strange as the building appears to be used also by a car dealer.

N620/13 H* Feria

Avda. de Ramón Pradera, s/n
Valladolid

📞 (983) 33.32.44

🅿 G	✗	✓
☕ ✓		🍴 ✗
🛏 6,300		🛏 4,000

Burgos: 131 km

In the town of Valladolid this hotel was opened in 1987 and is large and impressive. The restaurant looks particularly good and there are facilities for banquets and conventions.

N620/14 HR** Los Pinochos

Simancas, Valladolid

📞 (983) 59.02.57

🅿 VG	✗	✓
☕ ✓		🍴 ✗
🛏 5,000		🛏 3,800

Burgos: 138 km

Positioned well off the southbound carriageway – make sure to follow the signs carefully – this complex has everything, including its own *plaza de toros*.

N620/15 Hostal* La Barca

Simancas, Valladolid

📞 (983) 59.01.27

🅿 G	✗	✓
☕ ✗		🍴 ✗
🛏 2,200		🛏 1,200

Burgos: 138.6 km

This, and the Simancas, are accessed only from the southbound side. It is located right by a service station. It is smaller than and not as nice as the Simancas.

N620/16 HR* Simancas

Simancas, Valladolid

☎ (983) 59.03.63

🅿 G	✗ ✓
☕ ✗	🛏 ✗
🛏 3,500	🍴 2,500

Burgos: 138.6 km

See La Barca as the same comments apply.

N620/17 H** La Colina

Geria, Valladolid

☎ (983) 77.13.92

🅿 G	✗ ✓
☕ ✗	🛏 ✗
🛏 6,000	🍴 4,000

Burgos: 138.8 km

I did not see inside this modern hotel but from the other side of the road it looks nice. Access is only possible from the northbound side.

N620/18 H*** El Montico

Tordesillas, Valladolid

☎ (983) 77.04.50

🅿 VG	✗ ✓
☕ ✗	🛏 ✗
🛏 9,000	🍴 7,000

Burgos: 145 km

Another place I did not visit personally. This is accessed only from the northbound carriageway and is part of a complex, set in gardens.

N620/19 Hostal* La Luna

Tordesillas, Valladolid

☎ (983) 77.04.72

🅿 G	✗ ✓
☕ ✗	🛏 ✗
🛏 2,800	🍴 1,400

Burgos: 158 km

This isolated small hostal, close to a river, is even closer to the road and will be noisy.

N620/20 P* La Doba

Siete Iglesias de Trabancos, Valladolid

📞 (988) 85.00.19

🅿 G		✕	✓
☕	✗	🛳	✗
🛏 2,500		🛏	✗

Burgos: 180 km

Small and isolated but still pleasant and friendly, this might be a little expensive.

N620/21 P* Marcos

📞 (988) 86.70.95

🅿 G		✕	✓
☕	✗	🛳	✗
🛏 2,400		🛏	1,200

Burgos: 181 km

On the southern edge of town this is quite modern but the location is not that grand.

N620/22 Hostal* Galicia

Cañizal, Zamora

📞 (988) 60.30.23

🅿 G		✕	✓
☕	✗	🛳	✗
🛏 3,180		🛏	1,200

Burgos: 183 km

A nice small isolated place where inexplicably there is cane furniture in the bar.

N620/23

📞 ✗

🅿 G		✕	✓
☕	✗	🛳	✗
🛏 3,500		🛏	2,000

Burgos: 218 km

Above a garage this is apparently run by some old people who do not have a business card and who have not put a name on the outside. It is a very odd building and I think it is over-priced.

N620/24 Hostal** Carolina

Pedrosillo El Ralo, Salamanca

☎ (923) 35.44.04

P G	✗ ✓
☕ ✗	⚒ ✗
🛏 2,400	🍴 1,500

Burgos: 225 km

Laid well back off the road, quite, clean and rather nice.

N620/26 Hostal** Portal de la Armuñia

Pedrosillo El Ralo, Salamanca

☎ (923) 35.43.76

P G	✗ ✓
☕ ✗	⚒ ✓
🛏 4,000	🍴 2,500

Burgos: 225 km

This is on the road but still pleasant; the wooden shutters on the windows enhance the style.

N620/25 Hostal** Sol

Pedrosillo El Ralo, Salamanca

☎ (923) 35.4.95

P G	✗ ✓
☕ ✗	⚒ ✗
🛏 3,000	🍴 2,000

Burgos: 225 km

Near to the Carolina but much closer to the road, nice but noisy. The *menu del dia* is 900.

N620/27 Hostal** Mesón Castellano

Castellano de Moriscos, Salamanca

☎ ✗

P G	✗ ✓
☕ ✗	⚒ ✗
🛏 3,600	🍴 2,500

Burgos: 231 km

Quite a large two-floor hostal, this is nice and located just north of Salamanca.

18 N623 SANTANDER–BURGOS

The Route

There are no options on this route of about 160 km (100 miles), it is single carriageway all the way and passes through some splendid and interesting scenery.

The first few km take you through the dreary suburbs as the road heads towards distant hills, passing through an agricultural valley on the way. To English eyes it is peculiar to see huge palm trees in very green farmland; the two do not seem compatible.

After about 25 km it crosses the N634 San Sebastián to Oviedo road and from then on, as it gently climbs through a valley, the scenery is very reminiscent of parts of France and Switzerland. Before the Puerto de Escudo, at 1,011 metres the highest point of the route, there are beautiful views back down the valley. Beware though: even on an otherwise lovely August day this part of the road is high enough to be cloudcovered and it makes for severely restricted vision.

Just after the Puerto the second spur of the N232 begins. This is an unusual road and is detailed more thoroughly in Chapter 9. The road enters the Provincia de Castilla/León at 93 km from Burgos, and shortly after crosses a very barren plateau before descending into an attractive valley/gorge. About 40 km from Burgos it climbs out of the valley back up on to a wide open plateau and is much the same for the rest of the journey to Burgos.

Route Planner

REF	TOWN	NAME	PKG	KMs FROM SANTANDER
N623/1	Muriedas	Romano II	G	7
N623/2	Caranda de Pielagos	Ramon Fernandez Ruiz	G	25
N623/3	Vargas	Vargas	G	26
N623/4	Puente Viesgo	La Terraza	O/S	30
N623/5	Vilegar de Toranzo	Miralpas	G	40
N623/6	San Vicente de Toranzo	Posada del Pas	VG	42.5
N623/7	Luena	Ana Isabel	G	58.5
N623/8	San Felices del Rudron	Javier	G	103
N623/9	Covanera	La Trucha	G	110
N623/10	Sotopalacios	Sotopalacios	G	146
N623/11	Sotopalacios	Ubíerna	G	146
N623/12	Quintanilla Vivar	Tarve	G	148

The Hotels

N623/1 H* Romano 11

Muriedas, Cantabria

☎ (942) 25.48.50

🅿 G		✖ ✓
🍽 ✗		🛏 ✗
🛏 4,255		🛏 2,875

Santander: 7 km

A pleasant modern hotel that is unfortunately located close to a junction and therefore might be a little noisy in some rooms.

N623/2 Ramón Fernandez Ruiz

Caranda de Pielagos, Cantabria

☎ (942) 57.10.07

🅿 G		✖ ✗
🍽 ✗		🛏 ✗
🛏 2,500		🛏 ✗

Santander: 25 km

This is the Spanish equivalent of bed and breakfast. It is a rural environment and might well be interesting.

N623/3 Hostal* Vargas

Vargas, Cantabria

📞 (942) 59.82.43

🅿 G		✗	✓
☕ ✗		🛎 ✗
🛏 3,000		✉ ✗	

Santander: 26 km

This is located very close to the crossroads of the N623 and the N634. It might be noisy.

N623/4 Hostal* La Terraza

Puente Viesgo, Cantabria

📞 (942) 59.81.02

🅿 O/S		✗	✓
☕ ✗		🛎 ✗
🛏 1,855		✉ 1,166	

Santander: 30 km

A small hostal which as the name implies has an attractive terrace. The parking is in a public car park about 100 yards away. It is close to some prehistoric caves.

N623/5 HR** Miralpas

Vilegar de Toranzo, Cantabria

📞 (942) 59.42.09

🅿 G		✗	✓
☕ ✗		🛎 ✗
🛏 3,180		✉ 1,800	

Santander: 40 km

A nice-looking place in an isolated position with good views. The singles do not have a bath/shower.

N623/6 H** Posada del Pas

San Vicente de Toranzo, Cantabria

📞 (942) 59.44.11

🅿 VG		✗	✓
☕ ✓		🛎 ✓
🛏 6,000		✉ 4,000	

Santander: 42.5 km

In a lovely environment this is an impressive hotel, modern and isolated. There is a charge of 1,500 for an extra bed in a double room.

N623/7 Hostal Ana Isabel**

Luena, Cantabria

📞 (942) 59.41.96

🅿 G	✗	✓
🍴 ✗	🛏 ✗	
🛏 3,500	🛏 2,500	

Santander: 58.5 km

Located close to Puerto del Escudo in a high, isolated position, this is another place with attractive views. There is a long distance between this and the next hotel and I stopped here one night when it was getting dark. It is not bad but I was not overly impressed and consider it a little expensive.

N623/9 Hostal La Trucha**

Covanera, Burgos

📞 ((947) 15.00.12

🅿 G	✗	✓
🍴 ✗	🛏 ✗	
🛏 3,800	🛏 2,500	

Santander: 110 km

In the same valley as the previous place but in not such a nice location. Rather large and isolated. The morning I was there they had a huge pile of delicious-looking breads that were rather like a cross between giant rolls and pizza. The place is called The Trout.

N623/8 Hostal* Javier

San Felices del Rudron, Burgos

📞 ((947) 15.00.05

🅿 G	✗	✓
🍴 ✗	🛏 ✗	
🛏 2,200	🛏 1,500	

Santander: 103 km

A very small hostal located in a ravine-like valley, a very picturesque environment. The overhanging restaurant is notable and there is a terrace across the road by a river. This may be a little basic but it appeals to me and is on my list for a future occasion.

N623/10 HR** Sotopalacios

Sotopalacios, Burgos

☎ ((947) 44.10.33

🅿 G		✗	✓
🍷 ✗		🛠 ✗	
🛏 3,400		🚪 2,000	

Santander: 146 km

A reasonably sized hostal-residencia in a fairly isolated environment, with a large restaurant.

N623/12 Hostal Tarve

Quintanilla Vivar, Burgos

☎ ((947) 29.20.38

🅿 G		✗	✓
🍷 ✗		🛠 ✗	
🛏 3,180		🚪 1,590	

Santander: 148 km

Only 9 km from Burgos, a medium-size place in an isolated location. A double without bath is 2,120.

N623/11 Hostal* Ubierna

Sotopalacios, Burgos

☎ ((947) 44.10.41

🅿 G		✗	✓
🍷 ✗		🛠 ✗	
🛏 2,800		🚪 ✗	

Santander: 146 km

Situated across the road from the Sotopalacios this is smaller and plainer, but nevertheless pleasant.

The Route

This is probably the longest non-coastal road in Spain as it originates in Gijón on the north coast, and then proceeds southwards through Oviedo, León, Zamora, Salamanca, Cáceres and Mérida to Sevilla. For the purposes of this guide we join the N630 at Salamanca and all distances are from there. The scenery is dramatically different from the N620; although the road is smaller, the undulating hills with cattle farms everywhere are much more attractive than the flat country that proceeded them. After 48 km the road begins to climb and there are large mountains in the background: unusually there are many small fields here which are reminiscent of the UK. As the road approaches Bejar it is particularly scenic, and just after the town it passes through the Parque Nacional de Santa Barbara. It then descends into a wide agricultural valley with hills to the north and the Sierra de Gredos mountains to the south, and this continues to Plascencia where there is an interesting aqueduct. After Plascencia the scenery opens up much more but the countryside is very scrubby. There are ruins of a Roman bridge near 174 km and not far after a series of large lakes which make a nice change. The bridges over these lakes have two levels, the top for cars and the bottom for trains. Beyond Cáceres it becomes even more open and near 227 km there is a small castle/palace and four km further on the ruins of another castle.

The N630 crosses the NV in Mérida. This part of the world is extremely hot in the summer, temperatures of 46/47 Centigrade – about 115 Fahrenheit – are not uncommon, even in the early evening. From Mérida to Zafra, which is three to four km off the road, it is rather flat and very agricultural. In the summer there are many roadside stalls selling melons, tomatoes and other produce, and in early October the road is full of wagons carrying load after load of grapes into Almendralejo. There are direct outlets in this town and the range of wines is large; they even have Acorn liqueur. Surprisingly there is also a small zoo just north of this town. Zafra is worth taking a little time to see; it is commonly referred to as 'the Sevilla of the north'. Beware however of early October as it holds the provincial fair then and it is impossible to get a room anywhere close.

The scenery changes quickly as the road passes through the Sierra Morena, an attractive area, winding down to the wide Guadalquivir valley, and before entering Sevilla passes the Roman ruins (Ruinas de Italica) where two Roman emperors were born at Santiponce.

Warning

There are three places on this route that are particularly dangerous. They all involve places where the road passes under small bridges that are not wide enough for two cars. The first is on a hill and curve just south of Béjar and is even more dangerous because it is unexpected. The others near 122 and 174 km from Salamanca (464 and 516 km from Gijon) are not quite so bad but still dangerous.

Route Planner

REF	TOWN	NAME	PKG	KMs FROM SALAMANCA
N630/1	Salamanca	Lorenzo	G	1
N630/2	Mozarbez	Mozarbez	G	10
N630/3	Martinamor	Cuatro Calzadas	G	17
N630/4	Cabeza de Béjar	Jose-Carlos	G	55
N630/5	Ventorro Fresnedso	Los Rubios	G	60
N630/6	Bejar	Argentíno	G	68
N630/7	Cantagallo	La Plata	G	78
N630/8	Puerto de Béjar	Los Molineros	G	82
N630/9	Puerto de Béjar	Puerto	G	82
N630/10	Baños de Montemayor	La Glorieta	G	
N630/11	Hervas	Roma II	G	94.4
N630/12	Jarilla	Asturias	G	97.4
N630/13	Plasencia	Real	G	128
N630/14	Plasencia	Los Alamos	G	131.6

REF	TOWN	NAME	PKG	KMs FROM SALAMANCA
N630/15	Riolobos	Mirabel	G	148
N630/16	Malpartida de Plasencia	Mirabel II	G	150
N630/17	Malpartida de Plasencia	Santa Marta	G	151
N630/18	Cañaveral	Málaga	G	
N630/19	Casar de Caceres	Las Encinas	VG	202
N630/20	Casar de Caceres	La Granja	G	202
N630/21	Casar de Caceres	Richardson	VG	202.9
N630/22	Caceres	Pasaron	G	214
N630/23	Casas de Don Antonio	La Fortaleza	G	240
N630/24	Casas de Don Antonio	Medina	G	240
N630/25	Alcuescar	Los Olivos	G	249
N630/26	Alcuescar	Cruce las Herrerias	G	249
N630/27	Alcuescar	Canuto	G	249
N630/28	Merida	Los Milagros	G	278
N630/29	Torremejia	Flores de La Rosa	G	
N630/30	Almendralejo	España	O/S	310
N630/31	Almendralejo	Dulcinea	G	312
N630/32	Almendralejo	Espronceda	G	313
N630/33	Villafranca los Barros	La Marina	G	325
N630/34	Villafranca los Barros	Romero	G	326
N630/35	Zafra	Rafael	O/S	345
N630/36	Zafra	Huerta Honda	G	345
N630/37	Zafra	Zafra	VG	345
N630/38	Calzadilla los Barros	Los Rodrigues	G	354
N630/39	Fuente de Cantos	Vicenta	G	
N630/40	Monesterio	Puerta del Sol	G	382
N630/41	Monesterio	Extremadura	G	382
N630/42	Monesterio	Moya	G	383
N630/43	Monesterio	Los Conejos	G	395
N630/44	El Garrobo	Las Cumbres	VG	443
N630/45	Las Pajanosas	Puerto Blanco	G	446
N630/46	Guillena	Casa Vicente	G	463

G A L E R I A S

The Hotels

N630/1 HR* Lorenzo

Salamanca, Salamanca

☏ (923) 21.43.06

P G		✗	✓
☕ ✗		🛁	✗
🛏 2,900		🛏	2,000

Salamanca: 1 km

Just outside the city and quite large but the building is unattractive. There is a service station close by.

N630/2 Hostal* Mozarbez

Mozarbez, Salamanca

☏ (923) 30.82.91

P G		✗	✓
☕ ✗		🛁	✗
🛏 3,500		🛏	2,500

Salamanca: 10 km

In an isolated position this hostal has a pleasant style and rural views.

N630/3 Hostal** Cuatro Calzadas

Martinamor, Salamanca

☏ (923) 30.82.36

P G		✗	✓
☕ ✗		🛁	✓
🛏 3,000		🛏	1,900

Salamanca: 17 km

A very nice hostal that has an old fashioned atmosphere. There is a lovely open fireplace in the dining room.

N630/5 P* Los Rubios

Ventorro Fresnedso, Salamanca

☏ (923) 40.02.85

P G		✗	✓
☕ ✗		🛁	✗
🛏 1,600		🛏	900

Salamanca: 60 km

A small basic pension where the rooms do not have a bath/shower.

N630/4 Hostal* Jose-Carlos

Cabeza de Béjar, Salamanca

📞 (923) 59.11.93

P	G	✗	✓
☕	✗	🛏	✓
🛏 3,500		🛏 2,000	

Salamanca: 55 km

A very nice, isolated, hostal that is neat inside.

N630/6 HR** Argentíno

Béjar, Salamanca

📞 (923) 40.23.64

P	G	✗	✓
☕	✗	🛏	✗
🛏 3,200		🛏 2,200	

Salamanca: 68 km

Located just as the road enters the town this is rather a nice place. Although it is close to the road the rooms are set back somewhat and should not be that noisy.

N630/10 Hostal** La Glorieta

Baños de Montemayor, Cáceres

📞 (927) 42.80.18

P	G	✗	✓
☕	✗	🛏	✗
🛏 2,600		🛏 1,300	

Salamanca:

A little before the town, this is small and on a tight bend.

N630/7 Hostal* La Plata

Cantagallo, Salamanca

📞 (923) 40.20.24

P	G	✗	✓
☕	✗	🛏	✗
🛏 2,250		🛏 1,150	

Salamanca: 78 km

This is a two-storey hostal that is clean and ordinary.

N630/8 * Los Molineros

Puerto de Béjar, Salamanca

📞 (923)

P	G	✗	✓
☕	✗	🛏	✗
🛏 4,700		🛏 3,750	

Salamanca: 82 km

This hotel in the lovely surroundings of Santa Barbara National Park has pretty views but I would consider it a little expensive.

N630/9 H* Puerto

Puerto de Béjar, Salamanca

☎ (923) 40.20.06

🅿 G		✗	✓
☕ ✗		🛌 ✗	
🛏 3,000		🛏 2,000	

Salamanca: 82 km

In a traditional style building set above the north side of the road this is also in the lovely Santa Barbara National Park.

N630/11 H* Roma 11

Hervas, Cáceres

☎ (927) 48.43.44

🅿 G		✗	✓
☕ ✗		🛌 ✗	
🛏 3,600		🛏 1,900	

Salamanca: 94.4 km

A modern hotel in an open valley, it has pleasant views.

N630/12 Hostal* Asturias

Jarilla, Cáceres

☎ (927) 48.90.57

🅿 G		✗	✓
☕ ✗		🛌 ✗	
🛏 2,500		🛏 1,500	

Salamanca: 97.4 km

Located in an isolated position, with mountains in the background. There is a farm next door.

N630/13 Hostal Real**

Plasencia, Cáceres

☎ (927) 41.85.02

🅿 G		✗	✓
☕ ✗		🛌 ✗	
🛏 3,000		🛏 1,900	

Salamanca: 128 km

This is nicer on the outside than inside.

N630/14 Hostal** Los Alamos

Plasencia, Cáceres

☎ (927) 41.15.50

P	G	✗	✓
🍷	✗	🛏️	✗
🛏️	3,500	�101	2,300

Salamanca; 131.6 km

The hostal itself is quite nice but it is located in a horrible light industrial environment. The *menu del dia* is 750.

N630/15 Hostal* Mirabel

Riolobos, Cáceres

☎ (927) 45.30.22

P	G	✗	✓
🍷	✗	🛏️	✗
🛏️	3,500	�101	2,000

Salamanca: 148 km

A pleasant neat place in an isolated location, it has a brother just down the road.

N630/16 Hostal* Mirabel 11

Malpartida de Plasencia, Cáceres

☎ (927) 45.33.42

P	G	✗	✓
🍷	✗	🛏️	✗
🛏️	3,000	�101	1,800

Salamanca: 150 km

A little smaller than its brother, but also nice and in a rural environment.

N630/17 H* Santa Marta

Malpartida de Plasencia, Cáceres

☎ (927) 45.32.60

P	G	✗	✓
🍷	✗	🛏️	✗
🛏️	3,000	�101	1,500

Salamanca: 151 km

Although painted in a mustard colour this is an attractive hotel that is not spoilt, at least visually, by the pig farm behind it.

N630/18 Hostal* Málaga

Cañaveral, Cáceres

☎ (927) 30.00.67

🅿 G		✕ ✓
☕ ✗		🛏 ✗
🛏 2,000		🍴 1,000

Salamanca:

This is small and it is also in a small town. There is an old-fashioned atmosphere but it might be noisy.

N630/19 Hostal** Las Encinas

Casar de Caceres, Cáceres

☎ (927) 29.02.01

🅿 VG		✕ ✓
☕ ✗		🛏 ✗
🛏 3,000		🍴 1,500

Salamanca: 202 km

On the southbound side of the road this is quite large but a little bland.

N630/20 P** La Granja

Casar de Caceres, Cáceres

☎ (927) 29.05.21

🅿 G		✕ ✓
☕ ✗		🛏 ✗
🛏 2,000		🍴 1,000

Salamanca: 202 km

Directly opposite Las Encinas this is much smaller and quieter as it is well back from the road.

N630/21 M* Richardson

Casar de Caceres, Cáceres

☎ (927) 29.00.01

🅿 VG		✕ ✓
☕ ✗		🛏 ✓
🛏 5,000		🍴 3,000

Salamanca: 202.9 km

A most unusual and interesting place. The accommodation is air-conditioned and comfortable but the bar is a bodega that is more like a museum, with many ornaments exhibited as well as a stage for shows. If you fancy something a little different this is it.

N630/22 HR** Pasaron

Cáceres, Caceres

☎ (927) 22.28.50

🅿 G	✕ ✓
🍴 ✗	🛏 ✗
🛏 3,500	🍴 2,300

Salamanca: 214 km

A large busy hostal on the outskirts of Cáceres in a not very attractive building.

N630/24 Hostal** Medina

Casas de Don Antonio, Cáceres

☎ (927) 38.30.85

🅿 G	✕ ✓
🍴 ✗	🛏 ✗
🛏 2,700	🍴 1,700

Salamanca: 240 km

This is very modern and completely different from its neighbour, La Fortaleza.

N630/23 La Fortaleza

Casas de Don Antonio, Cáceres

☎ (927) 38.22.58

🅿 G	✕ ✓
🍴 ✗	🛏 ✗
🛏 2,250	🍴 1,750

Salamanca: 240 km

An old-style place both inside and outside, it is also isolated. The name means The Fortress.

N630/25 Hostal* Los Olivos

Alcuescar, Cáceres

☎ (927) 38.40.01

🅿 G	✕ ✓
🍴 ✗	🛏 ✗
🛏 3,000	🍴 1,000

Salamanca: 249 km

Despite the horrible two-tone green paint on the outside this is rather pleasant inside. It is in a rural environment.

N630/26 HR* Cruce de las Herrerias

Alcuescar, Cáceres

☎ (927) 38.40.66

🅿 G		✗	✓
☕ ✗		🌱 ✗	
🛏 3,300		🛏 1,800	

Salamanca: 249 km

Much larger than Los Olivos this, as the name implies, is on a crossroads and rather bland.

N630/27 Hostal* Canuto

Alcuescar, Cáceres

☎ (927) 38.41.97

🅿 G		✗	✓
☕ ✗		🌱 ✗	
🛏 1,800		🛏 1,000	

Salamanca: 249 km

The white paint on the outside is the opposite to the inside which is dark and dingy.

N630/28 Hostal** Los Milagros

Mérida, Badajoz

☎ (924) 31.76.61

🅿 G		✗	✓
☕ ✗		🌱 ✗	
🛏 4,000		🛏 2,000	

Salamanca: 278 km

This is a very nice clean medium-size place that is just to the north of Mérida and also close to the Roman ruins.

N630/29 H* Flores de la Rosa

Torremejia, Badajoz

☎ (924) 34.01.74

🅿 G		✗	✓
☕ ✗		🌱 ✗	
🛏 2,700		🛏 1,700	

Salamanca:

In a small town this is a very pleasant hotel.

N630/30 España

Almendralejo, Badajoz

☎ (924) 66.02.30

🅿 O/S		✗	✓
🍷 ✗		🛏 ✗	
🛏 3,500		🛏 ✗	

Salamanca: 310 km

This is a gem of a place, situated off the main road in a quiet street. Turn right at the Bodegas Iglesias/Bar Zara. Quite small but very dignified, it has a charming old-world style. A call ahead might be in order, especially in early October when the grapes are brought in and there are fiestas.

N630/31 Dulcinea

Almendralejo, Badajoz

☎ (924) 66.59.11

🅿 G		✗	✓
🍷 ✓		🛏 ✗	
🛏 6,000		🛏 4,000	

Salamanca: 312 km

A very new hotel that is situated a little off the road, just south of town. There are colour TVs in each room.

N630/32 Espronceda

Almendralejo, Badajoz

☎ (924) 66.44.12

🅿 G		✗	✓
🍷 ✓		🛏 ✗	
🛏 5,000		🛏 2,700	

Salamanca: 313 km

Another modern hotel that is just past the Dulcinea. Also set back from the road, it has a pleasant style about it.

N630/33 La Marina

Villafranca de los Barros, Badajoz

☎ (924) 52.07.48

🅿 G		✗	✓
🍷 ✗		🛏 ✗	
🛏 2,000		🛏 1,000	

Salamanca: 325 km

A very basic hostal but inexpensive and the food is not too bad.

N630/34 Romero

Villafranca de los Barros, Badajoz

☎ (924) 52.14.08

🅿 G	✗ ✓
☕ ✓	🍴 ✗
🛏 3,000	🛏 1,700

Salamanca: 326 km

Like other places on this part of the route it is quite large modern and set back from the road – though a little plain on the outside.

N630/37 Zafra

Zafra, Badajoz

☎ (924) 55.18.12

🅿 VG	✗ ✓
☕ ✓	🍴 ✓
🛏 4,000	🛏 2,700

Salamanca: 345 km

A very nice hotel located on the junction of the Córdoba/Sevilla road just outside Zafra. It even has a fur shop.

N630/35 Rafael

Virgen de Guadalupe, 7, Zafra, Badajoz

☎ (924) 55.20.52

🅿 O/S	✗ ✓
☕ ✗	🍴 ✗
🛏 3,300	🛏 1,750

Salamanca: 345 km

I can recommend this small family run pensión; it is very pleasant and the food is good also. The on-street parking is not a problem except during the fiesta in early October when it will be booked solid as will all others in this town. Rooms without bath are 1,100 and 2,200 respectively, and for three people the rate is 3,800 without bath and 4,100 with.

N630/36 Huerta Honda

Lopez Asme, s/n, Zafra, Badajoz

☎ (924) 55.08.00

🅿 G	✗ ✓
☕ ✓	🍴 ✓
🛏 6,500	🛏 4,500

Salamanca: 345 km

Part of the Best Western chain, and is very well decorated with every facility. However, having stayed here twice, there are things about it that I consider are just not right. There is only air-conditioning in double rooms and even then it is turned off automatically. They do not know how to keep the pool clean. In fact, on both occasions it was simply too dirty to get into, and this where the temperature is regularly over 100°F.

N630/38 Los Rodriguez

Calzadilla de los Barros, Badajoz

☎ (924) 50.07.01

🅿 G	✗	✓
🍴 ✗	🛏 ✗	
🛏 3,000		🚪 1,000

Salamanca: 354 km

This is a small hostal where the singles do not have a bath/shower.

N630/39 Vicenta

Fuente de Cantos, Badajoz

☎ (924) 50.02.27

🅿 G	✗	✓
🍴 ✗	🛏 ✗	
🛏 1,400		🚪 700

Salamanca:

Another very small place but it has a nice feel to it.

N630/40 Puerta del Sol

Monesterio, Badajoz

☎ (924) 51.70.01

🅿 G	✗	✓
🍴 ✗	🛏 ✗	
🛏 3,000		🚪 1,500

Salamanca: 382 km

Situated back off the road in a small plaza, this is a clean modern style place. Monastario is a small town and the hostal is across from the *mercado*.

N630/41 Extremadura

Monesterio, Badajoz

☎ (924) 51.65.02

🅿 G	✗	✓
🍴 ✗	🛏 ✗	
🛏 1,200		🚪 ✗

Salamanca: 382 km

A small place but I would expect that the rooms do not have a bath/shower.

N630/42 Moya

Monesterio, Badajoz

☎ (924) 51.61.36

P	G	✗	✓
☕	✗	🛏	✗
🏷 2,500		🛏 1,400	

Salamanca: 383 km

This is quite large and, very unusually, is set back from the road at a tangent. It has a pleasant atmosphere.

N630/43 Los Conejos

Monesterio, Badajoz

☎ (924) 51.61.58

P	G	✗	✓
☕	✗	🛏	✓
🏷 1,500		🛏 1,000	

Salamanca: 395 km

Named The Rabbits, this is a small place in the sierra about 40 miles north of Sevilla. There is a swimming pool and a shooting range; although it is a little on the basic side it is good value.

N630/44 Las Cumbres

El Garrobo, Sevilla

☎ (95) 413.00.28

P	VG	✗	✓
☕	✓	🛏	✓
🏷 9,000		🛏 5,000	

Salamanca: 443 km

This hotel has everything and is very nice indeed, but it is not cheap. Located at the top of a hill it is appropriately called The Summit. However if you approach from the north it is not well signposted and it is easy to pass.

N630/45 Puerto Blanco

Las Pajanosas, Sevilla

☎ (95) 413.00.09

P	G	✗	✓
☕	✗	🛏	✗
🏷 1,500		🛏 ✗	

Salamanca: 446 km

Located in an isolated position this appears to be nice and clean and it is reasonably priced.

N630/46 Casa Vicente

Guillena, Sevilla

☎ (95) 479.81.12

🅿 G		✗	✓
🍵	✗	🛏	✗
🛏 5,000		🛏 3,000	

Salamanca: 463 km

A small hostal in an isolated position, this is not all that pleasant and I consider it to be very expensive for what it is.

G   A   L   E   R   I   A   S

20 N634/N632/N634
SAN SEBASTIÁN–BILBAO–SANTANDER–GIJÓN–RIBADEO

The Route

This route is very attractive for the most part, as either the sea, hills or mountains are never very far away, and it is only spoilt by the occasional very ugly town. Between San Sebastián and Bilbao the A8 autopista, a toll road, runs parallel to and frequently crisscrosses the N634. It is more than likely that the closest hotels to the A8 will be located on the N634.

The first part of the route, between San Sebastián and Deba, is attractive. The road winds from lovely hilly landscapes to beach resorts and back again, a particularly interesting contrast. After Deba the road continues inland passing Eibar, an ugly industrial town, on the way to Bilbao. Follow the N634 Santander road signs through Bilbao. While avoiding much of the city traffic, the road goes through some grim suburbs. Between Bilbao and Castro-Urdiales there are sea views from high cliffs, and then at Alto-Laredo there is a wide panorama down and across the beach at Laredo.

The N634 then continues inland across a peninsula towards Santander where it splits, one part going towards the city and the other continuing onwards to Torrelavega where it again meets a road coming from Santander. From Castaneda, where it crosses the N623, the scenery is rather pretty and the road meets the sea again at San Vicente de la Barquera. This is a very attractive town and extremely popular in July and August, so much so in fact that the afternoon I passed, it took over two hours to get through the town. Between San Vicente and Llovio, just outside Ribadesella, the road is never far from the sea to the north and mountains to the south. At Ribadesella there is an option on this route. The N634 continues inland to Oviedo and eventually meets the coast again at Luarca while the N632, which is detailed here, follows the coastal route – via Gijón – before eventually rejoining the N634 at Luarca.

The initial section to Villaviciosa has an interesting mixture of hills, countryside and sea, and after, towards Gijón, the road climbs through scenic hills. Gijón itself is nothing special while Avilés is decidedly unattractive, even ugly. From Avilés, to where the two roads rejoin, the route is very dramatic as the road goes up and down through pine covered hills and bays and across rural countryside. The day I made the journey, in August, the weather was terrible and it poured with rain most of the time making driving very hazardous. These weather conditions are not unusual even in summer, and strangely it is one of the reasons that this area is so popular with Spaniards: it is a contrast to the usual relentless heat in most of Spain.

The final section on the N634 between Luarca and Ribadeo is different again; it is far more open with hills to the south and the sea to the north. It is interesting to take one of the small roads that run off the N634 at a tangent towards the sea; the tiny villages are similar to some in Cornwall. The view from the bridge over the river at Ribadeo gives a very good perspective of the holiday atmosphere of this town. All of this coastline is extremely popular with the Spanish and, as a result, during July and August it is very crowded and hotels are often booked solid. It is best to stop early or book ahead. It is also more expensive than most other areas in Spain.

For many Spaniards the greeness of the scenery and the unpredictability of the weather are a complete contrast to their normal environment and it makes the area very attractive to them. In many ways it is similar to the way that northern Europeans take their holidays on the sun-drenched beaches of the Mediterranean, only in reverse.

G   A   L   E   R   I   A   S

Route Planner

REF	TOWN	NAME	PKG
N634/1	Orio	Esnal	G
N634/2	Zarauz	Talaimendi Apart.	VG
N634/3	Zarauz	Zarauz	VG
N634/4	Zarauz	Norte	O/S
N634/5	Iciar/Deba	Iciar	G
N634/6	Deba	Miramar	E
N634/7	Abadiano-Celayeta	San Blas	G
N634/8	Bilbao	Avenida	G
N634/9	Castro-Urdiales	Vista Alegrel	G
N634/10	Islares	Arenillas	G
N634/11	Alto de Laredo	El Carro	VG
N634/12	Colindres	Monte Carlo	O/S
N634/13	Beranga	El Paso	G
N634/14	Hoznayo	Adelma	G
N634/15	Hoznayo	Mizmaya	G
N634/16	Santander	El Carmen	E
N634/17	Quijas	Hosteria de Quijas	VG
N634/18	Cabezon de la Sal	Conde de Lara	G
N634/19	La Revilla	Venta de Abajo	G
N634/20	Pesues	Baviera	G
N634/21	Unquera-Pesues	Rio Deva II	G
N634/22	El Peral-Colombres	Oyambre	G
N634/23	El Peral-Colombres	Casa Junco	G
N634/24	Colombres	San Angel	VG
N634/25	Llanes	Europa	G
N632/26	Ribadesella	Boston	G
N632/27	Ribadesella	Puente El Pilar	G
N632/28	Prado-Caravia	Caravia	G
N632/29	La Isla-Colunga	Monte y Mar	G
N632/30	Tornon	Nautico	G
N632/31	Villaviciosa	La Ria	O/S
N632/32	Concha de Artedo	Portobello	G
N632/33	Artedo-Cudillero	Yolimar	G
N632/34	Soto de Luina	Andurina	O/S
N632/35	?	Yendebarcas	G
N632/36	Santa Marina	Prada	G
N632/37	Barcia	El Redondel	G
N634/38	La Ronda	No Name	G
N634/39	Otur-Luarca	Casa Consuelo	G
N634/40	Villapedre-Navia	El Pinar	G
N634/41	Valdepares	Rego	G
N634/42	Tapia de Casariego	Chiquin	G
N634/43	Ribadeo	Voar	G

The Hotels

N634/1 Esnal

Orio, Guipúzcoa

📞 (943) 83.00.29

🅿 VG	✗ ✓
🍴 ✗	🛏 ✗
🛏 3,000	🛏 ✗

San Sebastián: 20 km

An old-fashioned place with a rural atmosphere. There are pretty views back over a wide river with hills in the background.

N634/2 Talaimendi Apartamenduak

Zarauz, Guipúzcoa

📞 (943) 83.01.32

🅿 VG	✗ ✓
🍴 ✓	🛏 ✓
🛏 8,500	🛏 ✗

A large modern apartment hotel where the prices are for four people.

N634/3 Zarauz

Zarauz, Guipúzcoa

📞 (943) 83.02.00

🅿 VG	✗ ✓
🍴 ✗	🛏 ✗
🛏 7,500	🛏 3,850

A large and impressive hotel which has a lovely style. The only drawback is that it is located on the main road through this resort town: the beach is only 200 yards away.

N634/4 Norte

Zarauz, Guipúzcoa

📞 (943) 83.23.13

🅿 O/S	✗ ✓
🍴 ✗	🛏 ✗
🛏 4,000	🛏 2,500

A relatively small place that is located on a busy corner close to the beach. Bad parking.

N634/5 Iciar

Iciar/Deba, Guipúzcoa

📞 (943) 60.13.94

🅿 G		✗	✓
☕ ✗		🍴	✗
🛏 1,800		🚪	✗

San Sebastián: 29 km

Located in an isolated position between these two towns, there are distant sea views. The rooms do not have bath/shower.

N634/7 San Blas

Abadiano-Celayeta, Vizcaya

📞 (94) 681.42.00

🅿 G		✗	✓
☕ ✓		🍴	✗
🛏 4,059		🚪 3,675	

San Sebastián: 87 km

A large hotel that is not far from the sea and has pleasant views to the mountains in the background.

N634/6 Miramar

Deba, Guipúzcoa

📞 (943) 60.11.44

🅿 E		✗	✓
☕ ✓		🍴	✗
🛏 7,745		🚪 3,630	

This lives up to its name, The Seaview, as it is located right on the beach as you enter Deba from San Sebastián. It is a large hotel and private garages are 500 a night extra.

N634/10 Arenillas

Islares, Cantabria

📞 (942) 86.07.66

🅿 G		✗	✓
☕ ✗		🍴	✗
🛏 4,000		🚪	✗

Close to a bay, this is a modern hostal that is very busy in the summer months.

N634/8 Avenida

Bilbao, Vizcaya

☎ (94) 412.43.00

🅿 G	✗ ✓
☕ ✓	🛏 ✗
🛏 8,250	🍴 6,490

Located on the San Sebastián side of Bilbao this hotel is more easily accessed from the eastbound carriageway. It is very grand, rather formal, and only a short distance from the centre of town. A room for three is 9,550.

N634/11 El Carro

Alto de Laredo, Cantabria

☎ (942) 60.61.75

🅿 VG	✗ ✓
☕ ✓	🛏 ✓
🛏 5,400	🍴 5,000

A new modern-style hostal that has spectacular views across the bay of Laredo. It is called The Waggon. Reservations must be made for the summer months.

N634/9 Vista Alegre

Castro-Urdiales, Vizcaya

☎ (942) 86.04.62

🅿 G	✗ ✓
☕ ✓	🛏 ✗
🛏 7,000	🍴 5,000

Just outside the resort town of Castro-Urdiales this is a large hostal with sea views.

N634/12 Monte Carlo

Colindres, Cantabria

☎ (942) 65.00.75

🅿 O/S		✗ ✓
☕ ✗		🍴 ✗
🛏 4,000		🦴 2,500

This is a pleasant hostal but at a busy location and likely to be noisy.

N634/15 Mizmaya

Hoznayo, Cantabria

☎ (942) 52.40.73

🅿 G		✗ ✓
☕ ✗		🍴 ✗
🛏 3,000		🦴 ✗

Close to but smaller than the previous place, this has much character. Also only has doubles.

N634/13 El Paso

Beranga, Cantabria

☎ (942) 63.50.47

🅿 G		✗ ✓
☕ ✗		🍴 ✗
🛏 4,000		🦴 2,000

Located in an isolated position on the peninsula approaching Santander, this is small and the people were friendly.

N634/14 Adelma

Hoznayo, Cantabria

☎ (942) 52.40.20

🅿 G		✗ ✓
☕ ✓		🍴 ✗
🛏 5,000		🦴 ✗

A pleasant hostal with an attractive restaurant that has views down to the beach.

N634/16 El Carmen

Santander, Cantabria

📞 (942) 23.01.90

🅿 E	✗ ✓
☕ ✗	🍴 ✗
🛏 4,200	🚪 2,000

Santander is a very large busy resort town where there are many hotels. This one is a short distance away from the beach areas and the street has a wide pedestrian walkway down the centre. The Capitol garage is next door and it costs 800 a day to park there.

N634/17 Hosteria de Quijas

Quijas, Cantabria

📞 (942) 82.08.33

🅿 VG	✗ ✓
☕ ✓	🍴 ✓
🛏 8,000	🚪 ✗

Located just 5 km west of the N623 Santander/Burgos road this is really a delightful place. The style is very much open brickwork and exposed wood done in a very traditional style. There is also a vine covered porch.

N634/18 Conde de Lara

Cabezon de la Sal, Cantabria

📞 (942) 70.03.12

🅿 G	✗ ✓
☕ ✗	🍴 ✗
🛏 4,000	🚪 ✗

This is a fairly small place in a pretty town. It has a nice atmosphere but could be a little noisy.

N634/19 Venta de Abajo

La Revilla, Cantabria

📞 (942) 71.01.00

🅿 G	✗ ✓
☕ ✗	🍴 ✗
🛏 3,900	🚪 2,000

A nice clean hotel with a pleasant atmosphere; there are very attractive views to the rear.

N634/20 Baviera

Pesues, Cantabria

📞 (942) 71.70.54

🅿 G		✗	✓
☕ ✗		🛏 ✗	
🛏 2,800		🍴 1,800	

Located at the summit of a hill just after San Vicente de la Barquera, it is small, basic, and the area is not so nice.

N634/21 Rio Deva 11

Unquera-Pesues, Cantabria

📞 (942) 71.72.83

🅿 G		✗	✓
☕ ✗		🛏 ✗	
🛏 4,500		🍴 2,300	

This is large and impressive from the outside: inside though it is not quite so nice. The location is interesting as it is by a wide basin where the river breaks through to the sea.

N634/22 Oyambre

El Peral-Colombres, Asturias

📞 (985) 41.22.42

🅿 G		✗	✓
☕ ✗		🛏 ✗	
🛏 3,000		🍴 ✗	

A pension that is much smaller and more basic than its two close neighbours.

N634/23 Casa Junco

El Peral-Colombres, Asturias

📞 (985) 41.22.43

🅿 G		✗	✓
☕ ✗		🛏 ✗	
🛏 4,500		🍴 3,750	

A very nice hotel that is close to a farm. There is a water fountain just outside.

N634/24 San Angel

Colombres, Asturias

☎ (985) 41.20.00

🅿 VG	✗ ✓
🍴 ✓	🛏 ✓
🛏 7,450	🚿 5,450

A splendid hotel, set well back from the road, with all the expected facilities.

N634/25 Europa

Llanes, Asturias

☎ (985) 40.09.45

🅿 G	✗ ✓
🍴 ✗	🛏 ✗
🛏 4,100	🚿 ✗

An interesting place to look at, quite large and has a nice bar.

N632/26 Boston

Ribadesella, Asturias

☎ (985) 86.09.66

🅿 G	✗ ✓
🍴 ✗	🛏 ✗
🛏 5,000	🚿 ✗

Located in a very busy spot by a junction, this could well be noisy. Apart from that, it is nice and close to the beach.

N632/27 Puente El Pilar

Ribadesella, Asturias

☎ (985) 86.04.46

🅿 G	✗ ✓
🍴 ✗	🛏 ✗
🛏 6,600	🚿 3,300

A rather small hostal just to the west of Ribadesella. It is close to the beach and all information can be obtained from the nearby bar.

N632/28 Caravia

Prado-Caravia, Asturias

☎ (985) 85.30.14

🅿 G	✗ ✓
☕ ✗	🍴 ✗
🛏 3,500	🛏 1,800

Quite a large hostal but rather plain inside. There is a *horreo*, a traditional building for storing hay, just outside.

N632/29 Monte y Mar

La Isla-Colunga, Asturias

☎ (985) 85.65.61

🅿 G	✗ ✓
☕ ✗	🍴 ✗
🛏 5,000	🛏 4,000

In a very rural environment with the sea close by, this is aptly named Hill and Sea. It is a very pleasant hotel even allowing for the pink paint on the outside.

N632/30 Nautico

Tornon, Asturias

☎ (985) 89.09.22

🅿 G	✗ ✓
☕ ✗	🍴 ✗
🛏 4,000	🛏 1,800

A rather small hostal in a very rural and attractive area, this has a plain bar.

N632/31 La Ria

Villaviciosa, Asturias

☎ (985) 89.15.55

🅿 O/S	✗ ✓
☕ ✓	🍴 ✗
🛏 6,200	🛏 4,750

Situated right in the centre of this town it is a modern hotel that also has a pizzeria. The parking is very bad here.

N634/32 Portobello

Concha de Artedo, Asturias

☎ (985) 59.02.02

🅿 G	✗	✓
🍺 ✓	🛋	✗
🛏 4,500	🍴 3,000	

A very nice modern oddly-shaped hotel, high up overlooking the sea.

N632/33 Yolimar

Artedo-Cudillero, Asturias

☎ (985) 59.04.72

🅿 G	✗	✓
🍺 ✗	🛋	✗
🛏 2,500	🍴	✗

I rather like this small old-fashioned and basic guest house. It is in a very attractive rural area.

N632/34 Andurina

Soto de Luina, Asturias

☎ (985) 59.61.12

🅿 O/S	✗	✓
🍺 ✗	🛋	✗
🛏 3,000	🍴 1,500	

This is also set in a very rural environment. It is a next door to a lumber yard.

N632/35 Yendebarcas

✗☎ (985) 59.62.98

🅿 VG	✗	✓
🍺 ✗	🛋	✗
🛏 6,000	🍴 3,000	

Apart from being painted in a ghastly shade of blue that is entirely at odds with its surroundings, this is quite a nice place. Perhaps a little expensive.

N632/36 Prada

Santa Marina, Asturias

☎ (985) 59.61.71

🅿 G		✕	✓
☕ ✗		🍴 ✗	
🛏 4,500		🛏 3,500	

A very strangely decorated house, though quite attractive and in a rural environment, it has been turned into a small hostal with parking in the front garden. Enquiries and extra rooms are at the Bar Goya across the road.

N632/37 El Redondel

Barcia, Asturias

☎ (985)

🅿 G		✕	✓
☕ ✗		🍴 ✗	
🛏 ✗		🛏 ✗	

Called The Ring, this is of medium size and directly across from a service station. It had not opened the morning I passed and therefore I could not get any more information.

N634/38 No Name

La Ronda, Asturias

☎ (985) 64.04.89

🅿 G		✕	✓
☕ ✗		🍴 ✗	
🛏 4,000		🛏 2,000	

A rather plain place that seems a little expensive.

N634/39 Casa Consuelo

Otur-Luarca, Asturias

☎ (985) 64.16.42

🅿 G		✕	✓
☕ ✓		🍴 ✗	
🛏 4,500		🛏 3,800	

Literally The House of Comfort, this is a very nice place that is large, clean, and has attractive views.

N634/40 El Pinar

Villapedre-Navia, Asturias

📞 (985) 47.22.21

🅿 G	✗	✓
🍷 ✗	🛏️ ✗	
🍽️ 4,000	🛏️ 2,500	

A small hostal that is located on the edge of a village in a typical rural area quite close to the sea. I have stayed here and although the rooms do not have a sink, bath or shower it is quite nice.

N634/41 Rego

Valdepares, Asturias

📞 (985) 63.70.20

🅿 G	✗	✓
🍷 ✗	🛏️ ✗	
🍽️ 2,000	🛏️ 1,500	

A very small Fonda that is basically just rooms above a bar. Being close to the road it will be noisy.

N634/42 Chiquin

Tapia de Casariego, Asturias

📞 (985) 62.40.39

🅿 G	✗	✓
🍷 ✗	🛏️ ✗	
🍽️ 4,240	🛏️ ✗	

A new isolated hostal that has sea views in the distance.

N634/43 Voar

Ribadeo, Galicia

📞 (982) 11.06.85

🅿 G	✗	✓
🍷 ✗	🛏️ ✗	
🍽️ 4,900	🛏️ 3,900	

This is on the outskirts of Ribadeo. It is fairly large and quite nice.

21 A TO Z OF HELPFUL HINTS

Accidents

In the unfortunate event of an accident:

a) Do not panic, wait for the police to arrive and then follow their instructions.

b) Follow the instructions supplied with your Green Card to comply with the legal requirements.

c) Telephone the Helpline number given by your Motor Insurance company. These people are very experienced, helpful and speak English, they usually give you a contact name and that person will then handle all aspects of your case. Being familiar with your policy and local conditions, they are in a position to advise on what options are available to you. When a choice has been made they will then co-ordinate between yourself and all other parties.

d) Methods of payment vary according to the Motor Insurer but generally do not involve cash.

Bail Bond

If you do not like the idea of going to prison in the event of an accident make sure you carry a Bail Bond document with you. This usually comes free with your Motor Insurance and/or Green Card.

Banks

These are generally open from Monday until Friday from 0900–1400. During Fiesta time, however, they are likely to open somewhat earlier and close as early as 11am.

Bank Cashpoints

These are very common in Spain and there are two main systems, Servired and Telebanco. However, both systems take Access, Eurocard, Eurocheque, Mastercharge and Visa cards and the pesetas you get are charged against your UK account.

Breakdowns

In the event of a major breakdown:
a) Telephone the Helpline number given by your Motor Insurance company. Give them your exact location, a telephone number at which you can be contacted (if possible) and as much detail as you can about the problem. If you are going to need towing emphasise that point. They will then arrange for a mobile unit to come to your assistance. Remember to get a contact name at the Helpline office.
b) Stay with your vehicle until that unit arrives.
c) If the vehicle can be fixed on the spot complete the necessary paperwork, strictly according to the instructions given by the Motor Insurance company, and continue your journey.
d) If the vehicle has to be taken back to the garage for further repairs, go with it. When the garage has estimated how long the repairs will take call the Helpline contact. If the people at the garage cannot speak English have them talk to the Helpline contact first.
e) At this stage there are a variety of options according to the damage to the car and the availability of spare parts etc. The Helpline contacts are very experienced, helpful and being familiar with your policy, and local conditions, they are in a position to advise on what options are available to you. When a choice has been made they will then co-ordinate between yourself and all other parties.
f) Methods of payment vary according to the Motor Insurer but generally do not involve cash.

Minor problems
Minor problems such as punctured tyres (*neumaticos*) etc. are best resolved, without involving the Travel Insurer, at garages with the sign *Talleres* – which means repairs.

British Consulate

The British Consulates exist to help British citizens abroad to help themselves and can, amongst other things, issue emergency passports, offer all kinds of advice and contact British nationals who have been arrested or are in prison. They are obliged, by Acts of Parliament, to charge fees for certain services. Do not, though, expect them to pay any sort of bills, give legal advice etc. or get you better treatment than is

provided to local nationals in hospitals or prison, for example.
Always contact the Consulate in the following circumstances:
a) If someone in your travelling party dies.
b) If you, or someone in your travelling party, is arrested on a
serious offence insist that the British Consulate is informed. A
consular officer will make contact as soon as possible.

Car Servicing

Obviously, before leaving on such a long journey, you will
want to be sure that your car is in good shape. Beware,
though, one of the clauses in the Insurance Policy is likely to
be that the car must be serviced to manufacturer's standards.
Failure to comply could mean that you will not be covered in
the event of an accident or breakdown.

Cash

Remember most insurance policies set a limit on the amount
of cash that is covered, usually it is around £250 to £300. In
any event it is always wise to carry alternative methods of
payment, possibly as many as two or three. Options include
Travellers Cheques (you pay more initially for peseta cheques
but save commission charges in Spain), Eurocheques (the
accompanying Eurocheque card can be used in Cash
Dispensing machines throughout Spain) and Credit Cards,
some of which can also be used in cash dispensing machines.

Clubs

When you see the sign 'CLUB' – which is usually accompanied
by bright flashing lights – on buildings by the side of the road,
beware, things are not what they might seem. These are
houses of ill repute.

Conversion charts

Length

Miles	1	5	10	15	20	25	50	100
Kilometres	0.62	8.05	16.1	24.1	32.2	40.2	80.5	160.9

Speed

Mph	20	30	40	50	60	70	80	90	100
Km/h	32	48	64	80	96	112	128	144	160

Temperature

Fahrenheit	32	41	50	59	68	77	86	95	104
Centigrade	0	5	10	15	20	25	30	35	40

Tyre pressure

Lbs per Sq inch	20	22	24	26	28	30	32	34
Kg/cm^2	1.41	1.55	1.69	1.83	1.97	2.11	2.25	2.39

Volume

Gallons	1	3	5	8	10	12	15	20
Litres	4.54	13.6	22.7	36.4	45.5	53.0	68.0	91.0

Weight

Lbs.	1	5	10	15	25	50
Kilograms	2.20	11.02	22.04	33.06	55.11	110.23

Currency

The peseta is the currency of Spain and is available in the
following denominations.
Coins: 1, 5, 10, 25, 50, 100, 200 and 500
Notes: 100, 200, 500, 1,000, 2,000, 5,000 and 10,000
The 1 peseta coin is now widely ignored. Generally the money
is just rounded up, or down, to the nearest 5.
The 5 peseta coin, like the new 5 pence piece in the UK, is very
small, and there is also an old, larger, one in circulation.
There are two 25 peseta coins in circulation. The new one is
easy to identify, since it is smaller and has a hole in the middle.
Beware of the 200 peseta piece. This is easily confused with
others of lesser denominations, so be sure to take extra care.
Although you might come across notes of lower
denomination, the lowest in common use is the 1,000 peseta
note.

Days in Spanish

Sunday *Domingo*	Wednesday *Miercoles*	Saturday *Sabado*
Monday *Lunes*	Thursday *Jeuves*	
Tuesday *Martes*	Friday *Viernes*	

Drink

There are some parts in the south and south-west where the
temperatures can be extremely hot; well over 100 Fahrenheit
and even as high as 120 Fahrenheit on occasion. This makes it
uncomfortable for adults, let alone children, and most people

are continually thirsty. With an accident or breakdown in an isolated location it could be dangerous for young children if you did not have any liquids available. The following hints might help:

a) Make space before you leave for a cooler. Most every service station sells bags of ice (*hielo* – don't pronounce the h) for about a £1. Buy water, or soft drinks, in a shop – much cheaper than at a service station or a bar – and keep them in the cooler.

b) Stop regularly for a drinks break.

c) Keep the empty bottles and when you see a sign on the side of the road saying *Agua Potable*, refill the bottles. This water is free and quite often is natural spring water.

d) Buy one of those small plastic bottles that, when squeezed, emits a fine spray. Fill it with water and use it to spray the face and neck every now and again – its amazingly refreshing.

Drinking and Driving

Anyone involved in an accident and found to have more than the equivalent of one and a half units of alcohol in their blood is liable to prosecution. There is only one safe answer and that is do not drink and drive.

Drinking Water

There are many myths about the quality of Spanish water but these days there are few problems with the regular mains water. However, bottled mineral water is immensely popular, especially in the heat of the summer months. This is produced by any number of different companies but there are only two main types. *Agua mineral sin gas* – non-carbonated water and *Agua mineral con gas* – carbonated water.

The Spanish for ordinary drinking water is *Agua potable*.

E111 GB Form

This entitles you, and your fellow travellers, to free medical treatment in other EC countries. However the conditions vary between countries and more details can be found in Leaflet T1 'The Travellers Guide to Health' and a copy can be obtained by calling 0800.555777. In Spain this can only be obtained from doctors and hospitals operating under the Spanish health care system which like with the NHS, often means long queues.

Information on where these services can be obtained are found at the local Instituto Nacional de la Seguridad (INSS) office. Do not expect to be able to reclaim any fees paid directly to a doctor when using this scheme, unless it is covered by your Travel Insurance policy.

The E111 GB Form is obtained at any main Post Office and the person who applies need know only their own National Insurance number and birthdate as well as the birthdates of the other travellers. There is however one small problem. When obtaining treatment the E111 GB Form can only be used once as it has to be handed in. To get around this either take several photocopies or, if you are a frequent visitor to Spain, go to any INSS local office on arrival and exchange the original for a book of ten vouchers.

Possession of this form does not mean that you do not need to take out Personal Travel Insurance; always take both as they are complimentary to each other.

Electricity

Electricity is generally 220/225 volts and the plugs are of the two round prong variety. Hotels often have a 110/125 volt socket in the bathroom for electric razors.

First Aid Kit

Although not compulsory always carry one in the car.

GB sticker

Don't forget to place a GB sticker in a prominent position on the back of your car.

Green Card

As with any other form of insurance this is not compulsory. However, any sensible person never leaves home without one. It ensures that the financial liability of your motor insurance meets the compulsory, legal, standards in the countries you are going to drive in. It is obtained from your regular car insurance company in the UK and, for a two week period, costs around £17.

Headlights

a) The flow of the headlight beam needs to be converted for right hand side of the road driving. Conversion kits, for all types of vehicle, are available from stores such as Halfords and the AA and RAC outlets.

b) Full headlights are prohibited in built-up areas.

Identification and other documentation

It is essential that when you are driving, even on short trips, you carry official personal identification, a passport for UK citizens, and all the necessary vehicle and Insurance documentation.

International Driving Permit (IDP)

This is a compulsory requirement for those with a Green UK driving licence and is highly recommended even for those with a Pink EC licence. They can be obtained at AA and RAC travel shops for a small fee. Remember to take two passport size photographs.

Light Bulbs

A replacement set of light bulbs for your vehicle is compulsory in Spain.

Motor Insurance

This is usually combined with Personal travel Insurance, and should be bought from an organisation that has the facilities to assist you in the countries you are going to.

The two best known companies in the UK are the AA and RAC though there are important differences as to how they calculate their premiums.

The AA allows you to choose what cover you want and calculates the premium according to the number of people travelling. The RAC, on the other hand, offers a set amount of cover at a given premium, at least for the top level of cover. The difference is negligible if there are four people travelling, but the RAC premium becomes proportionally more expensive the fewer people there are.

There is an economical alternative which still provide a quality service without the attendant costs. Europ Assistance launched a new kind of cover in 1991 that is fundamentally different from that of its competitors. Their Family Continental Motoring Assistance charges a flat premium of £19 plus £3 per day to cover you, your car and up to as many passengers as the manufacturers recommend, for all the motoring, medical, baggage, legal and personal insurance that you are ever likely to need. Direct billing means that there is no need to worry about vouchers – as with the AA and RAC – and a single telephone number gives access to all of their services. They have over 12,000,000 members and 15,000 garages throughout the Continent with over 4,000 of these recovery and breakdown specialists in both France and Spain. Financially, for a family of four motoring abroad for two weeks Europ Assistance charges £61 compared, at 1991 rates, to £104.95 for the AA's 5-Star Service. The rates, and accompanying levels of service, make Europ Assistance worth serious consideration.

Motorways

There are two systems of motorway:
Autovia: a road to motorway standards but toll free.
Autopista: a toll (*peaje*) road, and beware the tolls are high.

Mountain Passes

Contrary to popular opinion much of Spain is very cold in the winter months and snow is a major problem in the centre and north of the country. Many roads cross mountain passes and often, these can be blocked by snow. For information on the status of these passes call Teleruta on (91) 441.72.22.

Numbers in Spanish

0	cero				
1	uno	11	once	21	veintiuno
2	dos	12	doce	22	veintidos
3	tres	13	trece	23	veintitres
4	cuatro	14	catorce	24	veinticuatro
5	cinco	15	quince	25	veinticinco
6	seis	16	dieciseis	26	veintiseis
7	siete	17	diecisiete	27	veintisiete
8	ocho	18	dieciocho	28	veintiocho
9	nueve	19	diecinueve	29	veintinueve
10	diez	20	viente	30	treinta

From 30, numbers are structured *treinta y uno* (31); *treinta y dos* (32); *treinta y tres* (33) etc.

40	cuarenta	100	cien*	700	setecientos
50	cincuenta	200	doscientos	800	ochocientos
60	sesenta	300	trescientos	900	novecientos
70	setenta	400	cuatrocientos	1,000	mil
80	ochenta	500	quinientos		
90	noventa	600	seiscientos		

* *ciento* for all numbers between 101 and 199

Overtaking

The roadsigns in Spain that indicate where overtaking is allowed, or not, are put there for a reason, even if that reason is not immediately obvious.

Parking

On-street
a) Pay-and-display parking is allowed between the blue lines painted on the road. The tickets are bought from machines that are often located on the pavement – in San Sebastian though the tickets are purchased in Estancos (see Post Offices), and they must be displayed prominently. This normally applies Monday to Friday 0900–1400 and 1700–2000; and Saturday 0900–1400.
b) Parking is also allowed between white lines but expect an attendant to be on hand to request payment.
c) There are usually no restrictions in other places. Beware though of 'Protection Rackets'. In some places, outside the Cathedral in Sevilla and by the harbour in Algerciras are two examples, you will be approached by unseemly looking people asking for money to look after your car. Either pay, no more than 200 ptas or so, or park somewhere else.

Organised car parks
These are identified by a large blue sign with a white P. Most are open 24 hours and are attended but, even so, that does not guarantee security. The going rate is about 100 ptas an hour and between 1,000 and 1,500 ptas for 24 hours.

Passports

A lost or stolen passport can cause immense problems. So, before you leave, take photocopies of all passports and keep them separate from the real thing at all time.

The first thing you will be asked for when checking into a hotel is your passport. Certain details have to be entered on a registration card, which then has to be signed before the keys are handed over. After that the passport is generally kept at the reception. However there are no hard and fast rules about this and if you are a UK citizen it is advisable to reclaim your passport, and carry it on your person when you leave the hotel. Primarily this is because UK citizens do not have a national identity card and, in the event of an emergency, there may be no other means of identification. Also certain museums offer free, or reduced, admission for EC citizens on presentation of their passports.

Personal Health

Those people that require special medical treatment, or diets, should always carry a letter from their doctor, translated into Spanish, stating the nature of their condition and the medicines and/or diets required.

Personal Travel Insurance (also see Motor Insurance)

Personal Travel Insurance and Motor Insurance are usually purchased together, on the same policy, and no one should travel without it and an E111 GB Form. Personal travel insurance gives far greater cover than the E111 GB and would pay for such things as repatriation in the case of a severe emergency. It also insures against travel delay, loss of personal effects etc.

Remember, in the unlikely event that you are robbed a police report is a necessity and must be obtained within twenty-four hours of the theft.

Police

Police patrolling on motorcycles are the most common; they are always found in pairs. Often they will place themselves on either side of the road, sometimes in remote locations, whilst observing the passing traffic. If you see oncoming cars flashing their headlights, for no apparent reason, it is a warning of just such a circumstance – so slow down. The Spanish greatly appreciate it if you warn them in turn. If you are pulled over, for any reason, they are firm but polite and should you be charged with a traffic violation there is a 20% discount for payment on-the-spot. They will always, in such circumstances, want to see formal identification and vehicle documentation.

Post Offices

Each town usually has one main Post Office, Correos. Besides selling stamps (*sellos*) it also has a facility for sending telegrams and packages, etc.

There are also smaller Correos but these are generally located in the suburbs. There are many little shops that sell tobacco (*tabaco*), postcards (*postales*) and newspapers, etc.; these are called (*Estancos*). These are identified by a maroon and yellow Tabacos sign and, of more importance to tourists, also sell postage stamps.

Public holidays

Jan 01   New Year's Day
Jan 06   Epiphany
Feb 28   Dia de Andalucia (only in Andalucia)
          Maundy Thursday (Thursday before Easter)
          Good Friday
May 01   Labour Day
          Corpus Christi
Jul 25   St. James's Day
Aug 15   Ascension Day
Oct 12   Colombus Day
Nov 01   All Saints' Day
Dec 06   Constitution Day
Dec 08   Immaculate Conception
Dec 25   Christmas Day

It is likely that each town will have extra days during its own fiesta.

Red Cross

Red Cross (*Cruz Roja*) stations and ambulances are a common sight on Spanish roads. These volunteers are often first on the scene of an accident.

Roadblocks

Do not be panicked if you see police, heavily armed with sub-machine guns, manning roadblocks. These are not that common and you are very unlikely to be stopped.

Road Safety

Spain has a very high accident, and death, rate on the roads. This is particularly bad between the middle of July and early September; in 1991 over 1,200 people were killed in this period. There are literally millions of cars on the move all over Spain – so take care!

Roadsigns

Many of the roadsigns used are based on the International standard and others are self explanatory. There are some, however, where particular Spanish words need to be explained: *Aviso* means 'warning'. *Cambio de Sentido,* possibly one of the most common road signs in Spain, means Change of Direction. It is used, for example, in the following circumstances. a) When turning left, across oncoming traffic, on the open road. In Spain the sign directs you off the main road, to the right, and you then cross as though at a regular junction. b) When you want to get off a dual carriageway onto another road, or to go back in the other direction. *Camino* means 'road', however it is generally used to indicate a smaller road. *Camiones* means 'lorries' and is often used near roadworks to indicate that lorries are passing in and out. *Carretera* also means 'road', but a main one. *Obras* means 'works' and indicates that there are roadworks ahead. *Peligro* and *Peligroso* mean Danger and Dangerous respectively so, when you see either word, pay particular attention.

Security

Unfortunately, in this day and age there are many problems throughout the world and Spain is not an exception. It is always a wise policy to take adequate precautions so follow the following advice.

a) Never stop your car on the open road for anyone except the police. Be especially resistant to signals telling you to stop – for instance "because you've got a puncture" – coming from overtaking motorists. If you want to check do so after the signaller is way out of sight.

b) Never stop and sleep in any remote place on the road.

c) Never leave anything, of any value, on open display in your vehicle – especially when driving through large cities. One of the most popular crimes is to drive by on a moped, smash the window, grab what is on sight and then drive off.

d) Never leave your vehicle, with or without valuables, on the street overnight in large cities such as Madrid, Barcelona, Sevilla and Malaga etc. In my experience this is not a problem in smaller, provincial, towns where most people are very friendly and helpful.

e) Be careful with handbags, shoulder bags and cameras when you are walking around. As with c) youths on mopeds are adept at grabbing these and then disappearing.

Speed Limits

These vary according to different road conditions, and sometimes even on the same road, but they are all well signposted. The police use radar to check for speeders.

Summer Time

Spanish summer time, one hour ahead of the UK, is from the morning of the last Sunday in March to the last Sunday in September.

Telephones

There are four ways of making telephone calls.

Public telephones
These are located on the streets and in public places such as stations, airports and sometimes bars and restaurants. Usually they have instructions in several languages and display the national and international codes.

Local calls – those within the same province – start at 15 ptas, national calls – those to other provinces – begin at 50 ptas and international calls at 200 ptas. It is always wise to have a good supply of 100-peseta coins for international calls. Telephone rates are cheaper at night, Sundays and holidays.

Telefonicas
These are staffed telephone offices and there is usually at least one in every large city. They are run by the telephone

company and, as you go in, the attendant will tell you the number of the booth to use. Simply dial the number you want and when you have finished your call go back to the attendant, who will tell you the cost. If it is more than 500 ptas you can pay by credit card. Other advantages are the usual wide range of telephone directories and the fact that they are open until late at night.

Private telefonicas
These are run on the same basis as those above, but they are far fewer, much smaller and owned by individuals. They are identified by a large Telefono sign.

Hotels and other places with private phones
Beware: it may seem very convenient to sit in your hotel room and make your call but you will regret it when you receive the bill. Hotel phones cost much more than public ones. Likewise, a private phone in a bar or restaurant will be more expensive. Some have an attached counter and you pay a certain number of pesetas for each digit, which is very costly.

Telephone Codes

Internal
Each Spanish province has either a two digit (e.g. 91 for Madrid) or three digit (e.g. 958 for Granada) prefix. These are only used when dialling from one province to another and are not used for calls within the province.

International (calling from Spain)
To telephone the UK dial the International Code (07) first and wait for a new tone, then dial the Country Code (44) and the English number but remember not to use the initial 0. For example a London number becomes either 71 or 81.

International (calling to Spain)
To telephone Spain dial the International Code (010), the Country Code (34), the Provincial Code (excluding the initial 9) and then the number.

Triangles

A warning triangle, to be placed some distance behind the vehicle in the event of an accident, is highly recommended. Two triangles are compulsory for vehicles with over nine seats.

Unleaded Petrol

Unleaded petrol *Sin Plomo* is being introduced into service stations rapidly and, as at January 1992, many of the listed stations will sell it. Most of those that do not are in the process of being converted.

Vaccinations

Visitors from the UK do not need any vaccinations to enter mainland Spain or its Islands, according to the Spanish Health Authority and the World Health Organisation. Visitors from other countries should check with their local Spanish Consulate.

Valuables, Cameras and Money etc.

Do not leave any of these unattended in a public place or even in an unattended car. Almost every Insurance policy has a clause excluding cover in the above circumstances. Few people are likely to leave things in public places but many more would think little of leaving them in a car, especially if they are out of sight. The simple message is do not, as you will not be covered by most Travel Insurance policies. This can cause difficulties for those travelling alone, particularly if they are going to a beach, for example. The only option is that you might be covered under 'All Risks' and 'Money' clauses in your Household Comprehensive policy – check before travelling.

Visas

Visas, for visits to Spain (including the Balearic and Canary Islands, Ceuta and Melilla) of up to 90 days, are not necessary for citizens of the European Community, USA and Japan as long as the holders passport is valid for the entire period. As far as other countries are concerned the Spanish government, as at 1991, operated a reciprocal policy, so people from outside the EC should check with their own authorities before leaving.

22 PETROL STATIONS ON EACH ROUTE

This chapter has been compiled with the assistance of Repsol, the largest retailer of petrol in Spain who sell their products under three brand names – Repsol, Campsa and Petronor. The individual brand name of each service station is correct as at 1st January 1992, however it is possible that some of these will change in the future.

Chapter 3: NI Madrid–Burgos–Vitoria–San Sebastián–Irún (France)

Name	Location on road	Town	Kms from Madrid
Repsol	Both sides	Alcobendas	16.6
Repsol	Both sides	Fuente del Fresno	24.1
Repsol	Both sides	El Molar	40.2
Repsol	North side	La Cabrera	58
Campsa		Buitrago de Lozoya	74.7
Petronor		Sepúlveda	110
Repsol		Boceguillas (off the Autovia)	117
Petronor		Gumiel de Hizán	171.1
Repsol	Both sides	Lerma	203
Campsa		Villagonzalo de Pedernales	232.7
Campsa		Burgos	233.9
Repsol	North side	Burgos	245
Campsa		Burgos	245.6
Repsol	South side	Burgos	246.9
Repsol	North side	Burgos	248.5
Repsol	Both sides	Burgos (north of the city)	251.7
Repsol	Both sides	Briviesca	289.2
Repsol	South side	Pancorbo	302.5
Campsa		Miranda de Ebro	318
Repsol	North side	Palacios	333.8
Repsol	North side		341.6
Repsol	Both sides		346.5
Campsa		Elorriaga	353.4
Repsol	South side		354.6
Repsol	South side		360.6
Campsa		Quilchano	364.3

Campsa		Legorreta	429.8
Campsa		Iruerrieta	433
Repsol	South side	Villabona	444.7
Campsa		San Sebastián	461.9
Repsol	Both sides	Oyarzun	475
Repsol	Both sides		484
Campsa		Behobia	486
Repsol	Both sides	Irún (French/Spanish Border)	486.4

Chapter 4: NII Madrid–Zaragoza–Barcelona–La Junquera (France)

Name	Location on road	Town	Kms from Madrid
Repsol	Both sides	Madrid	12.7
Campsa		San Fernando de Henares	16.3
Repsol	North side		18
Repsol	North side		29.8
Repsol	South side		50.8
Campsa		Ledanca	94.9
Campsa		Algora	113.5
Campsa		Sauca	125.1
Repsol	South side		135.9
Campsa		Santa María de Huerta	180.4
Campsa		Cetina	202.2
Campsa		Calatayud	234
Repsol	Bopth sides	El Cisne hotel	309
Campsa		Zaragoza	315
Campsa		Zaragoza	315.2
Campsa		Puebla de Alfindén	321.7
Repsol	North side		331
Repsol	North side		334.7
Campsa		Osera de Ebro	354.1
Repsol	South side	Bujaraloz	390
Campsa		Candasnos	412
Campsa		Fraga	435
Repsol	North side	Fraga	436
Repsol	Both sides	Fraga	441.4
Repsol	Both sides		450
Campsa		Bell Lloch	475.1
Campsa		Bell Lloch	477.9
Campsa		Mollerusa	484
Campsa		Bellpuig	495.5
Campsa		Vilagrasa	504
Campsa		Tarrega	507.9

Repsol	Both sides		518
Campsa		Montmaneu	532.1
Campsa		Igualada	556
Petronor		Odena	588
Petronor		Martorell	593.3
Campsa		Martorell	595.8
Repsol	South side		599
Campsa		San Justo Desvern	615.9
Repsol	North side		616.2
Petronor		Badalona	626
Campsa		Mataró	654.7
Repsol	North side		667.6
Campsa		Calella de Mar	674.1
Campsa		Pineda de Mar	678
Campsa		Vilademuls	731
Repsol	Both sides	Vilademuls	731.4
Campsa		Medina	734
Campsa		Figueras	761
Campsa		Figueras	763

Chapter 5: NIII Madrid–Valencia

Name	Location on road	Town	Kms from Madrid
Repsol	Both sides	Madrid	7.1
Campsa		Vaciamadrid	19.5
Repsol	Both sides		23
Repsol	West side		39.2
Repsol	West side		56.8
Campsa		Fuentidueña de Tajo	62.5
Repsol	Both sides	Tarancón	82.5
Repsol	Both sides	Montalbo	116
Repsol	West side	Villares del Saz	131.2
Campsa		La Almarcha	154.4
Campsa		Alarcón	187.1
Campsa		Motilla del Palancar	199.8
Repsol	West side	Castillejo de Iniesta	211
Petronor		Minglanilla	225.6
Campsa		Utiel	262
Campsa		Utiel	263.5
Campsa		Buñol	305.6
Campsa		Chiva	311.6
Campsa		Ribarroja del Turia	329
Repsol	East side		335.7
Campsa		Mislata	338.6

Chapter 6: NIV Madrid–Bailén–Córdoba–Sevilla–Jerez–Cádiz

Name	Location on road	Town	Kms from Madrid
Repsol	Both sides	Madrid	6.7
Repsol	Both sides	Getafe	12.5
Repsol	Both sides		20.2
Campsa		Pinto	24.3
Repsol	Both sides	Seseña	36.4
Petronor		Aranjuez	46.6
Campsa	Both sides	Ocaña	62
Campsa		Dos Barrios	72.2
Repsol	North side	La Guardia	83
Campsa		Tembleque	94.1
Repsol	South side		124.6
Repsol	North side	Camuñas	129.6
Campsa		Puerto Lápice	135
Repsol	North side	Villarta de San Juan	145.3
Campsa		Villarta de San Juan	147.6
Campsa		Manzanares	171.1
Campsa		Manzanares	173
Repsol	Both sides	Villanueva de Franco	185.2
Campsa		Santa Cruz de Mudela	216.9
Campsa		Almuradiel	232
Campsa		La Carolina	269.1
Repsol	Both sides	Guarromán	280
Campsa		Bailén	296
Repsol	North side		346.6
Campsa		Alcolea	384.1
Campsa		Córdoba	394
Repsol	Both sides	Córdoba	398.3
Campsa		Córdoba	412
Campsa		La Carlota	433.1
Repsol	North side	Éjica (off the Autovia)	451.7
Campsa		Éjica (off the Autovia)	452.3
Repsol	South side	Éjica (off the Autovia)	455.5
Repsol	North side	Éjica (off the Autovia)	456.3
Repsol	South side		509.2
Repsol	Both sides	Sevilla	536.7
Repsol	Both sides	Sevilla	537.6
Campsa		Sevilla	545
Repsol	South side	Sevilla	549.7
Repsol	North side	Los Palacios	569
Repsol	Both sides	Jerez de la Frontera	635.8
Campsa		Jerez de la Frontera	641.5
Campsa		Puerto Real	668.6

Chapter 7: NV Madrid–Mérida–Badajoz (Portugal)

Name	Location on road	Town	Kms from Madrid
Repsol	West side	Madrid	3
Repsol	West side	Madrid	5.4
Campsa		Madrid	9
Repsol	East side		12.5
Repsol	West side	Valmojado	42.3
Repsol	East side		115.4
Repsol	West side		123.7
Campsa		Calzada de Oropesa	159
Repsol	East side	Navalmoral de la Mata	179
Repsol	Both sides	Navalmoral de la Mata	180.8
Repsol	West side	Romangordo	202.7
Campsa		Trujillo	253
Repsol	West side		268
Campsa		Miajadas	290.8
Repsol	West side		314.2
Campsa		Mérida	340.9
Repsol	East side	Mérida	343.3
Repsol	East side		381.4
Repsol	East side		395.7
Repsol	East side	Between Badajoz/Border	403.5

Chapter 8: NVI Madrid–Lugo–La Coruña

Name	Location on road	Town	Kms from Madrid
Campsa		Madrid	6.5
Campsa		Madrid	11.6
Campsa		Madrid	12.2
Campsa		Las Rozas	20.3
Repsol	North side		88
Campsa		Arévalo	123.4
Repsol	North side	Ataquines	141.5
Campsa		Medina del Campo	157.3
Campsa		Medina del Campo	159
Repsol	South side	Rueda	170.7
Campsa		Tordesillas	182
Repsol	North side		196.9
Repsol	South side	Mota del Marqués	202.2
Campsa		Villardefrades	215.8
Repsol	South side	Benavente	260.5
Repsol	South side		314.2
Campsa		Astorga	324.9

Repsol	Both sides		335.2
Repsol	Both sides		344.2
Petronor		Bembibre	369
Campsa		Ponferrada	393
Campsa		Portela	418.5
Campsa		Piedrafita del Cebrero	429.9
Repsol	Both sides	Corgo	488
Campsa		Lugo	493.7
Campsa		Lugo	497.8
Repsol	Both sides	Parga	533.6
Campsa		Guitiriz	539.6
Repsol	South side		583.5
Campsa		Oleirus	588
Campsa		Mino	591
Campsa		Fene	614
Repsol	South side		617

Chapter 9: A68/NI/N232 Bilbao–Logroño–Zaragoza

(The Kms shown here are from the beginning of the N232.
As described in the Chapter these do not always appear in the same manner on the actual road. Therefore, on this section it is necessary to identify them by the town. Also, as this is not a dual carriageway it is not necessary to detail the 'Location on road'.)

Name	Town	Kms on N232
Repsol	Salinillas de Buradón	439.1
Repsol	Logroño	413.1
Repsol	Logroño	404.5
Repsol	Agoncillo	393.1
Repsol	Rincón de Soto	346.1
Repsol	Pedrola	276.5

Chapter 10: N321/N331 Málaga–Códoba

Name	Location on road	Town	Kms from Córdoba
Campsa			167
Repsol	North side		162.3
Repsol	Both sides		138.4
Repsol	North side	Lucena	72

Chapter 11: N321/N334 Málaga–Sevilla

Name	Location on road	Town	Kms from Sevilla
Repsol	Both sides		85.4
Repsol	South side		69.7
Repsol	Both sides	Arahal	43.2
Repsol	Both sides	Mairena del Alcor	28.9
Petronor		Alcalá de Guadaira	9.2

Chapter 12: N321/N342 Málaga–Granada

Name	Location on road	Town	Kms on N342
Repsol		Loja	485.7
Repsol		Loja	483.4
Repsol		Santa Fé	446.7

Chapter 13: N323 Bailén–Granada–Motril

Name	Location on road	Town	Kms from Bailén
Campsa		Mengibar	14.4
Petronor		La Guardia	45
Repsol	North side	Campillo de Arenas	68.8
Campsa		Deifontes	106.3
Campsa		Caparacena	114.3
Repsol	South side	Dúrcal	154.9
Repsol	North side	Rio Vélez	187.5

Chapter 14: N340 Cádiz–Algerciras/Motril–Almería–Murcia

Name	Location on road	Town	Kms from Cádiz
Repsol	Inland side	Cádiz	3.3
Repsol	Inland side	Cádiz	6.7
Repsol	Inland side		59.7
Repsol	Coast side	Tarifa	84
Repsol	Inland side	Castell de Ferro	352
Campsa		Balanegra	406.9
Campsa		El Ejido	407.9
Campsa		El Ejido	408.2
Repsol	Coast side	Almería	445.5
Repsol	Both sides	Almería	452
Repsol	Coast side	Sorbas	492.6
Repsol	Coast side	Huércal-Overa	554.2
Campsa		Puerto Lumbreras	578.2

Campsa		Lorca	585.2
Campsa		Lorca	599.5
Campsa		Lorca	606.5
Campsa		Totana	611.2
Campsa		Alhama de Murcia	628.6
Repsol	Coast side	Sangonera La Seca	646

Chapter 15: N431 Sevilla–Huelva

Name	Location on road	Town	Kms from Sevilla
Repsol	East side		6.4
Repsol	West side		52.5

Chapter 16: N432 Córdoba–Granada

Name	Location on road	Town	Kms from Córdoba
Repsol	In the town	Alcalá la Real	114

Chapter 17: N620 Burgos–Valladolid–Salamanca

Name	Location on road	Town	Kms from Burgos
Campsa		Estépar	22.1
Repsol	North side	Quintana del Puente	55.9
Repsol	South side	Torquemada	61.5
Campsa		Magaz de Pisuerga	76.7
Campsa		Dueñas	88.9
Repsol	Both sides		102.4
Campsa		Cabezón de Pisuerga	112
Repsol	South side		120.4
Campsa		Valladolid	126.1
Repsol	North side	Valladolid	132.7
Repsol	South side		142.7
Repsol	South side		167.7
Campsa		Cañizal	203
Repsol	South side		223
Campsa		Villares de la Reina	234.8
Campsa		Salamanca	235.9
Repsol	Both sides	Salamanca	243.7

Chapter 18: N623 Santander–Burgos

(As this is a single carriageway road the 'Location on road' is not relevant here.)

Name	Town	Kms from Santander
Repsol	Villegar de Toranzo	44
Petronor	Valle de Valdebazana	84
Repsol	Escalada	100
Repsol	Vivar del Cid	150

Chapter 19: N630 Salamanca–Cáceres–Mérida–Sevilla

Name	Location on road	Town	Kms from Salamanca
Repsol	North side	Mozárbez	13
Repsol	South side		22.1
Campsa		Fresno Alhándiga	32
Repsol	South side		48.5
Repsol	South side	Béjar	72.3
Campsa		Béjar	73
Campsa		Aldeaneuva del Camino	95.8
Campsa		Villar de Plascencia	114.3
Campsa		Plascencia	132.5
Campsa		Plascencia	148.9
Campsa		Cañaveral	169.3
Repsol	South side		195
Campsa		Casar de Cáceres	202.6
Petronor		Cáceres	208
Campsa		Cáceres	214
Campsa		Alcuéscar	250.5
Campsa		Almendralejo	310.9
Campsa		Almendralejo	311.3
Repsol	North side		349.5
Campsa		Monesterio	382
Repsol	South side		405.6
Campsa		El Garrobo	443
Repsol	Both sides		459
Repsol	North side		469

Chapter 20: N634/N632/N634 San Sebastián–Bilbao–Santander–Gijón–Ribadeo

Name	Location on road	Town	Kms on N634
Repsol	East side		5.8
Repsol	West side	Zarautz	17
Campsa		Galdacano	102.3
Campsa		Bilbao	115
Campsa		Burcena Baracaldo	117.2
Repsol	West side		144.9
Petronor		Islares	154.9
Petronor		Laredo	171.3
Repsol	West side		173.3
Repsol	West side	Beranga	185.1
Campsa		Hoznayo	195
Repsol	East side		212.7
Campsa		San Roque del Acebal Llanes	299.1
Campsa		Posada de Llanes	310.1

Name	Location on road	Town	Kms on N632
Petronor		Villaviciosa	39.9
Petronor		Verina	74.3

Name	Location on road	Town	Kms on N634
Repsol	West side		443.6
Petronor		Navia	524.3
Repsol	West side		535.8
Repsol		Ribadeo	553.8